In the same series by Nigel Cawthorne:

Sex Lives of the Popes
Sex Lives of the U.S. Presidents
Sex Lives of the Great Dictators
Sex Lives of the Hollywood Idols
Sex Lives of the Great Composers
Sex Lives of the Great Artists

All published by Prion

SEX LIVES OF THE

HOLLYWOOD GODDESSES

NIGEL CAWTHORNE

PRION

First published in 1997
Reprinted 1998, 1999 and 2000
This edition published 2004 by

Prion Books
an imprint of the
Carlton Publishing Group
20 Mortimer Street
London W1T 3JW

A catalogue record for this book is available from the British Library

ISBN 0 85375 524 9

All the star portraits used in the picture inserts are reproduced
courtesy of the Vintage Magazine Company

Printed in Great Britain
by Mackays

CONTENTS

INTRODUCTION

I guess we always knew it – didn't we? – that those glim-
mering goddesses of the silver screen were not really content
with a chaste kiss and a cuddle in the arms of their leading
men. Back in the dressing-room the real action started off-
screen.

It was a regular occurrence for the screen goddesses to
fall in love with their leading men during filming. Many
thought that an off-screen romance often enhanced the on-
screen performance. But this could cause problems. The
attentions of one Hollywood goddess turned a very professional male lead on so much that he could not help but get an
erection during their love scenes. Decency demanded that he
only be shot from the waist up.

These romances were best forgotten once the film was in
the can though. On the next film, there would be a new leading man and a new lover. The golden rule was that a star
should only marry her male lead after they had fallen in love
on three films together.

The Hollywood screen goddesses, however, did not
confine their attentions to just their fellow actors. They
were much more democratic than that. They slept with producers, stunt men, lighting men, millionaires, playwrights,

politicians and even members of the general public and, of course, directors.

Many stories have been told about the casting couch. Indeed, during Hollywood's heyday, it was a revered institution. Most would-be actresses did not go unwillingly to the movie moguls' sofas. Most leapt at the chance. Even outside the enchanted realm of Tinseltown, few women can resist the lure of wealth and power.

The wayward appetites of the Hollywood goddesses, of course, had to be covered up. The League of Decency, the Hays Office and women's clubs across America saw to that. On-screen, even the sexiest siren had to appear virginal until she was married. Even when playing married couples on screen they had to sleep in separate beds and keep one foot on the floor during a clinch.

Off-screen, they could be seen going to glamorous night-clubs with handsome escorts, who were, of course, 'just good friends'. Rising starlets were kept in line publicly by the morality clauses in their contracts. Once a star got big enough to do what they liked, the studio had so much invested in them that they hired teams of lawyers, PR men, tame journalists, bent cops, corrupt judges and general 'fixers' to hush up anything their hot property got involved in – up to, and including, murder.

If all else failed, they could get married. The studio would handle that too, though, on the whole, they preferred their stars to stay single – or more accurately, married to their audience.

Marriage in Tinseltown was not like marriage in the rest of the world. The words 'till death do us part' had been cut by the script editor. What could be done, could easily be undone. Many Hollywood marriages were over in the blinking of an eye. And there was always another one right around the corner

'People in Hollywood think marriage is a game of musical chairs,' as Grace Kelly's father said.

INTRODUCTION

The vows of fidelity were most definitely cut from the script of the average Hollywood marriage. Vivien Leigh, star of *Gone With The Wind*, once told a friend: 'I am an actress, a great actress. Great actresses have lovers, why not? I have a husband and I have lovers. Like Sarah Bernhardt.'

The whole point about the Hollywood actress is that her success makes her an object of sexual fantasy for a large part of the population of the planet. Once having tasted that god-like status, who the hell could resist taking advantage of it? Faced with this temptation – a beguiling maelstrom of power and gratification at its most exciting and unpredictable – would you go home to the same old spouse or lover, no matter how wonderful they were, night after night?

With the whole world hankering for your body, it would be downright uncharitable not to spread it around a bit. It would be your moral, and immoral, duty to satisfy yourself with as many lovers as you could manage. You would owe it to your public.

For the sleaze-hungry public, one of the most fascinating aspects of the screen sirens is that despite their power and privilege, they made the same stupid mistakes we all do. Their divine status did not save them from the everyday pitfalls of love. These goddesses' feet – and other parts – were made out of clay.

And therein lies the human comedy. Those raised above us are as prey to human fallibility as the rest of us. But for the great stars their every fault and foible is magnified as large as their own image on the screen. We are lucky. We can hide behind our anonymity. Our blushes are our own. For a screen goddess, a minor mishap means, at the very least, the front page of *Hollywood Confidential*. And worse, in years to come, long after you were dead perhaps, some scurrilous author will come along and record every embarrassment, detail every gaff and expose every secret shame with almost indecent relish.

But then, if you have the money, the looks and the house

INTRODUCTION

in Beverly Hills would you care? Obviously not. In fact, the
sexual misdemeanours of Hollywood stars are so copious
that there are more than one can decently fit into one book.

1

THE SILENT SIRENS

Few of the names of the early movie stars are now remembered, though their images are preserved by the magic of film – forever young, sexy and, sometimes, naked. Former Olympic swimming star Anne Kellerman was the first Hollywood goddess to set America drooling when she appeared naked on screen in 1916. She was quickly followed by the delectable shape of June Caprice and Audrey Munson in *Purity*. D.W. Griffith's classics *Birth of a Nation* and *Intolerance* positively overflowed with nudes; and the silent star Alla Nazimova shocked the nation with her dance of the seven veils in *Salome* – even though she kept the seventh veil on.

This was an oversight that Nazimova planned to rectify at a two-day party in 1921, held at her place, The Garden of Alla. Realizing that Nazimova's striptease was to be the climax of the event, Hollywood's other screen goddesses were determined to distract attention from the movies' first stripper by turning up in a state of extreme undress. Betty Blythe wore the costume from her recent role as the Queen of Sheba, which covered her breasts with a few strategically placed strings of pearls. Pearl White, Colleen More, Dorothy Gish

1

and Constance Talmadge were also there similarly *déshabillées*, along with Paramount's pure young star Mary Miles Minter, whose career was to end in scandal after the murder of leading man William Desmond Taylor. Among Taylor's collection of knickers, pornographic photographs and love letters was some intimate correspondence with Mabel Normand, with Minter – and with her mother. Apparently, unknown to each other, both mother and daughter had been working fervently at night to further Mary's career. Her virginal image was shattered and she, along with Normand, was forced into early retirement.

Mary Pickford failed to get into the swing of the party turning up as Little Lord Fauntleroy; but America's 'The Girl Who Was Too Beautiful', Barbara LaMarr, knew how Hollywood worked. She hung a sign outside her pool-side bungalow at the Garden of Alla saying: 'Come one come all'. And Barbara was true to her word. By the age of sixteen she had worked her way via the Ziegfeld Follies to Mack Sennett's lot. In the next ten years, she went through six husbands and thousands of lovers.

'Lovers,' she said, 'are like roses – best by the dozen.'

She died at the age of 26, probably of exhaustion.

If this was not enough to upstage Nazimova's striptease, when Alla's music started twenty naked girls jumped shrieking into the swimming pool, which was shaped like the Black Sea to remind Nazimova, who came from the Crimea, of home, it is said. They were followed by every man who could swim and a few who could not. Nazimova retired, sulking, to her bungalow.

Although, as one of the first on-screen sex goddesses, Nazimova set men's pulses racing, she was, in fact, a lesbian. She even seduced Charlie Chaplin's first wife Mildred Harris, prompting their divorce. Her sexual preference did not stop Nazimova furthering her career on the casting couch, though. She would regularly be summoned by studio boss Lewis J. Selznick, David O.'s father. He was well known for his peccadilloes. When any attractive young actress turned up in his office, he immediately warned them not to waste his time. He never spoke to women with their clothes on. Once they were naked, he would produce a riding crop and ask them whether they were prepared to suffer for their art. Even his stars knew what was expected of them and, knowing Nazimova's sexual preferences, he took great delight in summoning her to his office in the afternoons and getting her to perform for him. In the light of this, Darryl F. Zanuck dubbed Nazimova the 'queen of the movie whores'.

Another graduate of the Sennett casting couch was Gloria Swanson – no woman was ever allowed in the Sennett lot without first satisfying him of their love of the movie business. Swanson had got into films through actor and female impersonator Wallace Beery, another devotee of the riding crop who became her first husband. But Gloria's star turn was as mistress of another movie mogul, Joseph Kennedy, father of Jack, Bobby and Edward – the bootlegger turned producer who had gone into the movie business with the sole intention of sleeping with his stars.

Swanson met Kennedy in 1927. Within two months, he had set up Gloria Swanson Productions Inc. and had taken control of her affairs. Then he decided to exercise his *droit de seigneur*, turning up uninvited at her hotel in Palm Beach.

According to Swanson: 'He just stood there, in his white flannels and his argyle sweater and his two-toned shoes, staring at me for a full minute or more, before he entered the room and closed the door behind him. He moved so quickly that his mouth was on mine before either of us could speak. With one hand he held the back of my head, with the other he stroked my body and pulled at my kimono. He kept insisting in a drawn-out moan, 'No longer, no longer. Now.' He was like a roped horse, rough, arduous, racing to be free. After a hasty climax he lay beside me, stroking my hair. Apart from his guilty, passionate mutterings, he had still said nothing cogent.'

Kennedy said that he wanted Gloria to have his baby and even introduced her to his wife. But the church stepped in when Kennedy asked permission to set up home with Swanson. Cardinal O'Connor begged Swanson to stop seeing Kennedy. He dropped her with the coming of sound, when he found she was no longer in demand. After two flops, Swanson discovered that the extravagant gifts Kennedy had plied her with had been bought with money rifled from her own company.

Swanson was a survivor. She made her last film in 1974 at the age of seventy-seven. One silent siren who was not was Olive Thomas. She came from a mining town in Pennsylvania where, at the age of ten, she started posing nude with her grown-up brothers for pornographic photographs. She was married at twelve to a twenty-six-year-old miner who liked to show Olive off naked to his drunken friends. Sometimes he would get her to give a demonstration of her sexual skills before an invited audience of pals.

At fourteen, she stole the bus fare and ran away to New York, where she made her way to the Ziegfeld Follies. Florenz Ziegfeld was well known for his taste for young flesh and no girl worked for him unless she graduated from the casting couch in his office. Olive had no problem with this. In the revealing costumes she had to wear for the shows, her transcendent beauty made her the star of the Follies and she was painted nude by the Peruvian artist, Alberto Vargas.

Olive's early life left her with a craving for rough sex. This presented Ziegfeld with a problem as make-up could not always hide the welts and bruises on the glorious young hide of his underaged star. The solution was to send her to Lewis J. Selznick.

Most girls found Selznick's manner intimidating, but Olive walked straight up to his couch and said: 'So this is where I get laid?' By that afternoon she was under contract and soon became a star as the virginal heroine of such movies as *Betty Takes a Hand*, *Prudence on Broadway* and

The Follies Girl.

A series of articles under her name counselled young girls to cultivate everything that was clean, wholesome and American. Meanwhile, she was dulling herself with booze and drugs, appearing naked and available as the star turn at the drunken orgies Selznick arranged for movie buyers.

To complete the fairytale image, Olive needed a husband. She found the perfect candidate in the clean-cut Jack Pickford, Mary's brother. He was cast as the 'ideal American boy' in such movies as *Seventeen* and *Tomboy*. Magazines wrote them up as the 'ideal couple'. Selznick promoted the match for all it was worth. However, Pickford did not quite live up to his mom-and-apple-pie image – he was a heroin addict.

It was not that she did not like sex with her husband, but there were so many other men in the world. So Olive set off on her honeymoon unencumbered by Jack. In Paris, she set out on a wild bout of drugs and sex. She was seen in the lowest dives of Montmartre with notorious French gangsters. On the morning of 10 September 1922, she was found naked, sprawled on the floor of her suite in the Hotel Crillon on the Place de la Concorde, clutching a bottle of bichloride of mercury capsules – a cure for syphilis which often proved lethal. The resulting scandal ruined Selznick. Though far from innocent, he was branded as the man who had corrupted the sweet young girl the world had seen flickering on the silent screen. Olive Thomas was just twenty when she died.

Marion Davies survived rather better, physically at least. She died in 1961 at the age of sixty-four. Her reputation has taken a mauling, though. She was the long-time mistress of William Randolph Hearst and unfairly portrayed as a talentless bimbette in the movie *Citizen Kane*. In fact, she was a talented actress and made more than forty films, co-starring with the likes of Clark Gable, Gary Cooper, Pat O'Brien, Bing Crosby, Leslie Howard and Robert Montgomery. Despite her childhood stammer, she was one of the few silent stars to make it through into the era of the talkies.

Born Marion Cecilia Douras in Brooklyn, she was another starlet who began her career on Flo Ziegfeld's casting couch. She was just fourteen. She attended parties given by Elsie Janis designed to introduce showgirls to wealthy men, and soon attracted a considerable following of stage-door Johnnies who bombarded her with expensive gifts. Among them was newspaper proprietor Paul Block. It was through Block that she met Hearst. At the time, she was seventeen; Hearst was fifty-two and married.

She was at a party with Block when she first met Hearst. She was getting ready to leave. When she went into the bedroom to get her wrap, Hearst followed her.

'I'd like to see you soon,' he said, pressing a Tiffany watch into her hand. She was impressed and eager to show her gratitude. The watch was far more expensive than anything Block had given her. Besides, Block had taken up with another showgirl, sixteen-year-old Dorothy Mackaill.

Then disaster struck, Marion lost the watch. It slipped from her wrist and fell into a snowdrift. She was too embarrassed to phone Hearst, but her friend, fellow showgirl Pickles St Claire, called him. Within twenty-four hours, another identical watch arrived by special messenger.

The course of true love never ran smooth and Marion's mother took against the match. In an effort to save her daughter from what she thought were the unsuitable attentions of a married man, Mrs Douras took Marion to Florida to stay with James Deering. However, Deering was another wealthy man with an eye for young girls, so it was a case of out of the frying pan into the fire.

Marion resisted his advances, temporarily slipped the leash and headed off to Palm Beach, where Hearst and his wife of twelve years were staying with their newly born son. She was out cycling with Gene Buck, a songwriter for Flo Ziegfeld, when she spotted Hearst's car. Marion swerved and fell off her bike. She lay sprawled in the road in an extremely provocative position. Hearst's car stopped. The great man got out and rushed to her assistance.

The chauffeur put Marion's bike in the boot and, despite the fact that his wife was in the car, Hearst took Marion to a doctor. Although Marion pretended to be a stranger, Millicent, Hearst's wife, twigged who she was. She knew of her husband's affair and tolerated it. Although she had once been a showgirl herself, she had endeavoured to transform herself into a socialite and looked down on Hearst's indiscretions. In fact, Millicent Hearst was much closer to the dumb peroxide blonde of Orson Welles's movie than Marion Davies ever was.

A mysterious 'Carl Fisher' began calling Marion at the Deering residence. There was no doubt in anyone's mind that this was Hearst. Assignations were arranged and Marion managed, every so often, to give her mother and Deering the slip to meet up with her bashful lover.

Marion knew that Hearst's attraction to her lay in the fact that she could stand up to him better than anyone else. She also knew that she would lose her power over him if he thought he could possess her completely. So she played on his fears by seeing other men. In response, in a futile attempt to prove his love for her, he showered her with gifts and filled her dressing-room at the Follies every night with peach-coloured roses.

He once sent her a diamond bracelet with a note attached, which said: 'Send me to Marion. I've heard a lot about her and I must see her.'

Marion was so touched by the note that she asked Hearst for the pencil he had used to write it. When he discovered that he had lost that particular pencil, he presented her with some shavings he had found in a pencil sharpener that he swore were from the same pencil. She sealed them in an envelope and kept them until she died. Over the next thirty-five years, she would amass a lot of such trivial keepsakes, which she treasured far more than the expensive gifts he gave her.

Although she continued to see other men, she took care not to alienate his affections. She sent a relative and a friend around to Block's apartment to purloin any evidence of their affair that Block, Hearst's rival in the newspaper industry, might be tempted to use at a later date.

Hearst naturally used his papers to promote Marion's career. Her picture began appearing in Hearst newspapers with captions saying that she was 'the type of chorus girl who marries captains of industry and coronets'. Another caption read: 'For every man there's "one dangerous girl"'.

Handwritten poems from Hearst would turn up in Marion's dressing-room. One read:

The Cynic's Love Song

I had a little lady whose name was May
Her eyes were bright, her teeth were white,
her smile was sweet and gay
She smiled at me and I was hers forever and for aye,
But she smiled at many others in the self-same way...
I had another lady love whose name was Ruth.
She told me all her secrets with the innocence of youth.
She said I was her only love but when I hired a sleuth,
I found she'd told me everything except the truth...

I love a girl named Marion, she holds me in the thrall
Of her blue eyes and gold hair and figure lithe and tall.
She loves me too, she tells me so – alas that isn't all.
She likewise loves Flo, Charlie, Henry,
Nealie, Joe and Paul.

Even though he knew about these other men in her life, Hearst went right on loving her. In 1920, she received another poem which read:

The Bungalow is on the bum
  the studio is stupid.
For life is slow unless there's some
  companionship with Cupid.

Mars is all right to strive and fight
  and from our foes to screen us
But there are times when thoughts and rhymes
  turn longingly to Venus.

So while I write with much delight
  of armies and of navies
The sweetest thing of which I sing
The Muse to whom my soul I fling
The idol to whose feet I cling
  is lovely Marion Davies.

Despite his image as a ruthless tycoon who was credited with starting the Spanish-American war to sell more newspapers, Hearst was just a great big softie and Marion began to fall in love with him.

When Hearst entered politics, he had to terminate their trysts. To get him back, Marion resumed her affair with Paul Block and other old boyfriends.

Hearst was so obsessed with her that her flagrant infidelity enflamed new passion in him. At the time, he was standing as the Democratic candidate for mayor of New York. His opponent, Al Smith, put it about that Hearst was the type of man who 'took up with young actresses'. Hearst was forced to withdraw from the race.

Marion went on Hearst's payroll in 1917, but she was not his full-time mistress and continued her career on the stage. Film offers began to roll in. Hearst himself had been producing short films and newsreels since 1913, but he did not encourage Marion in that direction. He still intended to divorce Millicent and marry Marion, and her duties as Mrs

Hearst would make it impossible for her to pursue a film career.

Nevertheless, through her brother-in-law, Marion got the leading role in a movie called *Runaway, Romany* which was bankrolled by Paul Block. To Marion's horror, Hearst burst into the first screening. The film was truly awful, but Hearst saw Marion's on-screen potential.

'I'm going to make you a star, Marion,' he said. It meant that she could never be Mrs Hearst.

Under Hearst's direction, Marion starred in a hastily conceived cliff-hanger serial called *Betty Fairfax*. It was a flop. Her next pictures were declared masterpieces by the Hearst press. Although the public saw through this, rival studio bosses slowly recognized that audiences were responding to Marion as a star and her movie career took off.

Marion repaid Hearst by taking a series of lovers. Although she enjoyed sex, her real pleasure came from the fact that she knew she was being watched, and, of course, Hearst and his spies were watching. So were movie audiences. Her films opened to critical acclaim and bumper box-office receipts.

In *Little Old New York*, Marion had to appear disguised as a man. Hearst enjoyed seeing her in men's clothes so much that cross-dressing scenes were written into half-a-dozen more films.

In order to further her film career, Marion was seen around town with the notorious stud Charlie Chaplin. She even got Chaplin invited to a party on board Hearst's yacht, the *Onedia*. The party was in honour of the producer Thomas Ince, who Hearst was trying to do a deal with. Also present was Louella Parsons, then a little-known journalist. The champagne flowed freely. Marion got a bit frisky and disappeared into a cabin with one of the guests.

When Hearst went looking for her, he found her half undressed making love to a man. Hearst took one look and went to get his gun. Marion began to scream and her lover beat a hasty retreat.

Hearing the screams, Ince came running. He put his arms around Marion and was trying to calm her down when Hearst returned with a pistol. Misreading the situation, Hearst thought that Ince was the man who had been making love to Marion and shot him in the temple, killing him.

Once they had time to reflect, everyone on board agreed that a scandal would damage them all. The story, they decided, was to be that Ince had never even been on board the yacht. He had suffered a bout of acute indigestion, headed back to Hollywood and had died of natural causes in his car. A compliant coroner, eager to do a favour for a man of the stature of Mr Hearst, confirmed this and Ince was cremated a few days later, no questions asked.

Ince's widow was squared with a $5 million trust fund provided by Hearst. Louella Parsons became a syndicated Hollywood gossip columnist on Hearst's newspapers, while Chaplin slipped quietly away. It has often been noticed that Ince bore a striking resemblance to Chaplin and many believe that it was Chaplin who Hearst had disturbed making love to Marion.

Marion enjoyed being hostess at San Simeon, Hearst's California castle. Guests there included Albert Einstein, George Bernard Shaw, Charles Lindbergh, Winston Churchill and the notorious satyr Joe Kennedy with his mistress Gloria Swanson. When the talkies came, Marion took a sound test and was one of the few silent stars to have her contract renewed – though her career at Warner's was to last only three more years.

She retired to San Simeon with Hearst, but refused to let him divorce his wife and marry her as it would give rivals a powerful weapon against him. In 1941, the gaff was blown wide open. Hearst's life and his relationship with Marion Davies were ruthlessly satirized in Orson Welles's film *Citizen Kane*. The scriptwriter Herman Mankiewicz had discovered, probably from Marion's confidante, silent star

Louise Brooks, that Hearst's pet name for Marion's clitoris was 'Rosebud'. It is the first word in the film. The whole movie is about reporters' attempts to find out what 'Rosebud' means. At the end of the picture, 'Rosebud', which is the name on the young Kane's toboggan, is seen blistering and burning in the furnace at Xanadu, Welles's version of San Simeon.

Marion Davies remained with Hearst until his death in 1951. Ten weeks later, she married Captain Horace Brown of the US Maritime Service. Eight months after that she filed for divorce. Horace heard about it on the radio; Marion had failed to tell her husband. Instead, in true Hollywood style, she had given the glad tidings to gossip columnist Hedda Hopper.

By this time Marion's health was failing. There was a reconciliation and Horace was at her bedside when she died on 22 September 1961. The funeral was a proper Hollywood affair. Telegrams of condolence came from three US presidents and the pallbearers included Joseph Kennedy, Bing Crosby, Glenn Ford, Dick Powell and Raoul Walsh. It was a send-off befitting a star and a woman whose clitoris has a unique place in movie history.

2

PANDORA'S BOX

Louise Brooks was one of the great cult stars of the silent era. The quintessential flapper, she quit Hollywood to become the sex goddess of the European film industry – where she made three masterpieces of the silent era.

Louise came from a normal, well-adjusted American family – her mother was a frigid man hater, while her father had a formidable reputation as a ladies' man. Well into his ninety-third year, he was still having his way with the family's maid and he had his hearing aid specially adjusted so that he could eavesdrop on the people next door making love. Louise took after him and her sexual curiosity soon got her into trouble. At the age of nine, she was molested by a forty-five-year-old house painter. At fourteen, she had a fling with an artist who wanted her to pose nude for him. Her diary entries show that there were a number of other boys on the scene at the time. At fifteen, she joined a contemporary dance troupe and had an affair with the company's publicist, who called her 'Hell Cat'. Soon rumours were circulating that she had slept with the entire backstage crew and she was dismissed.

She moved on to Broadway, appearing in George White's Scandals which was like Ziegfeld's Follies, only the

13

girls wore less clothing.

'There were large quantities of gorgeous costumes on the girls of the chorus,' wrote one critic, 'most of them from the neck up and the shoes down.'

Louise soon attracted the attentions of a large number of stage-door Johnnies and attended the parties laid on for the chorusgirls to meet wealthy men.

'In New York in 1924, there was a hand-picked group of beautiful girls who were invited to parties given for great men in finance and government,' Louise later wrote. 'We had to be fairly well bred and of absolute integrity – never endangering the great men with threats of publicity or blackmail. At these parties we were not required, like common whores, to go to bed with any man who asked us, but if we did the profits were great. Money, jewels, mink coats, a film job – you name it.'

One of the men she met at these parties who took a particular shine to her was the Canadian newspaper magnate Lord Beaverbrook, who she described as 'an ugly little grey man who went directly to his object with no finesse'.

Louise created a sensation by dressing as scantily offstage as on. One of her gowns was barebacked and slashed at the front to the navel.

'Sitting at a restaurant or nightclub table,' she recalled, 'I was a nearly naked sight to behold.'

Her revealing dresses and the goings-on in her room got her evicted from the Algonquin. She moved to another hotel but was asked to leave when people in the next building complained of seeing her exercising on the roof in flimsy pyjamas.

Louise quit the Scandals without notice and headed off to Europe, where she became, in popular myth, the first girl to dance the Charleston in London. Back in New York, Ziegfeld snapped her up for his new Follies. Although he paid well, Louise subsidized her income by posing for nude photographs.

She was also taken up by a millionaire named John Lock. Louise became his mistress and he moved her into an expensive apartment. Despite this lucrative arrangement, Louise found it impossible to confine her favours to just one man. When Lock dropped around one night, he found Louise naked in the passionate embrace of a screenwriter named Townsend Martin. Not only did they not stop, Louise invited Lock to join in. He refused.

Louise lost her apartment and her job. Ziegfeld could not afford to have any tasteless scandal touch his girls.

Martin suggested that she try out for the movies and introduced her to Walter Wanger, head of production at Famous Players-Lasky who were still making movies on Long Island.

At the interview in his office, Wanger asked Louise what made her think she had what it took to make it in the movies. She took off her clothes, lay down on the couch and showed him. He put her under contract and when Famous Players-Lasky, which later became part of Paramount, moved to Hollywood, Louise moved with them.

Her first film was *The American Venus*, which was set behind the scenes at the Miss America pageant and provided an opportunity to show off a great deal of naked female flesh. The film would make Louise an erotic icon.

Louise's first major Hollywood affair was with Charlie Chaplin. It lasted two months. They often spent the weekend naked in an erotic foursome with Louise's best friend and well-known lesbian Peggy Fears and film financier A.C. Blumenthal.

At the time, Chaplin was convinced that iodine prevented VD. One night at the Ambassador Hotel, he painted his entire genitalia and came charging at Louise and Peggy with a bright red erection.

'He was a sophisticated lover,' Louise recalled. 'But his passion for young girls, his Lolita obsession, left him deeply convinced that he could seduce a girl only with his position as a director and star-maker.'

When *The American Venus* was released, the New York photographer tried to cash in by selling the nude photographs he had taken of Louise when she was a Follies girl. Louise attempted to have them suppressed.

'I intend to be married eventually,' she told the newspapers, 'and what do you suppose my husband would say if every time he picks up a newspaper or walks up Broadway he is confronted with a photograph of his wife clad in only a lacy shawl.'

Justifying posing nude in the first place, she said that she had supposed it to be the only way to get her foot on the first rung of the ladder to success; and they were very artistic.

'I pictured myself in the Louvre trying to imitate various works of the old masters,' she said. 'Mr De Mirjian was very kind and as the poses necessitated the gradual removal of the kimono I had brought with me, he very delicately replaced it with other drapes, which he hung about my body. I was in the studio for about two hours and a half, and when I was dismissed, hurried into my clothes and felt none the worse for my experience.'

Even though De Mirjian hinted darkly that he had a number of pictures of prominent socialites similarly unclad, he was forced to withdraw his pictures from sale. As Louise spent much of her time in *The American Venus* virtually naked, the scandal actually helped advance her career.

In 1926, when Louise was in *It's the Old Army Game* with W.C. Fields, the director Eddie Sutherland fell in love with her. The two of them would sneak off the set between takes to make love. When shooting was over, Sutherland began bombarding her with proposals of marriage, although he was a well-known playboy whose recent marriage had ended in a lightning divorce. Louise accepted but while wedding plans were being made, she fell in love with Buster Collier, the twenty-four-year-old co-star of her next picture *Just Another Blonde* – 'the only actor I ever cared for'.

Although Collier was in love with another silent star, Constance Talmadge, they both abandoned their other loves during the making of *Just Another Blonde*. On the set, Louise and Collier spent every moment together and often posed for unashamedly candid shots.

Sutherland knew nothing of Louise's relationship with Collier. He had been out at the coast and flew back to New York for the wedding. Their honeymoon consisted of two days in the Ambassador's before Sutherland flew back to California, leaving Louise free to continue her infidelity. Her next film was called *Love 'em and Leave 'em*.

Pressure of work kept Louise and her husband apart almost constantly but that did not mean that Louise's sex life was on hold. She would regularly spend time in the Ambassador Hotel with Peggy Fears, A.C. Blumenthal and – to make up the foursome – the director George Preston Marshall. Louise even found time for secret assignations with Marshall in Havana.

On-screen Louise began to appear in men's clothing. Audiences were intrigued about her sexuality. She experimented with lesbianism, spending the night with Greta Garbo, and was often to be found in the company of homosexual men.

Louise had a one-night stand with Jack Pickford. This came to the attention of the notorious lesbian and gossip Pepi Lederer. Next morning, everyone in Hollywood – including Sutherland and Pickford's then girlfriend Bebe Daniels – knew about the affair. Sutherland complained that Louise's infidelity had driven him to impotence and headed for the psychiatrist's couch. Meanwhile, she filed for divorce. He attempted suicide but eventually recovered, as Louise put it, 'aided by a flow of parties and pretty extra girls'. Louise herself returned to the arms of George Marshall.

Louise was becoming increasingly popular at the box office but she had a reputation for being unreliable and difficult to work with, partly because of her hectic sex life.

Her contract with Paramount came up at a time when the talkies were coming in and the general jitters that were spreading though the industry meant the studios were being particularly hard on the actors. Paramount boss Ben Schulberg told Louise that she could stay on if she took a pay cut to $750 a week – a tenth of what Clara Bow was getting. Louise told him what he could do with his offer. The German film-maker George W. Pabst had already offered her $1,000 a week to come to Berlin and star in *Pandora's Box*.

In mid-Atlantic, a cable from Flo Ziegfeld arrived for Louise on board the S.S. Majestic. It offered Louise the part of Dixie Dugan in a Broadway production of *Showgirl*. The part could have been written for her. But Marshall intercepted the cable before it even got to Louise. He was intent on a long break in Europe and tossed the cable overboard without even showing it to her, then cabled back: 'You couldn't offer me enough money to do it.' He signed Louise's name to the cable and that was the end of her career in the US.

Louise was immediately at home in the decadence of Berlin.

'Sex was the business of the town,' she wrote. 'At the Eden Hotel, where I lived, the café bar was lined with the higher-priced trollops. The economy girls walked the street outside. On the corner stood the girls in boots, advertising flagellation. Actors' agents pimped for the ladies in luxury apartments in the Bavarian Quarter. Racetrack touts at the Hoppegarten arranged orgies for groups of sportsmen. The nightclub Eldorado displayed an enticing line of homosexuals dressed as women. At the Maly, there was a choice of feminine or collar-and-tie lesbians.'

Another American in Europe, Josephine Baker, had just caused a sensation there with her revue *Chocolatte Kiddies*. In it, she appeared nude except for a girdle of bananas.

Before filming even started, Louise had created a sensation simply by being offered the part of Lulu in *Pandora's Box*. It was probably the most famous female leading role in

German literature. Lulu is a woman whose brazen sexuality devastates middle-class society around her. When the playwright, Benjamin Franklin (Frank) Wedekind, had first introduced the character of Lulu in the play *Erdgeist* in 1898, he had been condemned by church and state as an 'arch-pornographer' and jailed for satirizing German society and thereby libelling the Kaiser. When Pabst decided to film the second of Wedekind's Lulu plays, *Pandora's Box*, he went on a two-year hunt for Lulu. Sixteen hundred girls were tested for the part. Pabst turned down Marlene Dietrich. He did not even consider Greta Garbo, who he had discovered in 1921. But when he saw Louise Brooks in Howard Hawks's *A Girl in Every Port*, he knew he had found his Lulu.

'Endlich die Lulu ist gefunden!' proclaimed the headlines – 'Lulu is finally found.'

Louise enjoyed the attention the film brought her. During filming, the intimate love scenes with her co-star Gustav Diessel were shot with only Pabst himself present. However, the picture fell foul of the censors – even in France – for its frank depiction of sex, lesbianism, incest and prostitution. More than a third of the film was cut. In America, the final scene where Lulu dies at the hands of Jack the Ripper, was reshot with Lulu joining the Salvation Army instead. The film, predictably, bombed.

Worse was to come. Back in Hollywood, Louise refused to reshoot her silent movies in sound to spite Paramount, despite the offer of a $10,000 bonus. In retaliation, Schulberg put the word out that her voice did not record well.

She returned to Europe with Townsend Martin to film *Prix de Beauté* with René Clair but arrived in Paris to find that the movie was not going ahead.

When in a Paris café Martin started paying more attention to Lady Fellowes than to Louise, she slashed his face with a bunch of roses. Pabst witnessed the scene and took Louise under his wing. She rewarded him with a one-night stand. Although a married man, Pabst had a lively interest in women and sex. He had one of world's greatest collections of nude pictures. Louise later commented that it was 'the best sexual performance of my career'. She then took up with a half-English, half-Swedish boy who she called the Eskimo. Nevertheless, Pabst cast her as the lead in his next movie, *The Diary of a Lost Girl*.

Pabst banned the Eskimo from the film set, so Louise took up with muscle-bound cameraman Sepp Allgeier, the boyfriend of her co-star and rival Leni Riefenstahl. Riefenstahl got her own back by making up to Pabst. In the movie, Louise played a prostitute who ends up in a reformatory run by a sadistic lesbian, played by Valeska Gert. In real life, Louise and Gert began going out together to gay clubs, which further irritated Pabst.

Again the censors butchered the film and it was ignored by critics and public alike, who now had no time for silent films. It was never released in the US. Louise eventually made *Prix de Beauté*, which met a similar fate. Cut off from Hollywood, unable to speak French or German, Louise could find no work in the talkies that had now spread to Europe. She had no choice but to return to the US. She was just twenty-three and at the height of her beauty, but she would never play a leading role in a movie again.

Louise began to be seen out again with Eddie Sutherland and there were rumours that they would remarry. But then she was seen out with a lot of people, both male and female. One of her escorts was Paul Bern, who committed suicide shortly after marrying Jean Harlow. Eventually, she was given a contract by Columbia, but mucked up this last chance by refusing to sleep with Harry Cohn. She was forced to sit in his outer office while other girls walked in and out for his afternoon sessions on the casting couch. The trouble was, a friend observed, she was too degenerate for one part of Hollywood and not degenerate enough for the other.

She turned down a small part in the first picture she was offered. Then she took a role in a film made by Fatty

Arbuckle, who was desperately trying to make a comeback. His career had collapsed after a girl had died as the result of a sexual encounter with Arbuckle at an orgy in his hotel room in San Francisco. Association with Arbuckle did Louise no good. Soon she was broke. In 1932, she went bankrupt and was saved from the gutter by George Marshall.

In a desperate attempt to get back on her feet, she started a dance act with Chicago playboy Deering Davis. Then she made the mistake of marrying him. They split up a week after the end of their first club engagement.

'I hate marriage,' she said. They never saw each other again.

Although she had a string of other lovers, male and female, George Marshall continued to support her. A brief affair with Humphrey Bogart brought her a bit part in *Empty Saddles*. A six-month affair with singing cowboy Jack Randall brought a few more walk-ons. She did her career no good by refusing to sleep with producer Raymond Griffith. Her last $2,000 was sunk in a swindle by conman Fletcher Crandall who used her to front his bogus Brooks-O'Shea Studios. When it collapsed, Crandall went to jail and Louise took the train back home to Kansas.

Even in the Midwest she could not behave. She teamed up with nude model Danny Aikman, who claimed to be the most outrageous man in Wichita.

She drank to excess and supported herself by teaching dancing, though she made the papers when she was caught by a jealous wife teaching her husband 'ballroom dancing horizontally in bed'. Then she was arrested under Kansas statute for 'lewd cohabitation'.

Run out of Kansas with just $10 in her pocket, Louise headed back to New York, where she got some work on the radio. She had an affair with Sam Colt, heir to the famous gun company, and hung out with Tallulah Bankhead. She subsidized her radio career with some discreet prostitution, entertaining rich, older men for a price; and she wrote a book, a thinly veiled autobiographical novel called *Naked on My Goat*. It detailed the heroine's erotic adventures with easily identifiable people, some of whom were still alive, which made publication impossible.

She spent the following years as a kept woman. She nearly married an Irishman named James Dunne, but he was a Catholic and she a divorcee. The affair broke up after she spewed up over him in a New York restaurant. She was neither ill nor drunk; it was just a tasteless practical joke. Then she started a sadomasochistic relationship with a Marine from Fort Dix while cultivating a lesbian relationship with a woman called Butch, whom her Marine had designs on too.

Her last great love affair was with James Card, the curator of the Kodak International Museum of Photography in Rochester, New York, who did much to re-establish her reputation as a screen actress by showing her films at the Museum. The affair was as torrid, passionate and fraught as any in her life. Her tempestuous presence at the Museum and their scandalous trips to Europe almost cost Card his job. But Card would not leave his wife and dropped Louise when he feared that keeping up with her ferocious capacity for drink was turning him into an alcoholic.

In the 1960s, thanks largely to Card, *Pandora's Box* became a cult movie and Louise Brooks was rediscovered as a sex goddess. Critic Ken Tynan called her the 'most sexual image of Woman ever committed to celluloid'. In her personal life, he said, she was an unrepentant hedonist – 'the only pure pleasure-seeker I have ever known'. She condemned Tynan's profile of her in *The New Yorker* as 'sex gossip', but it made her a celebrity again.

She took the opportunity to spill the beans on her own sex life and the debauchery of the film industry in her memoirs *Lulu in Hollywood*. Louise Brooks died of a heart attack in 1985 at the age of seventy-eight. Even now, some still think of her as the sexiest of all the Hollywood stars.

3

THE 'IT GIRL'

Clara Bow was another silent siren who fell from grace with the coming of the talkies. By the end of 1929, she was the highest-paid star in Hollywood. The most unashamedly sexy of Tinseltown's flappers, she became the 'It Girl' in 1926, when she starred in the movie version of Elinor Glyn's study of sex appeal called *It*. She was brought down, not by the broad Brooklyn accent which clashed hideously with her sophisticated on-screen image as is often assumed, but by the decade's most withering sex scandal. Given Clara's background, this was hardly surprising.

Clara Bow was born in the squalor of a turn-of-the-century Brooklyn tenement block. Her father, Robert Bow, was busboy in a cheap hash joint. He enjoyed drinking, whoring and wifebeating. Her mother, Sarah, was an asexual woman who hated men, but had to prostitute herself to survive during her husband's periodic walk-outs. While she entertained her clients, Clara was locked in a cupboard with her fingers in her ears so she could not hear the noises her mother and her new 'uncle' were making on the bed. There in the cupboard Clara, retreated into an imaginary world.

As a teenager, she became fascinated by the movies. They offered her all the glamour and romance her squalid existence lacked. When she was not actually at the movies, she was absorbed in one of the many celebrity magazines that detailed the glittering lives of the Hollywood stars.

Her mother condemned the stars Clara idealized as whores. At the age of sixteen, behind her mother's back, Clara entered a talent contest in a movie magazine. Her father paid for the photographs required. They were awful, but Clara delivered them to the magazine in person. The manager of the contest was impressed by her looks and offered Clara a screen test there and then. She went on to win the competition and was offered a part in the movie *Beyond the Rainbow* alongside a number of Ziegfeld girls.

When her mother discovered what was happening, she decided to kill Clara rather than let her become a 'Hollywood whore'. One night while Clara was asleep, she crept into her bedroom with a butcher's knife and tried to stab her. Clara awoke in time to defend herself, but it left her with a lifelong case of insomnia. Her mother was committed to a mental hospital where she died.

With his wife gone, Clara's father demanded that the sixteen-year-old undertake all the conjugal duties. Clara cooked and cleaned. He wanted more and when she refused, he raped her. She had a love-hate relationship with him ever after and never could quite get him out of her life.

Unlike the Ziegfeld girls, Clara had no idea what was required of her in the movie business. When she refused to sleep with the director, she found her part in *Beyond the Rainbow* on the cutting-room floor.

Clara soon realized her mistake and rectified it by falling for Arthur Jacobson. He was one of the founder members of the Film Guild and was shooting a movie version of the F. Scott Fitzgerald story *Grit*. Under his loving attention, she was scouted by Preferred Pictures, who gave her the train fare to Hollywood.

As she was underage, the studio appointed an agent, Maxine Alton, to look after Clara's interests and to act as a chaperone. When Artie Jacobson turned up in Hollywood,

Alton tried to prevent them seeing each other. She also prevented Clara bringing her father from New York to stay with her. When Clara caught Alton having sex with studio boss Ben Schulberg, she had her fired.

Soon Clara was well on the way to becoming a star. She hired a house on Hollywood Boulevard for herself, her father and Artie Jacobson. This arrangement caused all kinds of problems. Robert Bow spent his time getting disgracefully drunk and picking up young female extras. Although he tolerated Jacobson, he grew violently jealous of any other man around Clara. One night he tried to shoot a visiting director. Only Jacobson's intervention prevented Clara's father killing the man.

Then forty-nine-year-old Robert Bow picked up eighteen-year-old Ella Mowery and married her. When he brought her home, Clara threw her out. A month later in the divorce courts, Robert Bow, who admitted being dependent on his daughter, was ordered to pay $15 a month alimony.

On top of their mutual jealousy, father and daughter also fought like husband and wife. When Los Angeles columnist Grace Kingsley came to interview Clara, she found herself in a food fight, with Clara and her father throwing macaroni – the only dish Robert had mastered – at each other. Jacobson ushered the bespattered columnist out.

Clara, it must be said, had some pretty strange ways. She refused to let her dog out of doors, so she had the floor of one room in the house covered with soil for it to use as a toilet.

Although Robert Bow tolerated Jacobson as his daughter's lover, he refused to let her marry him. The two decided to elope to Santa Ana but they fell out on the way and returned to Los Angeles. Jacobson moved out of Clara's house shortly afterwards.

Under the direction of Ernst Lubitsch, Clara began to get sexier parts. Lubitsch had found a way to get round the Hays Office code by showing little on-screen but suggesting everything. Her Cupid's bow lips and her tight dresses soon became a trademark while, off-screen, she progressed her career by flirting shamelessly with anyone and everyone.

She made another career move by bedding Sam Jaffe, Schulberg's brother-in-law and Preferred's production manager. The affair ended when Schulberg's wife, Adeline, brought a nice Jewish girl over from New York for Jaffe to marry.

Clara then fell for her co-star in the movie *The Plastic Age*, handsome Mexican ex-bullfighter Gilbert Roland, whose real name was Luis Antonio Damaso de Alonso. She called him Amigo. The affair, Clara later admitted, was her 'first really big love experience'. Robert Bow was beside himself with jealousy.

The Plastic Age turned Clara into 'the hottest jazz baby in films', the *New York Times* gushed. While Clara was still under contract for $750 a week to Preferred, Schulberg had no difficulty hiring her out to other studios for $3,000 a week.

Preferred Pictures were taken over by Paramount. In exchange, Schulberg got to make any film he wanted. He chose to supervise Clara's career personally, hitching himself to her rising star. The first thing he did was plant a story that Clara was having an affair with another of his actors, Donald Keith. Clara, Keith and Roland all benefitted from the resulting publicity over their supposed love triangle – as, of course, did Schulberg, who had them all under contract.

With the might of Paramount behind her, Clara quickly became a big star and was given the female lead in *Mantrap*, directed by Victor Fleming. Fleming was fresh from an affair with Norma Shearer and a well-known womanizer. At the time he was going out with actress Alice White, but twenty-year-old Clara soon fell under the spell of the forty-three-year-old director. On the set, he treated her with the utmost respect, as if she were a talent of limitless potential. She responded, off the set, by giving him her body.

She had more or less moved in with Roland by this time,

who was driven half insane with jealousy. Not only did he have to contend with Fleming, her star status attracted a string of admirers. Yale drop-out Robert Savage travelled from New York and wangled an invitation to one of her parties. He boasted that Clara had kissed him and called him her 'poet lover'. Threatening suicide if she spurned him, he persuaded her to meet him for lunch. Afterwards, he drove her to the Marriage License Bureau, despite her protests. Fortunately, they were delayed in traffic and arrived five minutes after the Bureau had closed for the day.

Clara blocked any further contact. Savage responded with a mock suicide. When the police were called, they arrived to find him languishing on a sofa holding a picture of Clara and one last poem to his beloved, and dripping blood from two superficial wrist wounds.

At his sanity hearing, Savage admitted staging the whole thing for love of Clara.

'I'll get her yet,' he told the judge.

Clara called a press conference and declared: 'Real men don't slash their wrists. They use guns.'

This line could have come straight from the temptress she played in *Mantrap* and confirmed her position as America's favourite *femme fatale*. Gilbert Roland broke off their engagement which only paved the way for a very public reconciliation. The couple would marry, Paramount's publicity department said, after her next picture *Kids' Boots* – despite her father's disapproval.

The marriage was never to take place. During the filming of *Kids' Boots*, Clara had an affair with actor Larry Gray and her name was also linked with co-star Eddie Cantor.

The name of her character in the movie was changed to Clara McCoy so she could be promoted as Clara Bow, the real McCoy. The studio's publicists also pushed her as the girl 'responsible for many accidents' – because while she was around men did not look where they were going.

Kids' Boots was an enormous hit and opened in New

York while *Mantrap* was still on its first run there. Clara was now the biggest star Paramount had. She renegotiated her contract, even managing to get Paramount's standard morality clause dropped.

The Hays Office insisted that actors and actresses who were caught in compromising circumstances were immediately fired. Plainly Clara was too valuable to be dropped like that. However, she had already been involved in some sexual shenanigans, so the studio insisted that $500 be deducted from her pay for the first year of the contract. This would be put in a trust fund in her name, which she would forfeit if she got caught up in a scandal again.

Her next movie was *Wings*, to be shot in San Antonio. According to director William 'Wild Bill' Wellman, location work was practically an orgy. It took nine months. Wellman said he remembered this because the elevator girls at the hotel where they were staying were all pregnant by the time they finished shooting. He also reckoned that men were standing in line for Clara – including a young unknown called Gary Cooper. Clara had a run-in with the movie's costume designer who kept trying to hide her magnificent figure. Instead, Clara insisted on showing off as much naked flesh as possible. She even had a topless scene which sent the movies' ratings soaring.

The day after she started filming *Wings*, she announced her engagement to Victor Fleming. Gilbert Roland sent a telegram congratulating the happy couple. Clara promptly denied that she was engaged to Fleming and promised Roland that she was not seeing other men.

In 1925, Ben Schulberg had tried to promote Clara as the 'Brooklyn Bonfire' but the epithet had stubbornly refused to catch alight. Then in 1926, he read Elinor Glyn's novel *It*. Ben Schulberg knew an idea he could exploit when he saw one and paid Glyn $50,000 to say that Clara had 'it'. The book was promptly thrown in the bin and two of Schulberg's screenwriters from Preferred set to work on a script that incorporated the concept of 'it'.

The movie *It* was the story of a shopgirl who tries to live by the tenets of Glyn's book and ends up marrying her boss. The leading role was designed to be the perfect showcase for Clara. Soon the whole world proclaimed that Clara Bow had 'it' and she became the 'It Girl'.

In Clara's next movie *Children of Divorce*, she played opposite Gary Cooper. His sexual prowess was already the talk of Hollywood. It was said he had the endowments of Hercules and the staying power of Job. Although she was publicly engaged to Victor Fleming and privately promised to Gilbert Roland, Clara could not resist Cooper. The feeling was mutual and soon the couple were deeply in love.

This was the last straw for Roland. He finally broke off the engagement. Clara temporarily suspended her engagement to Fleming, believing that he would forgive her for her infidelity. She regaled friends with stories of Cooper bathing her every morning. He let her take her beloved dog into the bath too.

Clara was right about Victor Fleming. He did forgive her. Although she discussed marriage with Gary Cooper, she kept seeing Fleming on the side. Cooper was consumed with jealousy. When Clara learnt that Cooper's father, a supreme court judge from Montana, disapproved of his son's entanglement, she flaunted her romance with Fleming. After six months, Cooper broke off the affair. He lacked the courage to stand up to his father, Clara said. Nevertheless, the two of them met up occasionally for sly sex sessions for the next two years.

Eventually, Victor Fleming split from her too. Although he had tolerated Clara's infidelity for years, he eventually could cope with it no more. Clara was mortified when Fleming walked out on her. Although he was twice her age, he offered her the only stability she had ever known.

'Of all the men I've known,' she would say, 'he was a man.'

Marriage, Clara now decided, was out of the question. She began a series of casual affairs that earned her a reputation as a nymphomaniac. The most lurid story of all concerned her having sex with the entire University of Southern California football team.

In 1927, football fever was sweeping southern California. Los Angeles did not have a pro-football team at the time so the denizens of Hollywood supported the USC Trojans, popularly known as the Thundering Herd. The team captain and hero of the Trojans' 1920s winning streak was Morley Drury. Clara heard about him and went to a game to find out what all the fuss was about.

She was instantly captivated by the strapping football players in their crimson and gold uniforms. After the game she phoned the team's fraternity house and spoke to Drury. Fifteen minutes later, she turned up outside to take him out. Her friend Tui Lorraine was with her and she asked Drury to bring another member of the team for a double date. Drury maintains that the evening passed entirely innocently.

After that, after every home game, the entire team were invited to her new Spanish-style bungalow at 512 Bedford Drive in Beverly Hills. What exactly went on there is now the stuff of legend. In some accounts, the team innocently dance with Clara, Tui and other actresses Clara invited, including Joan Crawford. Others talk of nude football games in the garden and Clara gangbanging the entire team – including hunky running back Marion Morrison, who later dropped out of college, went into the movie business and changed his name to John Wayne.

The post-game party became so raucous one night that the police raided the house, but as the officers were also fans of the Trojans nothing more was said. It was Clara's father Robert who eventually put an end to the parties. He returned early one night from the popular Hollywood brothel Madame Frances's, and finding Clara with the Thundering Herd, flung them out in a fit of drunken jealousy.

The parties moved to the Garden of Alla, the former home of Alla Nazimova which had been converted into a hotel and renamed the Garden of Alla. They usually ended with Clara and the team skinny-dipping in the pool at sunrise. Robert Bow heard about the goings-on and put an end to that too, but this may not just have been another display of jealousy over Clara. By this time, Robert Bow was coming on to Tui Lorraine.

The end of the USC parties was a blow for Clara. She did not have many friends. Socially she was shunned because she was from Brooklyn and, therefore, considered lower class. Her lack of hypocrisy – and discretion – in sexual matters led other, less brazen women to consider her a slut. There were times when she reinforced that opinion. She was known to turn up at formal dinners in a figure-hugging swimsuit and once, while dancing with a distinguished judge, she publicly planted a big kiss on his lips and unbuttoned his fly. In some disarray, the judge fled back to his wife. Even her best friends had trouble trusting their husbands around Clara.

Although she was overworked, Clara was still the most underpaid star in Hollywood. The studio began giving her a bonus of $10,000, but it was not paid direct to her. It went into the trust fund that Paramount could withhold under the amended morality clause in her contract. Nevertheless, they continued to turn out pictures to a formula that inevitably involved a scene where she removed her clothes. The stress began to affect her and she started menstruating twice a month. A doctor recommended that she have her ovaries removed, but the studio stepped in. Hollywood's foremost sex symbol could hardly be robbed of her reproductive organs.

Clara did end up in hospital, though, to have her appendix removed. On one of her visits, Tui found Clara locked in a passionate embrace with a young intern named Earl Pearson who had already made several passes at Tui herself.

'He's your type,' she told Clara, 'short on brains and

long on other organs.'

Pearson's attentive bedside manner ensured Clara's rapid recovery and when Clara was discharged Pearson continued his attentive treatment at her home, despite the fact he had just got married. It was the first time Clara had dated a married man.

Clara was not short of proposals herself; many of the 30,000 fan letters she received a month were offers of marriage. Often would-be suitors just turned up at the house with gifts. One man arrived clutching the deeds to his farm in Iowa as a wedding present.

Pearson was not the only man in her life. Her old friend Artie Jacobson and an actor called Jack Oakie also had keys to her Malibu beach-house. Then she met Bela Lugosi, the Hungarian actor who became Hollywood's most famous Dracula. In private, he did more than just bite her neck.

Meanwhile Tui, a New Zealander, had been nabbed by the Immigration and Naturalization Service for entering the US with neither a visa nor a passport. To avoid deportation, twenty-one-year-old Tui married fifty-three-year-old Robert Bow, Clara's father.

Although Tui considered the marriage a formality, Robert insisted on exercising his conjugal rights frequently. Tui soon complained of exhaustion, but that was not the real problem. Everyone in Hollywood knew that Tui was not in love with Robert, but with Clara. She made frequent passes at Clara, who was too naive and too heterosexual to understand. This strange *ménage à trois* drove Robert paranoiac with jealousy which reached new heights when his wife and daughter started dating other men. Robert retaliated by luring young female extras to Clara's beach-house. Tui caught him there with a young hopeful and divorced him. Clara, however, was a loyal daughter and sided with her father. The relationship between Tui and Clara was also over.

On-screen, Clara became known as the Mountie of Sex – she always got her man. Unfortunately, that was true off-screen too and the doctor's wife, Mrs Pearson, heard about it. She threatened to sue Earl for divorce, naming Clara as co-respondent. The studio invoked the modified morality clause in Clara's contract, dissolved the trust fund and used it to pay off Mrs Pearson. Clara gave Earl a ticket back to his home in Texas and issued a statement denying all wrong doing. Mrs Pearson's grounds for divorce were 'failure to provide'.

During the production of her first talkie *The Wild Party*, Clara's name was linked with that of Fredric March, though she was actually living with one of the stuntmen from the movie, ex-prizefighter Jimmy Dundee.

At that time, Clara had also taken on a new hairdresser, Daisy DeVoe, who quickly became her best friend and personal assistant. Daisy moved into 512 Bedford Drive, sorted out Clara's finances and evicted Robert Bow who had been pillaging his daughter's bank accounts. Daisy also joined in the fun there. It was heady stuff for a working girl to wake up in the same bed as Clara Bow and Gary Cooper.

Next, Clara had a very public affair with Harry Richman, the self-styled king of Broadway. He had come to Hollywood with the intention of breaking into the movies the same way the previous king of Broadway, Al Jolson, had. The easiest way to become a big movie star was to be seen out and about with the biggest movie star of them all – Clara Bow. As he explained in his boastful autobiography *A Hell of a Life*: 'Don Juan himself never had more girls. Without bragging, I can say I had every single one I went after.'

Clara put up little resistance. Richman got her phone number from her producer, called her and invited her over for dinner that night. An hour later, she was at his front door. She was, he said, 'one of the most luscious, sexiest women I ever saw in my life'. Off-screen, he admitted, she was even more beautiful.

He flaunted her in public shamelessly, in restaurants and at the club he owned. When he appeared in the theatre, he would summon her to the stage during his curtain calls to boost the box-office takings. He practically caused a riot when he took her to the fair at Coney Island. Clara did not mind any of this. The attention she attracted boosted her confidence, which had taken a bit of a beating since the advent of the talkies. They got along pretty well in private too, according to his account.

He bought her a piano so he could serenade her and a bearskin rug that they could make love on. Their happiness was not to last long. On a gambling trip to Mexico, she picked up a handsome young croupier. Richman tracked them to her Malibu beach-house. When he pulled up outside, he could hear them making love.

Although he was terribly jealous, he still saw Clara as his ticket to movie stardom. In desperation, he began deluging her with expensive gifts, but it made no difference. He was not being invited over to 512 Bedford Drive. She would say that she was tired, but he knew that she never needed sleep. One night, he parked outside her house. When she left in her red roadster, he followed her. She drove over to Gary Cooper's house. When it was obvious that this was no quick visit, he went to find comfort with a prostitute.

The next evening, Richman confronted Clara. At first, she denied everything. Then she told him that she could do as she pleased. Nobody owned her. He could take it or leave it.

Richman took it. He bought her a $5,000 engagement ring. None of her former fiancés had bothered to buy her a ring. The newspapers were not impressed. As one editorial put it: 'Clara's engagements are about as frequent and enduring as the average girl's headaches.'

As newspaper speculation about the couple's wedding plans reached fever pitch, Clara called a press conference breaking off the engagement on the grounds that she was about to have a nervous breakdown. In fact, she was about to go into hospital, long overdue, to have one of her ovaries removed.

Clara was having an affair with Guinn 'Big Boy'

Williams when she met actor Rex Bell. Born George Beldam, Bell had been delivering building supplies to Fox when the studio 'discovered' him and put him under contract. He played her boyfriend in *True to the Navy* and instantly fell for her.

'She was the first girl I was ever in love with,' he said.

Meanwhile, her reputation was taking a hammering. Al Jolson made a quip about her promiscuity on national radio. A columnist on a student newspaper in the Midwest joked that he had fathered triplets by her. The studio used its muscle to cow the college, the newspaper and the columnist into apologies, but they could do nothing about the interview Clara had given St Louis newspaperman Harry Brundidge. In it, she listed her lovers and spilt the juicy beans on each of them. The resulting article portrayed her exactly as she was – feckless and unfaithful.

Then Clara turned up in Dallas. She went to visit Mrs Pearson, now six months pregnant, who slammed the door in her face. A sharp-eyed reporter spotted Clara in a restaurant and asked her what she was doing in Dallas.

'Straightening things out with a boyfriend,' she said.

'Would he be a young doctor with an appealing bedside manner?' he asked. She refused to comment.

'What about Mrs Pearson?' he persisted.

Apparently, Mrs Pearson had refused Paramount's offer of hush money from Clara's trust fund. Instead, Earl Pearson had taken it to set up a urology clinic in downtown Dallas. Was Clara going to steal Pearson from his wife a second time? Clara said she did not know and she was kinda sweet on a guy named Rex Bell. That night she was seen in a nightclub with Earl Pearson.

The next day, Clara's trip to Dallas made front-page news across the US. Richman called from New York, demanding his $5,000 engagement ring back. She kept it. Rex Bell called, asking whether she intended to marry Pearson if he could obtain a divorce. No, Clara said, adding that it was he, Rex, she intended to marry.

Meanwhile, the studio was issuing frantic denials. The Hays Office demanded that she marry Richman or quit films. She responded that she could choose the latter, but Paramount would not let her go. The studio actually exploited the scandal. In her next movie, *Her Wedding Night*, Clara played a sex-crazed movie star. Lying naked on a masseur's table, she delivers the memorable line: 'I've had enough trouble with men without marrying them.' The film was a huge success.

Despite the Pearson incident, Rex Bell continued seeing Clara. He knew she was running around with other men, he said, but it was okay with him as long as she told him the truth about it. Clara responded warmly to this promise of unconditional love.

There was a fly in the ointment though – a long-running feud between Daisy DeVoe and Rex Bell. Daisy suspected Bell of being another conman out for his own advantage, like Richman and Pearson. Bell thought Daisy was feathering her own nest at Clara's expense. Things came to a head when Daisy discovered that Bell was intending to sack her and take over control of Clara's finances. She took Clara's cheque-books, business documents and some of Clara's love letters back to her own home for safekeeping, she said, until she could warn Clara about Bell's plans. Bell claimed that Daisy was merely hiding the evidence and Clara sacked her.

Finding herself isolated and without a job, Daisy demanded $125,000 for the return of the documents, or she would sell Clara's love letters to the newspapers. This was blackmail, said Rex Bell, and he called the police. The studio could have hushed the whole thing up but, for them, it was one scandal too many. Clara was not the star she had once been. Now she was turning into a liability.

Daisy was charged with thirty-five counts of extortion. In court, the defence took the opportunity to reveal intimate details of Clara's correspondence, in the hope of blackening Clara as Daisy's accuser. It worked. The American public were shocked to discover that Clara was involved with three or four men at any one time, and by the salacious details of what she liked doing with them written in her own hand.

Daisy claimed that Clara had given her the money and jewellery that she was supposed to have stolen as gifts but had probably forgotten as she was often 'too drunk to write her own cheques or even to remember which man she'd just spent the night with'. She also revealed the goings-on at the Trojans' after-match parties, but most of all Depression-gripped America was appalled by the reckless extravagance of Clara's lifestyle while millions stood in line at soup kitchens.

The jury found Daisy guilty on only one count, picked at random. Knowing that Daisy had revealed only a fraction of what she knew about Clara's personal life, Clara begged the judge for clemency. Daisy went to jail for eighteen months, but the trial destroyed Clara completely. Her next film was a flop. Never at ease with the talkies, she began to get 'mike fright', missing her cue over and over again.

A scandal-sheet named the *Coast Reporter*, claiming that it had a deal with Daisy DeVoe, began a demolition job. It ran a long list of Clara's lovers, who were said to include her chauffeur and her cousin Billy. With Richman, the paper said, she liked to have sex in public, but Bell was her favourite as he was 'ambidextrous in the saddle'.

She swung both ways too, the paper said, having lesbian affairs with Tui Lorraine and actress Dorothy Carlson. She even put on a show with two hookers in a Mexican whore-house for her croupier lover. And, it said, she did it with animals. She preferred her pet koala bear to a man and Paramount was considering sacking her because she had been seen at a party having sex with Duke, a Great Dane bought for her by Harry Richman. All this sex had, naturally, led to syphilis. When it was diagnosed, the *Coast Reporter* said, Clara had laughed and claimed that she had always wanted to be a beautiful corpse.

These attacks could be halted, of course, for a price. The *Coast Reporter's* editor and proprietor, Fred Girnau, offered to sell Clara the paper for a mere $25,000. He also sent copies to the Hays Office, which resulted in him being charged with a Federal offence – sending obscene material through the post. The prospect of another trial made Clara ill. As she was unable to work, Paramount tore up her contract. She was twenty-five.

Bell took Clara to a ramshackle ranch called The Shack in Nevada. They married quietly in Las Vegas but the news got out and The Shack was soon besieged by reporters. They only left when Clara came out and begged them to give the honeymooners some privacy.

After all this, Clara was still good box office and all the studios, except Paramount, began vying for her services. Eventually she signed a two-picture deal with Fox for $250,000. She made her comeback in *Call Her Savage*, playing opposite her old flame Gilbert Roland. The film had everything – booze, sex, a whipping scene, rape and syphilis. There was even a scene where Clara rolled on the floor with a Great Dane. Her fans loved it.

Her reward was a trip to Europe. In Paris, she visited the Folies Bergères, which made her blush. She thought Hays Office boss Will Hays should visit it, as it would make him less hard on Hollywood.

Her next part, as a sexy dancer in *Hoopla*, was less well received and she decided to call it a day.

'I don't want to be remembered as somebody who couldn't do nothing but take her clothes off,' she said.

Retreating to private life, Clara had two children. She spent some time in a mental hospital, a fate she had feared since the age of sixteen and the incarceration of her mother. But Clara recovered. She spent much of her later life studying but she never wrote her memoirs which she was sure would be 'a shocker in more ways than one'. The reason she gave was her sons and their families.

THE "IT GIRL"

'There are many things in my life that might possibly cause them embarrassment,' she said.

She died in 1965 at the age of sixty.

4

THE PLATINUM BLONDE

Clara Bow met Jean Harlow when she turned up on the set of *The Saturday Night Kid* in 1929. Assistant director Artie Johnson recalled the scene: 'The closer she came, the more interesting she became, because she was wearing this black-crocheted dress with not a stitch on under it.'

Johnson concluded that Harlow was a natural blonde.

'Take her off this goddamn set and never bring her back,' Bow ordered.

'Why?' said Johnson. 'She's a nobody.'

'Are you kidding?' said Bow. 'If she dresses like that for the interview, how's she going to dress in the picture? Who's going to see me next to her?'

Although Clara Bow was then Paramount's biggest star, even she could not get Jean Harlow off the set of *The Saturday Night Kid*. Harlow had a 'friend' in high places. It was rumoured that she was sleeping with studio boss Ben Schulberg. Within a few days though, Jean and Clara became good friends. Clara let Jean wear a sexy bias-cut dress that she had grown too fat for and even posed for a photograph with her. When publicist Teet Carle pointed out that stars should never pose with bit players, Clara replied: 'She's going to go places.'

Jean Harlow was born Harlean Carpentier on 3 March 1911 in Kansas City. Her mother, whose maiden name really was Jean Harlow, separated from her dentist father when baby Jean was nine. Harlean, known as the Baby, was brought up by her maternal grandparents, a family of strict Christian Scientists, while her mother went off to find work in Chicago. There, Mama Jean met a small-time Sicilian hustler named Marino Bello. After a boring marriage to a dentist, Mama Jean was quickly overwhelmed by her Latin lover. She had never known such happiness but Mama Jean believed that the difference in race and religion was too great to allow them to marry. Bello threatened to kill himself if she refused him. So she dropped Christian Science and, in the teeth of her family's opposition, they wed. News of the marriage caused uproar in the Harlow household. Harlean was found hiding in a closet.

Mama Jean returned to Kansas for Christmas four years later and fell ill. Her husband was summoned and, despite the objections of paterfamilias Sam Harlow, moved into his wife's room. Mama Jean made a quick recovery. One day over lunch, Sam Harlow asked Bello if he was beating his daughter. When Bello asked him why he thought that, Harlow explained that he heard terrible moans emanating from their room at night. Baby Jean must be hearing them too, he said, and he would prefer her to think that Mama Jean was making those sounds because he was beating her than... well. Bello said he would have a word with his wife and ask her to try and make it sound as if she was snoring.

At fifteen, young Jean was sent away to school. Already she had a full bosom which made her popular with the boys at school dances. At one dance, she met Charles 'Chuck' McGrew, the son of a stockbroker, and they began exchanging love notes.

Despite her developing bust, Jean refused to wear a bra, saying that they made her feel that her breath had been cut off. Besides, women in the ancient world had not worn them.

'Chuck said that Etruscan women wore dresses that showed their boobies,' she told her mother.

Desperate to leave school and return home to the Harlows, Jean told her mother about what she called 'muzzling', boys who would not stop playing 'handsy' and asked her mother why you 'feel sort of hot in the tummy when he touches you in certain places?'

The family decided that she should leave school at the end of the semester, but that was not soon enough for Jean. She went missing from school one night and returned the next afternoon saying that she had married Charles McGrew. Sam Harlow was beside himself with rage, but Marino Bello tried to calm things down and went to fetch Jean from school. She came to resent Bello as the man who had taken her away from her beloved husband.

Back home, Jean told her mother that she had spent the night in a hotel room with Charles and left Mama Jean in no doubt about what had gone on.

'Chuck seemed to like it, but I thought it was awfully messy,' she said.

While talking to her mother, Jean suddenly stripped off her nightgown, saying that she refused to wear anything that reminded her of school. Her mother was shocked to see how mature her sixteen-year-old daughter's body was.

Jean assured her horrified mother that she was not pregnant as Charles had used a rubber, but what she wanted to know was whether there was anything more to sex. She said she had spent her time studying the pattern of the wallpaper on the ceiling and felt she had missed out on something. Mama Jean left the room in embarrassment.

Sam Harlow said that Jean had brought disgrace on the family and he paid for Marino Bello, his wife and stepdaughter to move to Los Angeles where Marino thought a man of his talents and vision could prosper. Jean enjoyed the free and easy atmosphere of California. She soon stopped writing to Charles and took off her wedding ring. The marriage was legally dissolved shortly after.

When the money Sam Harlow had given them dried up, Bello refused to work, so Jean had to support the family by working as a film extra. She managed to avoid the casting couch but, at sixteen, posed for nude photographs. Laurel and Hardy hired her for *Double Whoopee*. In the picture, she had to get out of a taxi cab. The door slammed on her dress, leaving her in only a thin chemise as she walked into a hotel without noticing she was half undressed.

On the lot, she was spotted by agent Arthur Landau. Along with everyone else, he noticed Jean's high, firm, bra-less breasts, but he was even more taken by her hair, which was so blonde that it was almost white.

Landau took her to lunch and arranged a screen test for the following day. But, Landau said, Jean must wear some sort of a bra – 'something that gives the idea without actually showing them.' He signed her to a three-year contract and she touched him for $50.

The test was shown to Howard Hughes, who was reshooting *Hell's Angels* as a talkie. At first he was not impressed, but those around him thought that Jean's platinum blonde hair was an original touch. Landau sold her to Hughes by arguing that Jean looked like a hooker on her first day in the brothel – still willing to try anything and not yet all dried up inside. She was perfect for the role. She looked like the type of girl who would put out for the fliers, knowing that they might be going to their deaths the following day.

In the end, Hughes not only hired her for the picture, he signed her to a three-year contract; and he gave her star billing on *Hell's Angels*. With the RKO publicity machine behind her, the critics and the public soon hailed her as America's latest 'blonde bombshell'.

Jean went on a nationwide tour to publicize *Hell's Angels*, appearing everywhere in low-cut dresses that showed off her breasts. Before making public appearances, she rubbed ice on her nipples, a trick she used on the set.

Press releases went out saying she slept in the nude and loved the feel of fur against her skin. Her bed, it was said, was a replica of the scallop shell in Botticelli's *Birth of Venus*.

Although Hughes recognized that Jean Harlow's raw sex appeal was selling his movie more effectively than the dog-fights he had spent millions on, he had no follow-up projects he could use her on. So he hired her out to other studios for 'bad girl' roles. When she was making a movie for Columbia, Hughes's publicist suggested they switch the title to *Platinum Blonde*. The name stuck.

When Jean's contract came up for renegotiation, the figures soared. Written into the contract was a clause specifying that RKO's publicity photographers pay special attention to promoting her breasts.

For a sex goddess, she was not getting much sex. Even marriage would not change that. In her rise to stardom, she had somehow managed to avoid the worst excesses of the casting couch; nor had her name been linked romantically with any of her hunky co-stars. In 1932, she married Paul Bern, an assistant to Irving Thalberg at MGM.

He was an odd choice for a woman who could have had her pick of the Hollywood screen idols. She was twenty-one. He was forty-two, short, balding with a weaselly moustache. He was also suave, intelligent and well liked. On the lot, they called him 'little father confessor' because he listened to everyone's problems.

He had been seen out with some of Hollywood's most famous sex symbols – Joan Crawford, Mabel Normand, Barbara LaMarr. It was rumoured that he tried to commit suicide after LaMarr got married for the fifth time. It was also well known that he kept a mistress whom he visited every afternoon. What was not known was that he did not have sex with her. His turn on was to get her to lie naked on the bed, while he read poetry to her. He had another dark secret. He had a common-law wife, but she had gone mad and was confined to an asylum.

Only a few hours after Jean married Bern, her agent Arthur Landau got an hysterical phone call from her. He must come and pick her up immediately. Landau sped across town to find her in her nightdress standing barefoot in the road outside Bern's house. When Landau got her home, she stripped off to reveal her snow-white body covered in welts and bite marks. Bern had beaten and bitten her savagely.

Landau went back to Bern's house next morning to find Bern asleep naked on the floor. Landau saw that Bern had the undeveloped penis and testicles of an infant boy. When Bern awoke, he told Landau that he was completely impotent but he had hoped that Jean, as Hollywood's number one sex goddess, might have been able to cure him.

'Every man I know gets an erection just by talking about her,' he sobbed. 'Didn't I have the right to think Jean could help me at least that much?'

When he found that she couldn't, he had lost his temper and attacked her.

It was vital that this story did not get out. The truth would have destroyed her career. So Jean and her ersatz husband had to stay together for the sake of appearances.

The situation soon became intolerable. Jean wanted more out of marriage than chit-chat. Bern grew jealous of the real men who surrounded her on the set. When he discovered that she was happily doing a nude scene on an open set, though the script did not really call for it, he grew desperate. He bought a huge artificial penis with massive testicles and a bulb which made water squirt out of the end. When he burst into the bedroom wearing it, Jean burst out laughing. The two of them had a good laugh as he pranced around the room, waving it about. Then they cut it up and flushed it down the toilet.

The next day, while Jean was out at the studio, Bern killed himself. His naked body was found sprawled in front of a full-length mirror. He was drenched in Jean's favourite perfume, Mitsuko. There was a .38 pistol in his hand and a

.38 hole in his head.

He left a note, saying:

Dearest Dear,

Unfortunately this is the only way to make good the frightful wrong I have done you, and to wipe out my abject humiliation. I love you.

Paul

PS. You understand that last night was only a comedy.

Three days later, the body of New York actress Dorothy Milette was fished out of the Sacramento River. She had claimed to be Bern's common-law wife. Ten years before, she had had a nervous breakdown and had been committed to a sanatorium in New England. She recovered enough to move into a suite at the Algonquin Hotel in Manhattan, which Bern paid for. He visited her there, but she was greatly disturbed by reports of Bern's marriage to Harlow. Fearing that he might stop supporting her, she moved to California. It is thought that she had been in contact with Bern. Perhaps the thought of being exposed as a bigamist, as well as the humiliation of his physical inadequacies, contributed to Bern's decision to commit suicide.

'How does a girl like Harlow, a temple of sex, wind up married to a fairy bigamist?' ranted Louis B. Mayer, fearing that the scandal would ruin Jean's career.

Not only did Jean survive, the studio shamelessly exploited the publicity her tragic marriage had generated. In Jean's next movie *Reckless*, she played a showgirl whose husband commits suicide when he discovers she is having an affair with a character played by William Powell. In reality, Jean was having an affair with Powell during the filming.

The studio hoped that they would marry, with the wedding coinciding with the launch of the film, but it was not to be.

The death of Bern had left Jean acutely concerned about her own sexuality. It had also left her penniless. Although he lived the lifestyle of a wealthy man, Bern died deeply in debt – debts that Jean was supposed to honour.

'No one ever expects a great lay to pay all the bills, so why do they expect it of me?' she lamented. 'Is it because I am not a great lay?'

Harlow, thought of as the most passionate and abandoned woman in America, unburdened herself to Landau. Why was it that everyone thought that sex was the greatest thing in the world, she asked. Her own mother enjoyed sex with her Italian husband so much that she forgave him his frequent infidelities. She admitted that the physical act made her sick and begged Landau to find her a man who would show her how wonderful sex could be. If he did not, Harlow said, she would have to go to bed with the man she hated most in the world – her own stepfather. After all, Bello made her mother cry out in ecstasy every time he made love to her. Surely, as a sex goddess, it was Harlow's right to cry out in ecstasy too.

Jean did not go through with her threat, though there is little doubt Marino would have been willing. Indeed, he made frequent passes at her, but Jean feared that if his love-making had the same effect on her as it did on her mother, she too would become his sex slave and would spend her life forgiving him for sleeping with other women.

Instead, Jean took to driving around the streets at night, trying to pick up men. When she spotted a goodlooking man, she would kerb crawl, but she always lost her nerve at the last moment. She knew she was bound to be recognized. What if her lover used the encounter to blackmail her? She already had one blackmailer to deal with – Bern's afternoon mistress who threatened to sell a lurid account of nude poetry reading to the newspapers unless Jean paid her off. The strain was telling.

Under sedation for her nervous condition, Jean even made an inept pass at a male nurse.

Something had to be done. Harlow hacked off her famous hair, borrowed a wig from wardrobe and took the train to San Bernardino where she picked up a door-to-door salesman. They spent two nights together in a small hotel near the station. The salesman praised Jean for her body. She was okay at lovemaking, he said, though she was a little tense. In fact, she could probably get a job in a whorehouse back east. He could arrange it, he said. Back in Hollywood, Jean related the encounter in lovely detail to Mama Jean, Marino and Landau.

Although the experiment had not been a complete success – the only moment she felt lost in passion he had stopped and asked her if she was enjoying it – Jean determined to try again. Deep inside, she blamed her mother. If Mama Jean had stayed married to her father, Baby Jean would have grown up a respectable girl in Kansas City, got married and known true love. As it was, she was a sex goddess who men lusted after and could never love. They saw her as a body, not a woman.

Then she realized that there was a way she could experience true love. She could have a child. If she got pregnant quickly, she could pretend that the father was Bern. The studio would have to give her time off. She could go to Europe. With the studio's money behind her, she could have the baby's birth certificate falsified and return to America in triumph – this time as a symbol of motherhood not sex.

In San Francisco, she picked up a taxi driver and took him back to her hotel room. After the deed was done, a jealous Marino threw him out. The taxi driver assured Marino of his complete discretion. After all, if he told the boys back at the garage that he had made love to Jean Harlow no one would believe him. This incensed Marino. He and the cab driver came to blows. When the cab driver downed Marino with a single punch to the stomach, Jean gave him an extra $20, a deep passionate kiss and sent him on his way.

This was the beginning of a sex spree. Jean took to drinking and she would forget who she slept with, what they did with her and where they went in the morning. More than once she awoke to find herself alone with her money and jewellery gone. She called Landau and asked for more money so she could continue her orgy of anonymous sex. Often she would not bother to remove her clothes, so that she could get on to the next one quicker in the frantic hope that she would become pregnant. She even picked up a man outside the theatre showing her latest movie – *Red Dust* with Clark Gable. Back at her hotel room, the man said that she looked so much like Jean Harlow she could get a job as her double.

Jean did not get pregnant. She feared she might be barren, but still the indiscriminate orgy of anonymous lovers continued.

During the filming of *Blonde Bombshell*, Jean got friendly with lighting cameraman Hal Rosson. He comforted her through what was to be a difficult picture for her. The story was painfully close to the truth. It told of a young girl who just wanted to settle down but was forced to become a sexy Hollywood star by a grasping family.

Harlow and Rosson eloped to Yuma for a quickie marriage. They flew back to Los Angeles to face a storm of reporters. Harlow became apoplectic with rage when one of the reporters pointed out the physical resemblance between Rosson and Paul Bern.

The happy couple's belated honeymoon was interrupted when Jean developed appendicitis. When she went into hospital to have her appendix removed, a well-known east coast gangster offered a large sum of money for the hair shaved from Jean's pubic region before the operation. He planned to have the hairs mounted in gold and sold as mementoes.

The marriage lasted eight months. When Rosson moved out, Jean's name was soon linked romantically with that of boxer Max Baer, who was well known for his predilection for blondes. This relationship faltered too. Jean tried to reconcile with Rosson, but he was struck down with polio and quarantined. She then filed for divorce on the grounds that Rosson read in bed, which kept her awake. The resulting loss of sleep harmed her performance on the set the next day.

In fact, quite another thing was harming her career. It was the animosity of MGM boss Louis B. Mayer, the king of the casting couch. Jean Harlow was the only one of his stars to turn him down. One day, in his office, he offered her a mink coat and told her to undress and try it on. Jean refused and said that the only way that she would sleep with him was if she had the clap – and then he could keep his mink coat. She would do it for free.

Meanwhile, Marino Bello had taken over as her business manager and was squandering her money recklessly. He also used his position to inveigle hopeful young actresses into bed, even bringing them back to the house, much to her mother's chagrin. Mama revenged herself by putting pinpricks in his condoms. Nevertheless, she always forgave his indiscretions. He was a hot-blooded man with an eye for beauty, she explained.

Jean decided that something must be done. With a private detective, she arranged to entrap Marino in a sleazy hotel with an ugly hooker, a Mexican who did not speak English. Jean arranged for her mother to burst in and catch Marino *in flagrante*. Confronted by this sordid scene, the scales fell from Mama Jean's eyes. She told Marino to leave. He demanded a pay-off of $50,000. He got $38,000, which Jean paid willingly. However, in despatching Marino, Jean had sown the seeds of her own downfall.

Deprived of the comforts of the flesh, Mama Jean turned back to Christian Science and spent her time reading *Science and Health* by Mary Baker Eddy, the sect's founder. In 1937, Jean became ill. It may have had something to do with kidney damage sustained during the beating Paul Bern had given her. As a Christian Scientist, Mama Jean refused to call a doctor. It was against the teachings of Mary Baker Eddy. By the time Landau got Jean to hospital, it was too late. Jean Harlow died on 7 June 1937. She was twenty-six.

5

QUEEN OF THE CASTING COUCH

Joan Crawford always had trouble keeping her clothes on. A couple of nights before they were due to work together on the film *Torch Song* in 1953, Joan Crawford, who was then fifty, summoned director Charles Walters to her home for drinks. When he arrived, he noted that she was wearing a housecoat. Once he was settled, she threw the housecoat open to reveal her naked body underneath. Walters was flattered and embarrassed.

'At a time like that, where do you look?' he said. Slowly he brought himself to run his eyes over her magnificent form. Then she covered up again.

'There was absolutely nothing sexual in what she was doing,' he said later. 'It was purely professional. This was our first film together and what she was saying was: 'Okay, you'd better see what you've got to work with.' She simply wanted to show me the equipment.'

He was impressed.

At sixty-five, she was going to try the same thing with a

young Steven Spielberg. She had just accepted a part in the TV series *Night Gallery* and invited the director over to inspect the goods. Who should turn up but twenty-year-old Spielberg. It was his first directing assignment. Joan was wearing a very revealing négligé, but when she realized that her director was young enough to be her grandson, she kept it on.

Joan Crawford had a hard life. The only advantages she possessed were a great body and a prodigious ability at sex. She was born Lucille Fay LeSueur in San Antonio, Texas. Her father had abandoned her mother, Anna LeSueur, and brother Hal before she was born. Five years later, Anna took up with Henry Cassin and Joan, then known as Billie, took his name. When Joan was eleven, Cassin ran off too.

Joan was lodged with nuns at St Agnes Academy in Kansas City. She was a forward child. As soon as she reached puberty, she would sneak out into the park to meet boys. She was soon known as the fastest girl around. The sisters knew what she was up to, but they preferred not to send her back to her mother as Anna was well known around town for the number of gentleman callers she entertained. However, when Anna married the man she was living with, Joan went back to live at home. Later, she claimed that her new stepfather often tried to seduce her, only backing off when she threatened to tell her mother. Before long Anna found a new lover anyway.

When Joan was fourteen, her older brother Hal took her to see the famous fan-dancer Sally Rand. Joan was greatly impressed and thought that this could point the way ahead for her.

Already Joan was a fanatical dancer and would go anywhere to do the Black Bottom. She was particularly popular on the campus of the University of Missouri, where she would entertain the boys of the Phi Delta Theta fraternity house. They would get her to do a 'hot dance' on the table and she did not seem to mind how high she pulled her dress up.

She was just as uninhibited about sex – sex and dancing were fun as long as they were done without a care for what came after. She had a regular boyfriend, but he was just the sap who paid for her to go to clubs where she could pick up more exciting men.

Joan began to enter dance contests and regularly won them. She got a job as a chorus girl and moved in with a man. He had some shady connections and, when the show she was in folded, he put her in touch with a company that made 'What The Butler Saw' machines. Joan Crawford made her movie début dancing the Charleston, nude, for a nickel-in-the-slot peep show. She was seventeen.

Reverting to the name Lucille LeSueur, Joan headed for Chicago. She had the name of an agent there, but when she arrived at his office it was filled with 'the most attractively dressed, beautiful girls I had ever seen, all slim and chic,' Joan recalled. She pushed past them and burst into the agent's inner sanctum in tears.

'I know I am not as tall or pretty as those other girls out there, but I have less than two dollars and no experience, and I can't go back to Kansas City,' she sobbed.

He agreed that she was not as pretty as the other girls, but he could get her a job in strip joints. When she asked whether she would have to take everything off, he asked did she like to eat?

By all accounts, Joan was a great stripper. She knew how to turn an audience on and keep them turned on. Her performance was always aimed at the wealthier gentlemen in the house. This led to intimate diners, presents and command performances at the private parties of some of Chicago's better-known gangsters.

She also entertained at conventions where it was understood that the girls were available to the clients after the performance. Around that time she contracted a venereal disease and underwent the first of a series of botched abortions.

Gradually Joan progressed from stripper to chorus girl. One night while high-kicking at the Oriole Terrace, she kicked a drink over a customer. He was impresario J.J. Schubert. Instead of being angry, he was impressed. He offered her a part in his Broadway musical *Innocent Eyes*. The other girls warned Joan not to take Schubert seriously. He was just trying to get into her pants. But as far as Joan was concerned sleeping with people was fun, so she had nothing to lose. He got into her pants, and his offer was serious. Soon she was on the train to New York.

Joan's experience as a stripper made her very sexy on stage and she attracted more than her share of stage-door Johnnies. Diamonds and slap-up dinners were the order of the day. She fell in love with a well-known Broadway actor. There was talk of marriage until Joan discovered that he was seeing another woman behind her back. She was broken-hearted.

On the rebound, Joan married saxophonist James Welton. The marriage did not last. Joan was running faster and wilder than ever. Desperate to get into the movies, she appeared in a number of stag films with names like *Velvet Lips*, *Coming Home*, *She Shows Him How*. The most famous of them was *The Casting Couch*. It tells the story of a young woman who turns up at a producer's office in the hope of getting a part in the movies. She has to remove her clothes, perform oral sex on him, then submit herself to full inter-course on the eponymous casting couch.

Performing in stag films, or for that matter on the cast-ing couch, was not a guaranteed route to movie stardom, witness would-be screen goddess Peg Entwhistle. A success-ful actress in London, she went to Hollywood to try her luck. She signed with the Starr Agency, who sent her along to Hollywood parties where, she was assured, a girl could get noticed. This turned out to be little more than casual prosti-tution. She had a series of nude photographs taken which, again she was assured, would attract the attention of casting directors.

The result was a bit part in a movie called *Thirteen Women*, but no further offers. In frustration, she decided to show off her acting ability in stag movies. These led to a series of live performances on casting couches. Talented though she undoubtedly was, no contract was forthcoming. Nevertheless she became a Hollywood legend. In desperation, she climbed to the top of the 'D' in the famous Hollywood sign, a relic of Mack Sennett's failed real estate venture, and threw herself off.

One can hardly imagine Joan Crawford travelling that route. She was a survivor. When the Broadway show she was in closed, she worked as a taxi dancer in the famous Roseland ballroom and supplemented her income with prostitution.

She was working as a dancer in the speakeasy owned by Clara Bow's beau Harry Richman, when she met Nils Granlund. Richman wanted Joan to mingle with the customers after her act and she needed a glamorous gown. Granlund gave her the money to buy one and Joan went around to Granlund's office to show it to him. She had just disrobed ready to slip into the new dress when MGM's Marcus Loew dropped by. He liked what he saw and arranged a screen test for Joan. Meanwhile, Joan was pregnant again. The resulting abortion left her ill and, she thought, unable to have children. She was back in Kansas City recuperating when she got a telegram telling her to report for work in Culver City. She had a five-year contract with MGM.

Once she arrived on the lot, Joan quickly learnt how the studio system worked. If you wanted a part you had to prove your suitability on the casting couch. This was not a problem for her. Joan was soon in *Pretty Ladies*, thanks to an afternoon interview with MGM publicist Harry Rapf.

She dated technicians at night and visited Rapf's office every morning. Soon she was making headway in the business. It was decided that her name Lucille LeSueur was okay for a stripper or the star of a stag film, but it was no good for an MGM girl. *Movie Weekly* held a competition to name the studio's newest hopeful. The winning entry was 'Joan Crawford', so that's what she became.

Off-screen, Joan soon acquired a reputation as the hottest girl in town. F. Scott Fitzgerald, a Hollywood scriptwriter at the time, described her as 'the best example of a flapper'. Out dancing every night, she came to the attention of the newspapers. Studio boss Louis B. Mayer took an interest and she was given a leading role in *Old Clothes*. Realizing that she was now a hot property, she burst into Mayer's office and told him that she had just seen a house that she had to buy. The problem was she did not have any money. The office door was locked. His calls were cancelled while Mayer gave due consideration to the problem. Half an hour later, he emerged from his office and ordered his secretary to raise a cheque for $18,000 so the studio's newest leading lady had somewhere to live befitting her status.

Before Jean Harlow came along, Paul Bern also took an interest. Joan began to see the wisdom of sleeping with the director of her current movie, so that he would pay proper attention to her part. She also found it hard to keep her hands off her leading men. Joan was named as the other woman in the divorce action brought against actor Neil Neeley. She liked leading ladies too, and had affairs with bisexual actresses Ruth Chatterton, Lilyan Tashman, Natasha Brent and Martha Raye. Her live-in maid used to take the precaution of locking her bedroom door at night and Marilyn Monroe claimed that Joan had made a pass at her.

Joan continued to use the casting couch to propel her career forward. She wanted the leading role in *Dancing Daughters* but producer Hunt Stromberg wanted Clara Bow for the role. Joan turned up at his office and took her clothes off to demonstrate beyond a shadow of a doubt that she was the girl for the part. Stromberg was certainly impressed with the magnitude of her talent, but informed her that casting for the picture was in the hands of director Harry Beaumont. Barely bothering to put her clothes back on, she headed to Beaumont's office where she repeated the performance. She got the part and it made her a star.

Joan got engaged to Mike Cudahy but the marriage did no go ahead because he was an alcoholic. She was also greatly attracted by the silent star John Gilbert, who was soon to be destroyed by the coming of the talkies – Mayer put it about that his thin falsetto did not match his manly looks. Their on-screen love scenes were sizzling, but Gilbert was involved with Greta Garbo at the time. Next she fell for Douglas Fairbanks Jnr. In the face of the opposition of his father and step-mother, Mary Pickford, the couple eloped and got married. It was eight months before they were invited to Pickfair where Hollywood's uncrowned king and queen, Joan's in-laws, held court.

Mary Pickford was barely civil. She warned Joan: 'If you ever make me a grandmother, I will kill you.'

Joan worked hard at the marriage, but her husband's career was waning and he was more interested in socializing than acting. After an exhausting week in the studio, Joan would be dragged to San Simeon for weekends. There, she felt out of her depth socially, except in the company of Marion Davies.

Her marriage was on the rocks when she met the man who she later described as the great love of her life, Clark Gable. She had followed his career with interest and picked him to co-star with her in *Possessed*. On the set, she was captivated. He had 'more sheer animal magic than anyone in the world,' she said. She defied any actress to play opposite him without feeling 'the twinges of sexual urge beyond belief'.

'I knew when Clark walked on set,' she said. 'I didn't know which door he came through, but I knew he was there. He had presence. I knew I was falling into a trap that I warned young girls about – not to fall in love with leading men or take romantic scenes seriously. Leave the set and forget about it because that marvellous feeling would pass. Boy, I had to eat those words, but they tasted very sweet.'

Years later she was asked by David Frost what Gable's attraction was.

'Balls,' she said. 'He had them.'

The offending word had to bleeped from the interview.

There was talk of marriage, but the studio put paid to any wedding plans as they were both married at the time. MGM could hardly afford to have both their major stars involved in messy divorce cases simultaneously. However, the affair proved enduring. It lasted from 1931 until Gable's death in 1960, despite numerous other affairs and marriages. Joan was even on hand to comfort him when his third wife, Carole Lombard, was killed in a plane crash in 1942.

As her marriage to Douglas Fairbanks Jnr was coming to an end, Joan found herself pregnant once again. She claimed that she lost the baby when she slipped on the deck of a ship during the filming of *Rain*; she may well have had another abortion.

They tried a trip to Europe as a last-ditch attempt to save the marriage but throughout the holiday, they were both impossibly unfaithful. When they returned to California, Joan rented a cottage on Malibu beach and went to live there without even telling her husband where it was. Fairbanks quickly became involved in a scandal when a Dane called Jorgen Dietz sued him for 'alienating the affections' of his wife Lucy, an extra at Warners.

The next man in Joan's life was actor Franchot Tone. He was a stage actor and a newcomer to Hollywood, but when he appeared in *Dancing Lady,* with Joan Crawford and Clark Gable, it is generally thought that he came off best.

Tone was very caring and supportive of Joan but she refused to marry him, saying she was convinced an actress should never marry. Besides, she was also seeing actor Ricardo Cortez, one of her two leading men in *Montana Moon.* However, she changed her mind about Tone's proposal in 1935, when she discovered that he and Bette Davis, his co-star in *Dangerous*, were rehearsing their love scenes alone in her dressing-room.

The wedding night was spoilt when she got a phone call from an anonymous 'collector' who claimed to have a copy of her stag film *The Casting Couch*. She called Louis B. Mayer who paid $10,000 for it. It is said that over the years the studio shelled out half a million dollars in an attempt to buy up every surviving copy. When one man refused to part with his copy, his house mysteriously burnt down. One full set of Joan's complete porno repertoire was thought to be in the possession of a Czech arms king. He was said to view them nightly. One clip appeared in a sixties compilation, but no one, not even the compilers, realized that the enthusiastic teenage porno starlet was the legendary Joan Crawford.

Joan found she had a rival in Loretta Young who had already had a brief affair with Clark Gable. Spencer Tracy had left his wife for her and when Joan fell for Tracy during the filming of *Mannequin*, Loretta was seen out with Franchot Tone.

The last straw came when Joan caught her husband making love to Loretta in his dressing-room. When asked why, Tone said: 'To prove to myself I am still a man.'

The divorce almost foundered when Joan was photographed dancing with Tone in a New York nightclub. The judge asked her how she could bear to dance with a man she was divorcing on the grounds of mental cruelty.

'I hope I am intelligent enough to be friendly with my husband,' she said. The divorce went through.

Meanwhile, the thirty-three-year-old Joan was having a brief fling with seventeen-year-old Jackie Cooper. He had heard people talk of her wild sexual appetite around the studio and decided to sample it for himself. He lingered around the house after a party. When he refused to go home, she simply closed the curtains and took off her clothes.

'I made love to Joan Crawford,' said Cooper, 'or rather

she made love to me.'

The performance was repeated eight or nine times over the next six months. After the first time, all their assignations were in the dead of night. Cooper would sneak out of the house after his mother and stepfather had gone to sleep and roll the car down the street until it was far enough away to start the engine without waking them. Then he would drive over to her house.

Cooper acknowledges that Joan taught him a lot about sex.

'She was a very erudite professor of love,' he said. 'She would bathe me, powder me, cologne me. Then she would do it over again. She would put on high heels, a garter belt and a large hat and pose in front of the mirror, turning this way and that.'

When she had finished with him, she would set a date for his next visit.

Finally, she decided that they were not going to see each other any more. They did not meet again for thirty years. Even then, they did not talk of what she told him would be their 'magnificent secret'.

Next came a brief romantic interlude with Charles McCabe, a married man from New York. She tried to seduce Glenn Ford, but he found her too aggressive in her attempts to get him into bed.

Meanwhile, she moved from MGM to Warner Bros where she ran up against Bette Davis, who was mourning her second husband. He had been fatally wounded by a friend who had found him in bed with his wife. Joan showed little sympathy.

'After all,' she said, 'her first husband caught her in bed with Howard Hughes. God knows how many times I turned him down.'

In 1942, Joan married actor Phillip Terry. Joan was extremely busy, not least because she had adopted two children; she was later to adopt two more. She ran her life on a strict schedule, setting aside an hour in the afternoon for her husband.

Unsurprisingly, the marriage collapsed and they were divorced in 1946, with Joan swearing once more that she would never get married again.

She found Henry Fonda very attractive and, during the filming of *Daisy Kenyon*, she sent him a jock strap encrusted with rhinestones and sequins. During a scene where he has to carry her upstairs, she asked him whether he would mind modelling the gift for her later. He almost dropped her.

Cowboy Don 'Red' Barry was the next man on the scene. As she frequently told the technicians, supporting actors were sexier than leading men: 'They may not get top billing, but they get the highest marks in the bedroom.'

Joan was also flirting with lesbianism again. She tried to sleep with her children's nanny and became so persistent that the woman had to leave. She also made passes at women journalists and other actresses. Her favourite ploy was to pull out dresses from her wardrobe for them to try on, in the hope that they would undress. It was also said that she had a secret hankering for Bette Davis. Nevertheless, she continued to entertain her men friends, including Yul Brynner, in her bedroom wearing only her undergarments.

'I was a highly sexed woman,' she explained later.

One night Don Barry made a joke about Joan in a bar. Greg Bautzer, Hollywood's 'attorney to the stars', leapt to her defence and, in the ensuing fracas, lost several front teeth. Joan paid for his dental work. After that, they would weekend in Palm Springs where they would dance until dawn and spend the rest of the day recovering in bed.

Bautzer flattered Joan by treating her like a star. In return, she treated him like a dog. Once, she asked him to get out of the car to check the tyres, then drove off leaving him stranded. He retaliated by taking up with Merle Oberon, then Ginger Rogers. When Joan came across Bautzer and Rogers dancing cheek-to-cheek at the Beverly Wilshire Hotel, she fled in tears.

Director Vincent Sherman replaced Bautzer, but their

relationship broke up after a series of brawls. Joan went back to Bautzer, though there was violence from him too. Once she appeared with a black eye, explaining it away by saying simply: 'He loves me.'

When Bautzer was seen taking lunch with Rita Hayworth two days running, Joan took up with Peter Shaw. Despite another reconciliation with Bautzer in a flurry of expensive gifts, he was soon seeing Lana Turner and she was seeing director Charles Martin. When Joan dropped Martin, she invited Lana Turner to her house and simply informed her that Turner's affair with Bautzer was over.

'Greg doesn't love you,' she said. 'He hasn't for a long time. I couldn't let you go on believing it. What Greg and I have is real. It's me he truly loves, but he hasn't figured out how to get rid of you. So why don't you be a good little girl and tell him you're finished. Make it easy on yourself.'

The tactic worked, but Joan's renewed relationship with Bautzer continued to be as tempestuous as ever with him smashing up her car and her flushing the $10,000 cufflinks she had given him down the toilet. The plumber charged $500 to retrieve them. Once, after being brushed off by Bautzer's secretary, Joan stormed into his office to find it empty. Bautzer had climbed out of the window and was hiding on a narrow ledge twelve storeys above Hollywood Boulevard.

'I hated him and loved him at the same time,' she once explained. The affair lasted for ten years.

Joan was jealous and fiery. She dated producer Bill Dozier and walked out on him when he danced with another woman. The fact that she was dancing with another man at the time made no difference. When she thought a man had done her wrong, she would make him get down on his knees and beg her forgiveness.

'There was always a steady flow of men,' said a former servant. 'They came and went at all hours. If she had a date, I used to see her take him by the hand at the end of the evening and lead him upstairs. I don't know if she was sexy in a playful way or playful in a sexy way, but Miss Crawford always succeeded, and, as I recall, a few gentlemen were a bit reluctant.'

Marilyn Monroe was named 'Fastest-rising Star of 1952' by *Photoplay* magazine. At the award ceremony, she appeared in a sheer figure-hugging gown with a *décolletage* to her navel. Crawford told Bob Thomas of Associated Press cattily: 'There is nothing wrong with my tits, but I don't go around throwing them in people's faces.'

Marilyn wondered whether this comment was Joan's revenge for her having spurned her lesbian advances. Her response was subtle.

'I've always admired her for being a wonderful mother,' Marilyn, an orphan herself, told reporters, 'for taking four children and giving them a fine home. Who better than I knows what that means to homeless little ones.'

It was well known around Hollywood that, to facilitate her 'steady flow of men', Joan had sent her adopted children away.

Joan also riled Elizabeth Taylor. In *Torch Song*, she played opposite Michael Wilding who was Taylor's husband at the time. Joan casually boasted to Taylor that she always slept with her leading man.

She had an affair with Milton Rackmil, president of Universal Studios. Then she met Alfred Steele, a former college football star who had become president of Pepsi-Cola. For their first date, Steele, a married man living in New York, flew to Los Angeles to take Joan out for dinner. She was greatly impressed. When Steele divorced, they married.

Both Joan and her new husband were strong-willed people and, consequently, fought like cat and dog. Steele particularly objected to Joan sleeping over at the studio when she had had a long day. Once during a row, he gave her a black eye and she could not film the next day. Nevertheless, though stormy, the marriage turned out to be happy.

'It's heaven to find love and be loved,' said Joan. 'There are things you learn in a good marriage. I learned that you don't use sex. You give it.'

They stayed together until Steele's death in 1959. He was fifty-eight.

His death left Joan penniless and she went back to work. On *Whatever Happened to Baby Jane?*, Joan and her old rival Bette Davis fought for the affection of director Robert Adrich. Joan had had a brief affair with him during the filming of *Autumn Leaves* in 1956, but Bette finally won out during the sequel *Hush, Hush, Sweet Charlotte* and Joan was replaced by Olivia De Haviland.

During the filming of her last film, *Berserk* which was shot in England, Joan got up to her old tricks, showing off her naked body to director Herman Cohen in her dressing-room. He never revealed if she succeeded in seducing him.

After Joan's death in 1977, aged sixty-nine, her adopted daughter Christina Crawford tried to destroy her mother's reputation with the book, and subsequent film, *Mommie Dearest*, in which she detailed the beatings and cruelty she suffered at Joan's hands. Christina catalogued her own collapse into alcoholism in a follow-up called *Survivor*. In the end, Joan seems to have come off best – a screen goddess of her stature is not easily tarnished.

6

I (DON'T) WANT TO BE ALONE

In the early days, many of Hollywood's imported screen sirens brought their decadent European ways with them. The Russian star Alla Nazimova surrounded herself with other lesbians in her notorious Sewing Circle. She acted as mentor to many of the young girls drawn to Hollywood.

She also took a platonic interest in Hollywood's gay male stars, providing them with partners if their sexual orientation threatened to become public. When rumours of Rudolph Valentino's preference for young boys started to circulate, false as it turned out, Nazimova arranged for him to marry Jean Aker, one of her own girlfriends. The marriage, of course, was in name only; there was no necessity for anyone to change their sleeping arrangements.

Although the press were satisfied, in Hollywood the marriage was considered a joke. Aker grew tired of being a figure of fun and shocked women the length and breadth of America when she inexplicably divorced the Great Lover. Nazimova dragooned another of her girlfriends into a marriage of convenience with Valentino. Winifred Hudnutt's name was changed to Natascha Rambova to make her seem exotic enough to marry the virile hero of *The Sheik*. Nazimova made the ultimate sacrifice for gay star, Ramon Navarro, when she married him herself.

Greta Garbo swung both ways. As a young girl, she had physical encounters with other girls and, possibly with her older sister, Alva. Her early letters hint at lesbianism.

At fifteen, she was working in a milliner's shop in Stockholm when she met a wealthy man-about-town called Max Gumpel. He invited her home for dinner. She accepted and was a little disconcerted when he served her artichoke. She had never seen such an exotic vegetable before.

She began to visit Gumpel often. He bought her a gold ring with a stone set in it, which she told companions was 'as beautiful as a diamond in the English Royal Crown'. A year or so later, they married. The marriage didn't last but they parted amicably. Later, when she was a big movie star, she would dine with him when she returned to Sweden. One of the shrewdest businessmen in Europe, he advised her on real-estate investments.

Garbo got her start in the movies in 1922 in Sweden in a slapstick comedy called *Peter the Tramp*. She played a sixteen-year-old bathing belle in a less than revealing swimsuit. A theatrical stretch gave her the chance to show off her well-developed bust but for years Garbo, a keen swimmer, swam in the nude. David Niven said that the first naked female his sons ever saw was Greta Garbo swimming happily in their pool in Hollywood. When Garbo's co-star in *Wild Orchid* and *The Single Standard*, Nils Asher, informed her that one of her servants was letting paying customers watch her nude swims from a certain window, she just laughed.

On holiday with her lesbian lover, Mercedes de Acosta, at Silver Lake in the Sierra Nevada, or in the South of France with Aristotle Onassis, she was happy to go topless, even in the most public place. At home she would regularly garden nude, even though people could see her.

In her second film *The Saga of Gösta Beling*, the story of a much-sinning defrocked priest redeemed by the love of a countess, Garbo's infatuation with fellow starlet Mona Mårtenson was the talk of the set. Garbo told Mona that she loved her. Her affection was reciprocated. The two of them shared a hotel room when they were on location. Even when Garbo was a star in Hollywood, she hankered to return to Stockholm to appear on stage with Mona.

The director of *The Saga of Gösta Beling* was Maurit 'Moje' Stiller, a closet homosexual whose first film, The *Broken Spring Rose*, was banned by the liberal Swedish censors for excessive kissing and the fondling of the heroine's breasts. His sex comedy *Erotikon* was a big hit in Germany in 1920. It was Stiller who came up with the name Garbo for his young progetée. He was her Svengali, wringing from her the ambiguous sexuality of her screen performances. The eighteen-year-old Garbo spent so much time with the forty-year-old Stiller that people called them Beauty and the Beast. He took her everywhere with him, told her what to wear and what to say. Although he pursued his own sexual agenda, he liked having beautiful young women around him and coached Garbo to fulfil his vision of the 'ultimate woman'.

After *The Saga of Gösta Beling*, Stiller cast Garbo in the role of a Russian princess fleeing the Revolution, who is drugged and sold into a Turkish harem, in *The Odalisque from Smolna*. The film was to be shot in Constantinople. It was there at the Pera-Palace Hotel that the socialite Mercedes de Acosta, later Garbo's lover, first set eyes on her.

'One day in the lobby of the Pera-Palace Hotel, I saw one of the most hauntingly beautiful women I have ever beheld,' de Acosta wrote later.

Unfortunately, Stiller ran out of money halfway through shooting and the film was never finished. He and Garbo headed for Berlin where they threw themselves into the decadent nightlife. Stiller already had a contract with

Louis B. Mayer in Hollywood and he managed to get Garbo a part in Pabst's latest production *The Joyless Street*, which was the story of a young woman lured into prostitution but saved by an American lieutenant.

The film was a great success, though it was savaged by the censors. On the strength of that film, Garbo got a contract from Mayer too and she headed off to Hollywood with Stiller. There, they both immersed themselves in the homosexual subculture. Rumours circulated that Stiller and his openly gay colleague, the German director F.W. Murnau, were picking up young male prostitutes on Santa Monica Boulevard. Garbo was shocked. She told a friend: 'Moje only had the best in Berlin.'

Murnau later returned from shooting *Tabu* in the South Seas with a fourteen-year-old Polynesian boy who Murnau said was his 'valet-chauffeur'. The boy was not a good driver, though. During a momentary lapse of concentration on a trip from Los Angeles to Monterey, he swerved to avoid a truck and plunged down an embankment killing them both. Only eleven people were brave enough to turn up for Murnau's funeral. One of them was Garbo.

Meanwhile, Garbo hitched up with Lilyan Tashman, a lesbian actress notorious for her outrageous pick-ups in the powder room.

'Lilyan was one of the first women I ever heard use obscene language,' said silent-film actress Lina Basquette. 'She tried to corner me in the ladies' room when I was seventeen.'

Irene Mayer Selznick said: 'When Lilyan had some drinks, it was best not to go into the powder room with her. I did once and was never so startled in my life. I'd known Lil from way back, but nothing like that had ever happened to me in my life. So overt. I'd never seen anything like it – couldn't believe it was happening. Didn't know it ever happened.'

A former Ziegfeld girl, Tashman covered her tracks with

marriages of convenience. Her second husband was the actor Edmund Lowe, one of Hollywood's most overt homosexuals.

Tashman and Garbo were frequently seen shopping together and Tashman spoke openly of their relationship, even to the press. Paranoid about publicity, Garbo was furious and ditched Tashman for the 'Parisian sex symbol' Fifi D'Orsay. In fact, Fifi had never set foot in France. She was from Montreal and had become famous on the burlesque circuit for her catchphrase: ''Allo, beeeg boy.'

Garbo saw her in the 1929 movie *Hot for Paris* and wanted to meet her. A date was arranged. They met at the Russian Eagle and were frequently seen out in public together.

In February 1930, a Los Angeles daily reported: 'Greta Garbo and Fifi D'Orsay have become inseparable friends. Everywhere that Greta goes, Fifi is sure to tag along and vice versa. Greta stays in her shell and is so reserved that Hollywood has been greatly amused and interested in the dalliance. Fifi is Greta's first pal since Lilyan Tashman and Greta parted company. Greta sings the songs Fifi sang in *They Had To See Paris* (1929) and Fifi retaliates by trying to talk Swedish. Just how long it will last no one knows, but the two 'gals' are certainly a colorful pair – so different and both so foreign.'

The implications were clear. The source of the story was Fifi herself. Furious, Garbo dropped her and went back to Tashman.

Mayer was horrified by these stories. The woman the newspapers were talking about was the Swedish sex goddess the studio had invested millions in. She was the star of such heavy-breathing romantic classics as *The Temptress* (1926), *Flesh and the Devil* (1927), *Love* (1927), *The Divine Woman* (1928), *The Mysterious Lady* (1928), *A Woman of Affairs* (1928) and *The Kiss* (1929). They had to do something about it.

Louise Brooks takes up the story: 'After finally freeing herself from Stiller's disgusting homosexual games, she relaxed happily among the Hollywood lesbians until stories spread by those notorious gossips Lilyan Tashman and Fifi D'Orsay forced [MGM publicity chief] Howard Diez to yank back Garbo with a Gilbert–Garbo romance.'

Brooks should know. She, too, moved in Hollywood lesbian circles. She claimed that Garbo made a pass at her and they spent the night together.

'She was a completely masculine dyke, which makes her films even more wonderful,' Brooks said. 'She did the chasing, except for Mercedes de Acosta, whom she took on for snob reasons and gave a hell of a beating – the daughter of a butcher abusing a descendant of the Duke of Alba! But when someone like Dietrich or Bankhead went after her, Garbo took it on the lam.'

Naturally, the way to counter the lesbian allegations was to find Garbo a man. Fortunately, the studio had one to hand.

John Gilbert was one of the great stars of the silent movies. In 1925, after Valentino's death, he was the hottest thing in Hollywood. He earned a thousand dollars a week, drank with carpenters, danced with waitresses and made love to prostitutes and movie queens alike. But he had one great enemy, Louis B. Mayer.

During a script conference, Gilbert expressed interest in playing opposite Garbo in both *Anna Christie* and *Camille*. Mayer took exception to the scripts on the grounds that the heroines in both stories were essentially whores.

'What's wrong with that?' quipped Gilbert. 'My own mother was a whore.'

Mayer, taking this to be an affront to American motherhood, jumped up and launched himself at Gilbert who, Mayer considered, had already brought disgrace on MGM. He had split with his wife, the popular actress Leatrice Joy, three weeks before the birth of their daughter.

However, Gilbert was allowed to co-star with Garbo in *Flesh and the Devil*. Their love scenes, some of the hottest ever shot, were done with no rehearsals and no retakes. In the movie, Garbo seduces Gilbert. She did the same in real life. At the time, she was still a newcomer to Hollywood while he was an old hand who knew the ropes.

'She did what every actress has done since the word whore has been changed to the word actress,' said Louise Brooks. 'She went out with him and gave him a casual lay from time to time for the sake of her career.'

Soon after shooting finished on *Flesh and the Devil*, Garbo moved in with Gilbert. He built her a small cabin in his backyard, made an artificial waterfall and planted Swedish pines to comfort her when she felt homesick.

He swore his undying love to her. She was cooler but one day she actually agreed to marry him. The proposal took place at Marion Davies's hacienda in Beverly Hills. Garbo and Gilbert had been invited to dinner. The other guests included actress Eleanor Boardman and director King Vidor, both neighbours of Gilbert's, who were planning to marry two weeks later. After a drink or two, Gilbert suggested that they make it a double wedding. To everyone's surprise, Garbo said yes.

But on the morning of the wedding Gilbert saw Garbo pulling out of the driveway. She did not return. The wedding was to take place at Marion Davies's house, so Gilbert went there on the offchance that she would turn up. Mayer was there and made a typically crass comment.

'What's the matter with you, Gilbert?' Mayer said. 'What do you have to marry her for? Why don't you just make love to her and forget about it?'

Gilbert turned on Mayer who fell, banging his head on the floor and smashing his glasses.

'You're finished, Gilbert!' screamed Mayer as he struggled to his feet. 'I'll destroy you if it costs me a million dollars.'

Garbo later admitted that she was in love with Gilbert, but found him overbearing.

'I was afraid he would tell me what to do and boss me,' she said. 'I always wanted to be the boss.'

She hated his drunkenness and Stiller was furious that she should fall for anyone 'so half-witted as Gilbert'. Garbo had not told Gilbert that Stiller was gay and he assumed an on-going affair between the two of them was the reason she would not marry him.

Despite the marriage that never was, the studio continued to pump up the Gilbert–Garbo romance whenever lesbian allegations surfaced. Years later, the *New York Mirror* carried a story about Gilbert luring Garbo to the marriage licence bureau in Santa Ana but she 'broke away from him and hid in the railroad station until a train for Hollywood arrived'.

Hearst's Hollywood gossip columnist Louella Parsons reported: 'Garbo and Gilbert slipped quietly out of Los Angeles last Friday and were married in a nearby village. San Jose or Ventura are mentioned as the county seats where the license was obtained.'

It was all hokum, of course. Garbo was actually spending time with Nils Asher, her co-star in *Wild Orchid* and *The Single Standard*.

In his distress, Gilbert married actress Ina Claire on 9 May 1929. They separated on 31 August 1930 and divorced 4 August 1931. Meanwhile, Mayer lived up to his threat. Gilbert was given leading roles in a string of lousy pictures. He was wiped out by the Wall Street crash, but he still had an unbreakable contract with MGM to fall back on. When the talkies came along, Mayer took the opportunity to fix Gilbert once and for all. Gilbert's first talking picture release was *His Glorious Night*. Mayer got the MGM sound engineers to turn Gilbert's mellifluous tenor into a warbling falsetto – hardly an asset for a male romantic lead. Audiences tittered at the tinny whine and the critics dubbed the movie a 'shriekie'. Fans deserted him in droves. He took to the bottle and drank himself to death at the age of 39.

The writer and socialite Mercedes de Acosta had been obsessed with Garbo since she had first seen her in Constantinople in 1924. Before de Acosta discovered that

Garbo was an actress, she thought that she was so distinguished and aristocratic looking that she must be a Russian princess.

'Several times after this I saw her in the street,' she recalled. 'I was terribly troubled by her eyes and I longed to speak to her, but did not have the courage.'

She did not even know what language to use and no meeting took place then.

'As the train pulled out of the station which carried me away from Constantinople, I had a strong premonition that I might again see that beautiful and haunting face on some other shore.'

De Acosta had been confused about her sexual identity from an early age. She thought she was a boy until she was seven. Her family encouraged her in this delusion. Her mother had wanted a boy, so she called Mercedes 'Rafael' and dressed her in an Eton suit. As Rafael, de Acosta played with the other boys until one day, she said, 'the tragedy occurred'. One boy said that she could not throw a ball as far as them because she was a girl. She challenged him to a fight. Instead of fighting, he took her behind the bath house and showed her his penis. She thought it was horrible and said he was deformed.

'If you are a boy and you haven't got one, you're the one that's deformed,' he said.

The other boys came around the back of the bath house and showed her their penises too.

'Prove that you're not a girl,' they challenged.

Mercedes ran back home to her mother and forced her to admit that she was, in fact, a girl. She was sent to a convent where she vexed the nuns by claiming that she was not a girl and not a boy either – 'or maybe I'm both'.

Garbo, too, would refer to herself as a man.

Later in life de Acosta would say: 'Who of us are only one sex? I, myself, am sometimes androgynous.'

Mercedes certainly swung both ways. From 1920 to

74

1935, she was married to artist Abram Poole, which did not stop her picking up women. She even claimed to have taken a girlfriend on their honeymoon.

'I can get any woman from any man,' she used to boast.

She liked to hang out in drag clubs and also seduced men. Novelist Truman Capote developed a game he called 'International Daisy Chain'. The idea was to link any two people via the least possible number of sexual partners. He used to say that Mercedes was the best card you could hold: 'You could get to anyone – from Pope John XXIII to John Kennedy – in one move.'

Lesbian writer Alice B. Toklas was also fascinated.

'You can't dispose of Mercedes lightly,' she said. 'She has had affairs with the two most important women in America – Greta Garbo and Marlene Dietrich.'

Mercedes was invited to meet Garbo in New York in 1925, but was unable to go. Then, in 1931, de Acosta was summoned to Hollywood to write a script for Pola Negri. She did not have to be asked twice.

'The whole world thought of it as a place of mad night life, riotous living, orgies, careers that shot up like meteors and crashed down like lead, uncontrolled extravagances, unbridled love affairs and – in a word – SIN,' she wrote in her memoirs, *Here Lies the Heart*. It was, in short, her spiritual home.

Three days after arriving on the West Coast, de Acosta was invited to tea by Salka Viertel, a German actress whose home was the centre of émigré life. Garbo was also there. De Acosta was impressed by Garbo's eyes 'which held in them a look of eternity' and by the fact she wore trousers.

Two days later, they met for breakfast and spent the morning dancing at the beach-house of a Paramount screenwriter. Garbo invited Mercedes to come back to her house for lunch but de Acosta already had a luncheon engagement with Pola Negri which she could not break as it was 'an intimate lunch for six'.

Garbo laughed.

'More like six hundred,' she said. 'You don't know Hollywood.'

In the middle of the lunch, de Acosta got a telephone call. It was Garbo.

'Are there six or six hundred?' she enquired.

'More like six thousand,' de Acosta said.

She sneaked out of the party and sped over to Garbo's house. Garbo was waiting for her outside in a black silk dressing gown and men's slippers.

At sunset, she said: 'You must go home now.'

Later, they would spend nights together on the beach, locked in deep and meaningful conversations.

Garbo had planned a long vacation on an island in Silver Lake in the Sierra Nevada mountains because she wanted to be alone, but after two days, she returned to Los Angeles to fetch de Acosta. When they got back to the island, Garbo said: 'We must be baptised at once.'

She threw off all her clothes and plunged into the water. De Acosta was impressed and joined her even though the water was cold.

'How to describe the next six enchanted weeks?' de Acosta wrote in her memoirs. 'Even recapturing them in memory makes me realize how lucky I am to have had them. Six perfect weeks out of a lifetime... In all this time there was not a second of disharmony between Greta and me or in nature around us.'

Garbo and de Acosta moved into adjoining houses on Rockingham Road in Brentwood and spent time together every day. Mercedes also involved herself with what was left of Alla Nazimova's lesbian Sewing Circle. Most of the girls were now bisexual.

De Acosta was one of the most visible lesbians in Hollywood and frequently wore men's clothes. She encouraged Garbo to do the same. The two of them were famously pictured striding down Hollywood Boulevard, under the headline: 'GARBO IN PANTS!'

Garbo immersed herself in lesbian literature and had a short-lived affair with Eva von Berne, the so-called 'second Garbo' whom Irving Thalberg discovered in Vienna. She always dressed in men's clothes at fancy-dress balls and often expressed a desire to play men's parts in films. When she asked Aldous Huxley to write a screenplay about St Francis of Assisi for her, he replied: 'What, complete with beard?'

De Acosta attracted the wrath of Thalberg when she wrote a screenplay in which Garbo would be disguised as a boy for most of the film. Thalberg said: 'You must be out of your mind. We have been building Garbo up for years as a great glamorous actress. Now you want to put her in pants and make money out of her.'

When that project was canned, Garbo insisted that de Acosta write a screenplay based on *A Picture of Dorian Gray* for her. De Acosta said: 'You go and tell Irving the idea and have him throw you out of the window – not me.'

Director George Cukor saw another side of Garbo. He told Cecil Beaton: 'Of course she's a sensuous woman, will do anything, pick up any man, go to bed with him, then throw him out, but she reserves her real sensuousness for the camera.'

And the audience responded. At the height of her fame, she received fifteen thousand fan letters a week, many of them pornographic. She read none of them.

She met the charismatic conductor Leopold Stokowski at the Santa Monica home of Anita Loos and the two of them travelled together in Europe for several months.

'There will be no marriage for at least two years, owing to contracts and engagements in Hollywood,' Garbo told reporters. Soon after, Stokowski married heiress Gloria Vanderbilt.

In 1939, Garbo starred opposite Ina Claire, John Gilbert's ex-wife, in *Ninotchka* and made a pass at her which was declined. It was Garbo's last film. She was thirty-six and retired to seclusion in New York, saying famously: 'I want to be alone.'

By this time, the relationship between Garbo and de Acosta had cooled. De Acosta was involved in a torrid affair with the actress Ona Munson, a one-time protegée of Alla Nazimova. Garbo was having a brief affair with the health expert Gayelord Hauser, who she had met through de Acosta. He suggested they escape from this sexual hothouse and visit New York. There, Hauser took Garbo to the Russian dress designer, Valentina. George Schlee, Valentina's husband, turned up at his wife's saloon to find Garbo posing stark naked for a simple fitting. Schlee, Valentina and Garbo were soon seen out and about everywhere together. It was not unusual for Schlee to turn up to a party with his wife and Garbo both wearing identical blue sailor suits.

There was a lot of speculation about who was doing what to whom. Schlee is supposed to have told his wife that he was in love with Garbo, 'but she will never want to get married, and anyway you and I have so much in common'.

Others said that it was Valentina that Garbo really loved. However, Garbo was often seen alone with Schlee and they travelled widely together. Around that time, Garbo found time for a brief affair with Eric von Goldschmidt-Rothschild, but despite her outside interests, she maintained her uneasy ménage with the Schlees, always living close to them and eventually moving into the apartment above theirs on East 52nd Street.

In the spring of 1946, Schlee took Garbo to a small party given by Margaret Case, an editor at *Vogue*. The celebrity photographer Cecil Beaton was there. Beaton was a long-time friend of Mercedes de Acosta and had met Garbo in Hollywood in 1932. He was deeply attracted to her, but she was wary of him because 'he talks to newspapers'.

It was true that Beaton was a shameless self-publicist. At Cambridge, he sent stories about himself to the London newspapers, which was not considered at all the done thing in the 1920s.

Beaton's attitude to women was ambiguous. At school at Harrow, he had a homosexual affair and wore make-up. At Cambridge, he had an affair with Ben Thomas, who went on to become the Controller of the Central Office of Information. Many of his other homosexual chums went on to marry well and lead respectable lives. Beaton wanted that too. He could not accept his homosexuality, nor could he face the idea of having sex with a woman.

He enjoyed female company but, he admitted in his diary, 'I've never been in love with a woman and I don't think I ever shall be the way that I have been in love with men. I'm really a terrible homosexualist and try so hard not to be.'

On his second visit to New York in December 1929, he admitted that he had never been to bed with a woman to Marjorie Oelrichs, later the wife of bandleader Eddy Duchin. She offered to break his duck. Two days later, Adele Astaire, Fred's sister and dance partner, gave him a second bite of the cherry. She commended him for his modesty – while she was naked, he chastely covered himself with a towel. When he left for California a few days later, she turned up at the station with a gold pen which she gave him as a souvenir of their intimacy.

Beaton then played the heterosexual as hard as he could, condemning 'fairies' who, he said, 'frightened and nauseated' him. Dress designer Charles James accused him of merely posing as a part of the heterosexual world and it was true. Beaton was more comfortable in the company of homosexuals and lesbians. Within days of arriving on the West Coast, Beaton was doing the rounds with a black boxer called Jimmy. He later claimed to have had an affair with Gary Cooper on his first visit to Hollywood.

In Vienna in 1930, Beaton fell in love with Peter Watson. He was the lover of designer and decorator Oliver Messel, who Beaton saw as a lifelong rival. Beaton and Watson travelled extensively, but on a strictly 'look but don't touch basis'. Beaton found this tormenting and fell into black despair.

Watson suggested that Beaton take a lover, so Beaton attached himself to the glamorous Viscountess Castlerosse. The whole of London was soon chortling about the affair. Even Lord Castlerosse found it amusing.

Next Beaton bedded socialite Lilia Ralli. This led to invitations to photograph Princess Olga of Yugoslavia, the Duke and Duchess of Kent and, later, Queen Elizabeth. Actor John Gielgud attested to Beaton's growing heterosexual prowess: 'An actress friend of mine said Cecil was the best lay she ever had.' Nevertheless, Beaton still hung out in Turkish baths and attended homosexual orgies, and was so well known on the gay scene that few of his homosexual friends believed the stories of his heterosexual conquests.

Beaton was smitten with Garbo when he met her in Hollywood in 1932 and he found her just as beautiful when he met her again in New York in 1946. He steered her out on to the roof terrace and, while caressing her spine, made her promise to call him.

They began taking walks together in Central Park. One day, out of the blue, she said: 'My bed is small and chaste. I hate it.'

She went on to explain that, up to that point in her life, she had never really thought of settling down with one person in a marriage. Now she realized that had been a mistake. As she got older, she was getting lonely and now she thought she needed 'some permanent companionship'. Beaton immediately proposed.

Garbo chastised him for being so frivolous. A few days later, she admitted that she was in love with him. However, she had already booked a trip to Sweden so there was nothing to be done. She asked him to come round and take her passport photograph. Once he started snapping, Garbo got into the swing of being a model. She struck poses for him in different outfits.

While she was away, Beaton took the shots to *Vogue*. In Sweden, Garbo got wind of their imminent publication and cabled Beaton saying that she would never forgive him if the pictures appeared. Beaton frantically called *Vogue*, but it was too late. Copies were already on their way to the news-stands.

When Garbo returned to New York, she refused to take Beaton's calls. A month later, he managed to contact her in Hollywood, but she was frosty. For a year and a half, he bombarded her with letters, phone calls and telegrams. It did no good. In October 1947, he wrote in his diary: 'I am in complete despair.'

A mutual friend, Mona Williams Harrison, advised him to give up chasing her. If he stopped calling, it would make her worry. He had to play it cool and casual.

Four days after he stopped phoning, his telephone at the Plaza rang. It was Garbo.

'Can I come round now?' she asked.

He replied diffidently: 'It is too rainy and I've got to go out.'

She took no notice.

'I'll be right over,' she said.

He continued to play hard to get, intimating that he was seeing other women and other men – he was 'stepping out in both directions,' he said.

Then on 3 November 1947, she came to his room in the Plaza and he began massaging her back. She got up and drew the curtains. Suddenly, he found scenes that he had long rehearsed in his dreams were taking place in reality.

Garbo's greatest concern was that Schlee should not find out. On 14 November, she was upset when she was spotted by a hotel employee sneaking up the backstairs to Beaton's room. A cup of tea calmed her down.

'Do you want to go to bed?' she asked him after a while. Beaton felt, he said, like he was merely being used for his body.

On one occasion, Garbo began criticizing him for his effeminate manner and said she wanted to make a man out of him. He responded by saying that he could never marry her because 'you're not serious about me'.

'What a rebuff,' she said, then tenderly admitted, 'I love you, Cecil... I'm in love with you.'

They spent a lot of time together that December and talked seriously about their relationship. They found they shared an interest in cross-dressing when Beaton showed her pictures of himself dressed in women's clothing at Cambridge. He used to talk about the first time they had met and how glad he was that they postponed their relationship until he was more experienced. She said she worried that she had left it a little late to get married.

Garbo would still not spend the entire night with Beaton, and all their activities were confined to weekdays. She reserved her weekends for Schlee.

Mercedes de Acosta turned up in New York that Christmas Eve. In front of de Acosta, Garbo called Cecil 'Mr Beaton'. Beaton called everyone 'darling'. Garbo whispered under her breath: 'Don't you dare call anyone darling but me.'

On Boxing Day, Beaton invited Garbo, Schlee and a few others for drinks. The atmosphere was tense and Schlee could not bring himself to look Beaton in the eye. Beaton tried to kiss Garbo while Schlee was putting on his snow boots. This made Garbo both angry and frightened.

Garbo planned to spend New Year's Eve with Schlee, while Beaton went to a party with Mona Williams Harrison. Around 10.30, Beaton got a call from Garbo. She had had a row with Schlee. Beaton slipped out of the party without saying goodbye and took a taxi down Park Avenue to meet Garbo. They saw in the New Year together in Beaton's room with a bottle of 1840 whiskey. Beaton proposed a toast to their marriage and their life together. Garbo said nothing. That night, their lovemaking was 'wild and tender', but hopefully not noisy. Beaton said he was deeply disturbed by the 'most agonising sounds' the woman in the next room made while making love.

'Ecstasy is revolting,' he wrote.

Beaton begged her to come to England with him and be his wife but Garbo could not shake Schlee. They bumped into him one afternoon as they were coming out of the cinema together. With scarcely a nod to Beaton, Garbo took off with him. On another occasion, Beaton found himself in the theatre, staring at the back of Garbo and Schlee's heads.

One day, Garbo took Beaton to lunch with Mercedes de Acosta without warning her. She was so agitated that Garbo had to take over in the kitchen. Later, at dinner alone with Beaton, de Acosta begged him to marry Garbo. Gayelord Hauser, Stokowski and 'the little man' – Schlee – were not suitable for her.

Garbo, for her part, was upset when Beaton went to a first night with Leonora Corbett rather than spend the evening with her. At the interval, Beaton searched for a phone box to call Garbo. When he found one, it was occupied by Schlee, who was plainly on the same errand.

When Garbo headed back to California to sell her house there, Schlee told her that he did not want Beaton accompanying her. Beaton told Garbo that he had to go to Hollywood anyway to discuss the design work he was doing on a picture with Hitchcock and there was nothing she could do about it.

In fact, he covered his tracks better than that. When she left for Los Angeles, he followed on the pretext of doing a photographic assignment for *Vogue*. When he arrived, she met him and took him to her home in Benedict Canyon.

Beaton returned to England where he continued to fantasize about marrying Garbo. He wrote to her, addressing her as 'Dear Sir or Madam', 'Dear Boy' or 'Dear Young Man'. She called him 'Beattie' or 'Beattie Boy'.

In the summer of 1951, she came to England and stayed with Beaton for six weeks. She enjoyed life in Wiltshire and got on with his friends, including Princess Margaret, although she had a battle with his mother who found her a threat. The holiday ended when Garbo received a long letter from Schlee, which concluded: 'There is nothing left now but to announce your good news.' Garbo quickly headed back to New York.

Beaton finally realized how much control Schlee had taken over Garbo's life. There was no way that he was going to let her slip from his clutches. The following year Schlee was so confident of his hold over Garbo that he brought her to England and delivered her to Beaton himself.

Despite his years of persistence, Beaton's patience began to fray. One night in New York, in 1956, she brought up a row they had had long ago.

'If after all these years you can't forget that, then I'm a failure,' he said as he stormed from her apartment.

'Then you won't marry me?' she called after him sarcastically.

Before he returned to England, she told him: 'I do love you, and I think you are a flop. You should have taken me by the scuff of the neck and made an honest boy of me. You could have been my Salvation Army.'

All Beaton could muster as a reply was: 'Thank you for telling me that.'

The affair dragged on. In 1959, he phoned to tell her that he was planning to marry June Osborn, widow of pianist Franz Osborn.

'I'll come right over to cut her head off,' Garbo said. 'Give me another chance.'

But she was still seeing Schlee. Beaton had changed allegiance too. Sometimes when he was in New York, he would call on Valentina Schlee without bothering to visit Garbo in the apartment above. Beaton continued to pester Garbo about marriage after Anthony Armstrong-Jones married Princess Margaret.

Garbo was with Schlee in Paris in 1964 when he had a

heart attack and died. The following year she met Beaton again on board Cécile de Rothschild's yacht. They did not get on. There were rumours that Garbo and Cécile de Rothschild were lovers and her name was also linked with that of the actor Van Johnson. By the mid-1970s, after an impromptu visit to a sex shop, she was able to confide to a friend that she was glad that part of her life was over.

In 1972 and 1973, Beaton published his diaries, which included long passages about his affair with Garbo. Everyone turned on him for his disloyalty. He admitted that he had not asked the permission of this publicity-shy lover. When he had called her in New York, she had simply put the phone down on him. He told a friend, he considered that it would have been dishonest to leave out a major part of his life because of 'this woman's neurosis'.

Beaton was partially paralysed by a stroke in 1974 but she still blanked him. Sam Greene, a mutual friend, finally persuaded Garbo to visit Beaton in January 1980. On seeing her, Beaton began to weep. She sat on his lap and said: 'Beattie, I'm back.'

'Oh Greta,' he said. 'I'm so happy.'

Next morning, she made a tearful departure. Beaton died four days later, leaving her a painting of a single rose. Garbo died on 15 April 1990 in New York, leaving behind her $32 million and the reputation for being the gloomiest Scandinavian since Hamlet.

7

FALLING IN LOVE AGAIN (AND AGAIN, AND AGAIN...)

Garbo's greatest rival in Hollywood was Marlene Dietrich, another European screen goddess whose ambivalent sexuality held the rapt attention of the world.

She was born Marie Magdalene Dietrich on 27 December 1901 in Schöneberg, Germany. Schöneberg was swallowed up by the suburbs of Berlin in 1920. Her father, a policeman, left her mother and died before Marlene was ten. Marlene explained later that she wanted to take her father's place 'against my mother's will'.

She began to call herself Paul and at school, developed a crush on her French teacher – 'my secret love' – Mademoiselle Marguerite Breguand. This gave her rather ambivalent feelings when the First World War broke out.

Like all German schoolgirls, she was in love with Henny Porten, Germany's first great movie star. On a school trip to Mittenwald, the opportunity arose for her to take hero-worship a stage further than most girls her age. She discovered that Porten was staying in nearby Garmisch. She climbed out of the window of the boarding house where the school party was staying and, carrying her violin, she took a tram to Garmisch where she serenaded Porten early one morning. The star was not pleased.

At school, Marlene was famed for her 'bedroom eyes'. With the war on, most men were away at the front, so there were few to practise on. By the age of sixteen her looks were so provocative that she managed to get a young faculty advisor dismissed. At school pageants, Marlene would seize the opportunity to dress up as a boy and she had a 'special friend', Hilde Sperling, who worshipped her.

After the war, Marlene was sent to a boarding school in Weimar, where she entertained her room-mates with a risqué routine that involved her wearing only a bedsheet and doing an impression of a Chinese pagoda. She was already voluptuous and insisted on going to her private violin lessons with Professor Reitz, wearing a dress of the sheerest chiffon that left nothing to the imagination. Forty years later, Marlene told her daughter that she lost her virginity to the Herr Professor. Marlene did not win a place at the academy of music, but in Weimar she did meet influential members of the newly formed Bauhaus group.

To escape malicious gossip about her affair with Professor Reitz – who shortly left his wife and children for another woman – Marlene headed for Berlin to stay with an aunt and uncle and where she decided to try her hand at acting. To support herself meanwhile, she played the violin in a cinema, then in a theatre. Her legs soon got her out of the orchestra pit and into the chorus line at the Girl-Kabarett.

Marlene failed the audition to Max Reinhardt's acting school, but she began working in his theatres anyway. Her career was helped by her exotic Aunt Jolli who lent her outrageous clothes to wear around town. Wealthy Uncle Willi knew movie directors and used his influence to get her a part. When she met Rudi Sieber, an actor turned casting director, she threw herself at him. He may have been a well-known womanizer, but Marlene decided that this was the man she wanted.

At the age of twenty-one, Marlene Dietrich married Rudi Sieber in a registry office in the Berlin suburb of Friedenau. They remained married for the next fifty-three years until Rudi's death in 1976.

Rudi's former fiancée, Eva May, promptly slashed her wrists. She recovered, but shot herself in the heart the following year.

Marriage to Sieber did not give Dietrich the entrée into the movies she had hoped for. Instead, she got theatre roles as sluttish schoolgirls and French maids. In the movies, she played bathing beauties and scantily clad circus performers. Everything she did was overshadowed by Garbo's performance as a would-be prostitute in *The Joyless Street*. In 1924, Dietrich had a baby daughter, Maria or 'Heidede', and took a year off acting.

After the Wall Street crash, Berlin was flung into a pit of divine decadence. Every perversion imaginable was available on the streets. Dietrich and Sieber went clubbing. With Jolli's clothes, a handsome escort and her own dazzling beauty, Dietrich was bound to get noticed.

She was cast as a Parisian courtesan in *Leap into Life* and won good reviews. Although some producers thought her too beautiful to use, she found some success on the stage.

In *Duel on the Lido* (1926), she made her first movie appearance wearing trousers, which drew comment even from the newspapers of pre-war Berlin. Marlene continued to get roles as Parisian playgirls and jazz-age vamps, sometimes wearing a monocle which was to become something of a trademark. These bit parts helped Rudi fund an affair with a showgirl named Tamara 'Tami' Matul. It was an affair that was to last the rest of his life. Meanwhile, Dietrich was developing a relationship with the lesbian comedienne Claire Waldoff who helped Dietrich hone her distinctly masculine performing style.

Rudi had proved a bit of a flop when it came to helping Marlene with her career, so Marlene became the bosom pal of Betty Stern who hosted an influential salon. There, Marlene met matinée idol Willi Forst and followed him to Vienna where he was making a film. The director, Karl Hartl, made a solo screen test with her, which was no good.

'So we made more with Willi Forst in a love scene,' Hartl said. 'In view of their romance, it wasn't especially hard.'

Marlene got the part in *Café Electric*, which gave her a chance to show off her legs and play a good girl turned bad. Next she took a part in *Broadway*, a backstage love story in which she played a dancer, in a minuscule costume, opposite Peter Lorre. In Vienna, she also met Otto Preminger who tried to put her under contract.

Dietrich worked hard on her sexy image. She acted at the front of the stage, very close to the audience. Robert Klein, the artistic director of the Reinhardt theatres, saw her in Vienna and called her to Berlin to audition for a revue called *It's in the Air* that needed some added sex appeal. At the audition, he asked her whether she had any special talents. She said she could play the violin and the saw. He had never seen anyone play the saw and asked her to demonstrate. She got the part.

Marlene had nine major scenes in the show, including a lesbian duet with Margo Lion. They played two young matrons exciting each other with luxurious undies in the lingerie department. For the climax of the song, they were joined at the peek-a-boo counter by Oskar Karlweis.

One elderly gentleman came to see the show twenty-five times. Each time he insisted on front row seats and confirmed that Fräulein Dietrich was playing that night. Even Max Reinhardt turned up. Suddenly Marlene and her legs were everywhere. Stocking companies used her to advertise their wares. It wasn't long before Marlene's picture was appearing in magazines in America.

It's in the Air led to the title role in the movie *Princess*

O-la-la, in which she taught a young prince and princess, the victims of an arranged marriage, all about love. German movie magazines were soon calling her the new Garbo and insisted that G.W. Pabst give her the role of Lulu in his film *Pandora's Box*. Dietrich had actually made her stage début in the play. Pabst was on the point of signing her, even though he considered her too old and too sexy for the role, when Louise Brooks agreed to play the part.

Marlene went on to play another of her French girl parts in *I Kiss Your Hand, Madame*. Assistant cameraman Fred Zinneman remembers her as 'a good-time girl, especially with the crew'. She also began an affair with her co-star, the tenor Richard Tauber.

In 1929, Josef von Sternberg turned up in Berlin to film *The Blue Angel*. He was going to make two versions, one in German and one in English. Every actress in Berlin was tipped for the female lead of the sleazy nightclub singer Lola Lola. Hundreds traipsed through von Sternberg's office. Leni Riefenstahl, who later made the Nazi propaganda film *Triumph of the Will*, was privately convinced that she had the part, when she heard von Sternberg mention Dietrich's name.

'I've only seen her once,' said Riefenstahl, intending to put her down. 'She was sitting with some young actresses and my attention was drawn by her deep, coarse voice. Maybe she was a little tipsy. I heard her say in a loud voice: 'Why must we always have beautiful bosoms? Why can't they hang a little?' With that she lifted up her left breast and amused herself with it, startling the young girls sitting around her.'

Von Sternberg had already seen Dietrich's free-floating bosoms in a German movie called *Three Loves*, which had opened in New York to some acclaim. *The New York Times* particularly drew attention to Dietrich's 'Garbo-esque' beauty.

At the time, Dietrich was starring in Berlin's hottest revue. Von Sternberg went to see her and concentrated so intently on her that actor Hans Albers found it offputting.

FALLING IN LOVE AGAIN (AND AGAIN, AND AGAIN...)

Dietrich knew that von Sternberg was interested in her and feigned indifference. He was not impressed by the seventeen films she had already made, but he was convinced his direction could do her justice. At the screen test, she sang 'My Blue Heaven' in her inimitable style. This convinced him that he had found a star.

When Riefenstahl heard that Dietrich had got the part, she was so distraught that she cancelled an interview with Germany's leading movie magazine. Marlene was relaxing in a transvestite bar when the film's music direct Friedrich Holländer brought the news.

'She ordered so much champagne that you could have bathed in it,' he said.

During the shooting, Marlene gave the part everything she had got. Once, while she was singing 'Falling in Love Again', von Sternberg went crazy.

'You sow,' he yelled. 'Pull down your pants. Everyone can see your pubic hair.'

This may have been simply a display of jealousy. His discreet lunches *à deux* with his discovery in her dressing-room were the talk of the set.

When the film finally came out, one critic called her 'the new incarnation of sex'. That was not necessarily seen as a good thing. When the German company UFA, who had produced the film, saw the final cut, they were terrified and pulled the film from distribution.

This did not hamper Marlene's career. Even before the end of shooting, news of von Sternberg's discovery had reached America. Universal's man in Berlin, Joe Pasternak, turned up in her dressing-room to be greeted by Marlene 'wreathed coolly in a sheer peignoir and nothing else'. Paramount's Ben Schulberg had seen the rushes. Sales manager Sidney Kent saw her on the set. Jesse Lasky signed her and on 26 February 1930, Marlene Dietrich arrived in Hollywood.

Von Sternberg set about making *Morocco*, in which

91

Dietrich plays a nightclub singer much given to dressing up in men's clothes. He wanted John Gilbert to play opposite her, but was forced to use Gary Cooper instead. From the first day of shooting there was an enormous sexual chemistry between Dietrich and Cooper. Von Sternberg, who was obsessed with Dietrich, could scarcely conceal his jealousy.

In an attempt to build a barrier between his love and Cooper, von Sternberg would direct her in German.

'You goddamned kraut,' complained Cooper. 'If you expect to work in this country you'd better get on to the language we use here.'

Cooper knew perfectly well that von Sternberg had been brought up in New York city and was almost as American as he was.

Cooper's current lover, the tempestuous 'Mexican Spitfire' Lupe Velez, was no happier and insisted on doing a wicked impersonation of Dietrich around Hollywood, which she eventually took to Broadway after her affair with Cooper was over.

In Dietrich's next picture *Dishonored*, Marlene played a prostitute, recruited as a spy. Von Sternberg wanted to pair her with Cooper again, but Cooper refused to work with him. Von Sternberg's wife had also had enough.

'Why don't you just marry her?' she said. 'Maybe that will make her happy.'

'I'd sooner share a telephone booth with a frightened cobra,' von Sternberg replied. A few days later he kicked his wife out. Mrs von Sternberg retaliated with a $500,000 suit against Dietrich and the press branded her a 'love pirate'.

Maurice Chevalier found himself in an adjoining dressing-room while she was playing Shanghai Lily and they became lovers. Even the arrival of her husband Rudi and her child Maria did not cool her ardour. Tamara was left behind in Paris, in a luxury apartment financed by Marlene.

His affair with Dietrich later caused Chevalier embarrassment back in France. On the eve of the Second World

War, he blew a kiss to Marlene during a concert at the Casino de Paris. The audience booed. He only saved the situation by blowing another kiss to his discoverer and earlier lover, the legendary French music hall star Mistinguett who was also in the audience.

Cary Grant played opposite Dietrich in *Blonde Venus* and Brian Aherne co-starred in her next movie *Song of Songs*. He was to play an artist who sculpted her in the nude. The use of a statue of her nude throughout the movie was a skilful way around the morality codes of the Hays Office. Paramount even went so far as to put replicas of the famous nude in the foyer of their theatres. Otherwise, Dietrich and Aherne agreed it was a silly little picture, although after the crew went home each evening, they stayed the night together in her dressing-room.

The rapid turnover of men in Dietrich's life was an embarrassment to her daughter Maria. Dietrich explained that it was romance she craved, not sex, which was an 'inescapable burden that women had to endure'. Most of all she liked impotent or gay men.

'They are nice. You can sleep and it's cosy,' she said.

Marlene was not always so frank with her daughter. When Tamara Matul arrived in Hollywood, Marlene, Tami and Rudi would play musical bedrooms every night, so that the child would not discover the real sleeping arrangements.

One night Dietrich spotted Mercedes de Acosta with Cecil Beaton and was immediately love-struck. The next morning she turned up at de Acosta's house with a huge bunch of white roses, explaining that she knew few people in Hollywood and no one would introduce them. She had brought the flowers 'because you looked like a prince last night'. Dietrich also mentioned that Mercedes looked sad. De Acosta explained that Garbo was out of town.

'I am sad, too,' said Marlene, 'sad and lonely. You are the first person here to whom I have felt drawn. Unconventional as it may seem, I came to see you because I just could not

93

help myself.'

Marlene bombarded Mercedes with flowers – first tulips which de Acosta rejected as too phallic, then dozens of roses and carnations, sometimes twice a day. On one occasion she had ten dozen rare orchids flown in from San Francisco. When de Acosta's maid complained that Dietrich was sending so many flowers they were running out of vases, Marlene sent Lalique vases – and more flowers.

'The house became a sort of madhouse of flowers,' complained de Acosta. 'I was walking on flowers, falling on flowers, and sleeping on flowers. I finally wept and flew into a rage.'

She sent the maid off to the hospital 'with every damn flower in the house' and threatened to throw Dietrich in the pool if she sent any more. So Marlene began sending other gifts. Box upon box arrived from Bullock's on Wilshire Boulevard containing dressing gowns, pyjamas, slacks, sweaters, lamps and lampshades.

'Bullock's Wilshire moved into my home,' said de Acosta and she sent the gifts back to the store.

Marlene poured out her heart in a series of letters and telegrams. Finally, on 16 September 1932, Mercedes succumbed. They spent the afternoon in bed together. That evening, when de Acosta dropped Marlene home, she jumped hurriedly from the car and ran indoors, frightened that her daughter might see her.

Marlene and Mercedes spent a lot of time together at the Santa Monica beach-house Marlene rented from Marion Davies and romped on the beach with actors Martin Kosleck and Hans von Twardowski. Marlene would cook for Mercedes, while Mercedes encouraged Marlene to go without make-up and wear slacks.

When the studio began to get worried about rumours of Marlene's lesbian affair, she set Schulberg straight.

'In Europe,' she said, 'it doesn't matter if you're a man or a woman, we make love to anyone we find attractive.'

Marlene continued to buy gifts for Mercedes from Bullock's, but began to concentrate on items from the men's department. De Acosta wrote love poetry and letters to Dietrich, calling her Golden One and promising to 'kiss you all over – everywhere. And I kiss your spirit as well as your lovely body.'

She chastised Marlene for saying that she would love her 'always'.

'Don't say 'always', for in love it is blasphemy,' Mercedes wrote. 'One never knows if, from now on, one truly loves or if one is making oaths and one simply forgets them. Don't say always, for in love nothing binds you.'

Marlene's letters became more matter of fact. They would apologise for being late, tell Mercedes to go to bed and await her there. Gradually, Dietrich was getting fed up with de Acosta's constant talk about Garbo. It was true Garbo had a place in Mercedes' heart that no other could attain – 'Dietrich was a pro, but Garbo was an artist,' she wrote in her memoirs.

Dietrich stuck around to comfort de Acosta when Irving Thalberg fired her from MGM, but in May 1933, Marlene, Maria, Rudi and Tami took off on a family holiday in Europe. Then it was Mercedes who took to sending flowers as she tried to cling on to the relationship.

'I will bring anyone you want to your bed,' de Acosta wrote in desperation. 'And this is not because I love you so little, but because I love you so much, my beautiful one.'

In Paris, Dietrich recorded some songs but then, instead of going to London to meet Brian Aherne as planned, she headed to Vienna where her old lover Willi Forst was directing his first feature film which, it was rumoured, Dietrich was financing. She immediately fell in love with the star of the movie, twenty-eight-year-old matinée idol Hans Jaray. They were inseparable and were often seen around Vienna in the company of Forst or with the ever-tolerant Rudi.

Meanwhile, de Acosta had fallen into a black depression.

SEX LIVES OF THE HOLLYWOOD GODDESSES

Even the return of Garbo did not cheer her up. While she was out driving with her maid, she said that she wished a car would hit them and kill her. She almost got her wish. She was thrown from the car and landed on her head. Recovering in Santa Monica Hospital, she got a call from Marlene offering to pay her medical bills.

After renewing her relationship with Garbo, de Acosta wrote to her husband in New York suggesting that he take a model he had always fancied as his mistress. He wrote back protesting at this 'immoral suggestion'. In fact, he had already done so and, the following year, he asked Mercedes for a divorce. She was devastated.

Marlene returned to Hollywood to be cast as the insatiable Catherine the Great in a film entitled *The Scarlet Empress* after the Hays Office had banned the original title *Her Regiment of Lovers*. While she was there, Dietrich took up with another of Garbo's cast-offs – John Gilbert.

Garbo had tried to resurrect Gilbert's career by insisting he play her lover in *Queen Christina*, after rejecting both John Barrymore and Laurence Olivier. Mayer eventually relented, but the film was a commercial failure. The public now wanted macho actors like Clark Gable and Gary Cooper, not the effete mannerisms of the silent stars, and Gilbert set off once more down the slippery slope.

Marlene turned the full sunshine of her love on Gilbert. She put him in analysis, took him dining and dancing, and spent time sunbathing with him at the pool side. Under her influence, he dried out and she got him a job in her next movie *Desire*. He was to play the loser in a love triangle with Dietrich and Gary Cooper.

Legend has it that Dietrich dropped Gilbert after she saw Garbo's car in his driveway. In fact, there was no romantic reunion between Gilbert and Garbo. The shooting of *Desire* rekindled Dietrich's passion for Cooper who had now freed himself from Lupe Velez. Alcoholism had left Gilbert impotent, so there was no way he could compete with Cooper.

He began drinking again.

Heavy boozing brought on seizures and he was dropped from the picture. Marlene returned to his side, but it was too late. On 9 January 1936, Gilbert swallowed his own tongue and died. He was thirty-six. According to her daughter, Dietrich was with him when it happened, but realizing that he was dying she vamoosed. She knew that her career would be finished, by virtue of the studios' morality clause, if she was found with him. She instructed the servants to remove all trace of her from his bedroom. After calling a doctor and wetting a face flannel, she fled. Marlene collapsed with grief at his funeral.

Later, in London playing a countess in the film *Knight Without Armour,* she fell for her co-star, Robert Donat. Although she confided to a friend that he was romantically off limits because he was happily married, it was an open secret that she went to great pains to nurse him through a heavy bout of asthma that almost lost him the picture.

Having no luck with Donat, she took Douglas Fairbanks Jnr as her lover. Fairbanks would be seen sneaking out of Claridge's at five or six in the morning, still wearing his evening suit. CBS's young mogul William S. Paley was also pursuing Dietrich. He would call her and tell her what a mistake she was making choosing Fairbanks over himself. Once Paley bumped into Fairbanks outside Dietrich's suite at dawn.

'I know where you've been,' said Paley.

Fairbanks was a gentleman. He raised his finger to his lips and whispered: 'Yes, but don't tell Marlene.'

At first, Fairbanks was a little phased by Dietrich's relationship with Rudi, especially as he understood no German, but he soon realized that it posed no threat. He was also perturbed by Marlene's habit of swimming in the nude, after taking her to house parties with friends in the English countryside. Later, Fritz Lang explained that nude bathing was a German custom, as they relaxed on the patio of

Fairbanks's Beverly Hills home which had a wonderful view over Marlene's swimming pool next door. Her nude dip that afternoon must have been a trip down memory lane for Lang, who had had a brief affair with Dietrich when he first arrived in Hollywood.

Marlene moved into Fairbanks's flat in Grosvenor Square. He found her 'a wonderfully unconventional lover' and 'very naughty'. He sculpted her nude, giving her the original and keeping a plaster copy for himself. .

Back in Berlin, she met Erich Remarque, author of *All Quiet on the Western Front*. Marlene said that he looked much too young to have written such a classic. They talked until dawn and Marlene was delighted when he announced that he was impotent.

'Oh, how wonderful. What a relief,' she said.

She explained that she hated having sex. She was so happy because they could talk and sleep and love each other – 'all nice and cosy'.

Fearing the Nazis, Remarque escaped to Paris. Marlene followed. They travelled on to Hollywood where they stayed together in a bungalow at the Beverly Hills Hotel. He began to write a novel about his exile called *Arch of Triumph* which he dedicated to 'M.D.'

By this time, Marlene was in her late thirties and no longer a hot property. According to her daughter Maria, Dietrich's famous breasts began to sag from going for years without a bra. Soon all her costumes, even her dressing gowns, had flesh-coloured bras sewn into them. From then on she would entertain lovers only in the dark and they would never again get the chance to see her completely naked.

Dietrich made her comeback with Jimmy Stewart in *Destry Rides Again*.

'After a week's work on the picture, I fell in love with her,' Stewart admitted later. 'She was beautiful, friendly, enchanting and as expert at movie acting as anyone I'd ever known. The director, cameraman, cast and crew felt the same way. We all fell in love with her.'

Maria claimed that Stewart made her mother pregnant during the filming of *Destry* but, when she confronted him, the unmarried Stewart said nothing and walked away. Marlene, her daughter said, took care of the matter in the usual way.

Dietrich was filming *Seven Sinners*, when she spotted the up-and-coming John Wayne in the Universal commissary. She walked past him as if he was invisible. Then she stopped, half turned, ran her eyes over him from head to toe and whispered: 'Daddy, buy me that.'

Wayne got a small part in *Seven Sinners*, which was the movie where Marlene wore her first 'nude dress'. These were creations of sheer, transparent fabrics with the odd sequin sprinkled in strategic places. Wayne was mesmerized by her. She thought he was not exactly bright or exciting, but she enjoyed going hunting, fishing and drinking with him. They made two more pictures together.

Hitler was a great fan of Marlene's. Leni Riefenstahl surprised him watching a private showing of one of her movies at Berchtesgaden. The Führer had begged Marlene to return to Germany. She refused. On 6 March 1937, she took US citizenship and during the war she enthusiastically sold US War Bonds. Her favourite ploy was to sit on the laps of drunks in nightclubs while Treasury agents called their banks to make sure their cheques would clear. When President Roosevelt heard about her methods he summoned her to the White House.

'We're grateful to you,' the President said. 'But I won't allow this sort of prostitution technique. You will no longer appear in nightclubs.'

She did as she was told.

Marlene had met the French film actor Jean Gabin in Paris before the war. When he turned up in exile in Hollywood she moved with him to a house in Brentwood.

'He had the most beautiful loins in the world,' she told friends.

They were also appreciated by the woman next door who peered through the shrubbery during their nude swimming and sunbathing sessions – Greta Garbo. This disturbed Gabin. He also grew increasingly jealous of Marlene's Sewing Circle friends, who including Claudette Colbert and Lila Damita.

Aware of his feelings, Marlene transformed herself from a sex goddess into an ordinary German *hausfrau* and started cooking and cleaning for him.

'For that woman to put on an apron and cook a great meal was an absolute thunderbolt,' said her friend Orson Welles.

Gabin simply took it for granted. Like an old-fashioned French peasant, he would sit, puffing on a cigarette and reading the paper, waiting for the most glamorous woman in the world to put his dinner on the table in front of him.

Unhappy with the films he was offered in America, Gabin joined the Free French Army and sailed for North Africa. He left three valuable paintings with her – a Renoir, a Sisley and a Vlaminck – as a token of fidelity. After the war he said he intended to return to America, collect his paintings and make Marlene his bride.

Their paths crossed several times in Europe, when she was there entertaining the troops, and when he was demobbed, they moved into Claridge's in Paris together. They made movies together in Paris, where she met up with some of the lesbian friends she had known in Germany before the war. Gabin was a jealous man and began to beat her. She gave as good as she got.

Gabin had good reason to be jealous. Marlene was having several discreet lesbian affairs, including one with Edith Piaf. When it was over, Marlene acted as Piaf's bridesmaid. She also had a very public affair with General James Gavin, whom she had first met during the Battle of the Bulge.

The joke went around Paris that all that separated Gabin and Gavin was a French letter. The general's wife did not think this was funny and promptly sued for divorce, naming Marlene as co-respondent. The general asked Marlene to marry him. She refused.

'I can't be an army wife,' she said. 'What would I have to say to the other army wives?'

When she moved out of Claridge's to the Elysées Parc Hôtel, Gabin asked for the return of his paintings, which were still in California. Marlene said she thought he had given them to her. He said he had, but he wanted to live with her and the paintings – and he wanted to get married and have children. Marlene didn't want more children at her age and didn't see why her career should take a backseat to his. With an offer from Paramount in her pocket, she headed back to Hollywood. He never spoke her name again.

Even though she had run away from him, Dietrich remained in love with Gabin. She cherished all his love letters. She bought an apartment in the Avenue Montaigne near his, which she kept for the rest of her life. When she heard that he was getting married, she rushed to Paris, but he would not see her. He bought a plot in a graveyard in Normandy not far from his birthplace but when she bought the adjoining plot, he sold up. Years later, when Jean Gabin died – some years after the death of her husband Rudi – she said wistfully: 'Now I am a widow for the second time.' Gabin was the love of her life.

That did not mean she pined after their separation. She had a brief affair with Kirk Douglas and a long-running one with a New York businessman who wanted to marry her. She also slept with Ed Murrow, whose wartime broadcasts from London during the blitz had inspired her. Otherwise, her diaries were full of Michaels, Johns, Joes and Jimmys.

In *Stage Fright* (1950), Jane Wyman walked off with an Oscar but Dietrich walked off with co-star Michael Wilding, who was a dozen years her junior. They were separated when

Marlene became a grandmother and rushed to New York to give Maria a hand with the new baby. Shortly afterwards Dietrich flew to Paris to buy some clothes. At Balmain, she bought the most expensive mink they had ever sold, charging it to Darryl Zanuck, and took Balmain's *directrice* Ginette Spanier home with her. They became intimate friends. For years, Marlene would sleep over at Spanier's apartment when she was in Paris, until a small row over scrambled eggs escalated into a full blown fight. Women are wonderful, Marlene concluded, but you cannot live with one.

Marlene returned to Hollywood to find that Wilding had inexplicably developed an interest in Elizabeth Taylor.

'What's Taylor got that I haven't?' she demanded of producer Herbert Wilcox, who was far too gallant to mention that Taylor was just nineteen, while Dietrich was forty-nine. Marlene consoled herself with the young Yul Brynner, who found himself being unfaithful to his wife with a woman he had admired since he was a child. She was the most determined, passionate and possessive lover he had ever known – and the least discreet. He secretly rented a studio apartment where he could spend nights with Marlene, but an anonymous studio apartment did not suit a woman of Marlene's stature. She moved into an apartment in Park Avenue and covered the walls with mirrors so she could get an all round view of their lovemaking. She liked to smear his body with paint to arouse him and praised his inexhaustible virility.

When a friend criticized her Park Avenue apartment by saying it was a bit 'Hollywood', she said: 'What's wrong with Hollywood?'

The affair with Yul Brynner continued, though he treated her badly and her friends chastised her for chasing after him. During the filming of *The Monte Carlo Story,* Dietrich dreamt up an excuse to fly to Paris for the weekend. She returned to Monaco at noon on Monday, looking radiant.

'Yul was in Paris,' she admitted to the director Samuel A. Taylor.

The affair ended when Marlene became insanely jealous of Brynner's wife.

During the filming of *The Monte Carlo Story*, Dietrich spent a lot of time with a young French girl. Taylor recalled how he had spotted her in the bar of the Hôtel de Paris, while his wife was away, and had asked her to dinner the next night. That morning, he got a call from Marlene, inviting him up to her suite to talk about the script. When he arrived, he found the girl in Marlene's room. She just sat there saying nothing while Dietrich and Taylor had a meaningless conversation. Neither of them acknowledged the girl's presence. It was simply Dietrich's way of saying 'hands off, she's mine'.

After the picture was over, Taylor said: 'Marlene understood sex was the ruling physical thing in human life, but I don't think she was personally a very sexy dame. Sex may have been the guiding force in her life, but intellectually. She was fascinated by sex, all kinds, everybody's. She could have written a book.'

Back in New York, Marlene had an affair with an actress who had had no experience of sex with a woman before. In bed she described Marlene as 'expert and unfailingly considerate'. After one particular weekend, Marlene introduced the woman to a Hollywood producer who took a shine to her. When she went out on a date with the producer, Marlene lent the woman some of her jewellery, so that she would not look like a gold-digger. Later, the two got married. At the reception Marlene took the bride aside and said: 'I knew what would be best for you.'

Meanwhile, Marlene's career as a Hollywood star was at an end. In 1952, she had a flop with *Rancho Notorious*, produced by Howard Hughes and directed by her former lover Fritz Lang. It was her last star vehicle.

Ernest Hemingway, who had first met Marlene in the 1930s, wrote a fitting epitaph for her screen career in *Life* magazine. He said that Dietrich was a great actress because she 'knew more about love than anyone'. Director Samuel A.

Taylor said what Hemingway meant was she knew more about sex than anyone.

Marlene complained that 'Hemingway never asked me to go to bed with him'. He constantly made jibes about her 'girls' and wrote her off as a lesbian. However, his remark about knowing 'more about love than anyone' inspired *The Ladies' Home Journal* to run a column called 'How To Be Loved' under her byline.

In an attempt to boost *Rancho Notorious* at the box office, Dietrich went on a publicity tour, which convinced her that there was still a life for her on the stage. In December 1953, against the advice of Maurice Chevalier and Noël Coward, she opened at Sands Hotel in Las Vegas. She stood on stage and let her cape slip from her shoulders. Underneath was another of her 'nude' dresses. Tallulah Bankhead quipped: 'She told me she didn't have a thing to wear. And, to think, I didn't believe her.'

The show was an instant success and those 'nude' dresses soon made her the highest paid cabaret artist in the world.

Dietrich dedicated herself completely to the stage after a new man came into her life. She met Burt Bacharach at the Beverly Hills Hotel. He had a cold and she decided to play Florence Nightingale – though the way she told it she diagnosed gonorrhoea and said she had found a cure. Soon he was working on new musical arrangements for her and expanded her repertoire. He also became, as she put it, her *amitié amoureuse*.

After seeing the work of Alberto Giacometti in New York's Museum of Modern Art, Marlene became obsessed with the sculptor. She bombarded him with roses and sat on a stepladder in his dusty studio while he worked. Eventually he found he could not resist her, but returned home to his wife afterwards. Marlene consoled herself with a new 'throb', as Noël Coward put it, the Italian film star Raf Vallone.

Despite these affairs, Bacharach stayed with her until 1965. By then he had a burgeoning career as a composer and he longed to have a settled life with a wife and children. This Marlene could not provide. The woman he turned to was movie actress Angie Dickinson. Dietrich was furious that he was leaving her for someone who was not a star.

Soon after, Tamara Matul died, murdered by another patient at Camarillo, the California state mental hospital where she had been confined after a breakdown. Dietrich and her factotum Bernard Hall flew to California to comfort Rudi at the chicken farm in the San Fernando Valley where he lived. Rudi was in his sixties by then and Marlene still referred to him as divine.

Some time later, while touring Australia, Marlene was pestered for an interview by a young journalist named Hugh Curnow. Although he was married with three children, he was well known on the Sydney singles scene. Marlene snapped him up and took him back to Paris, where he was to ghost-write her memoirs. Curnow complained that Marlene, by then bound in bandages to keep her body trim, had to be unwound like a mummy. He also complained about her love-making.

'She made love the French way,' he said, 'hated to have me on top of her.'

If that was not bad enough, he did not even feign interest in her scrapbooks. So she sent him back to his wife and kids. She saw him once more, briefly, in Sydney when she was on her way to Adelaide. Later that day, he was killed in a freak accident, decapitated by a helicopter's rotor blade.

Fritz Lang said: 'When she loved a man, she gave herself completely, but still looked around for another. That is the great tragedy of her life. Maybe she has always to prove to herself that because one man loves her, there'll always be another.'

In May 1967, Rudi had a heart attack, followed by a stroke. Marlene rushed to his bedside to look after him twenty-four hours a day. He survived and returned home. He had a housekeeper to look after him and kept a picture of Tamara which was never out of his sight.

Dietrich continued to tour the world with Ginette Vachon, a former Canadian Olympic tennis player who was still in her twenties. Vachon was there to cradle Marlene in her arms when she broke a leg on stage in Sydney. Dietrich was flown to Los Angeles and checked into UCLA Medical Center, in the room next to Rudi who had returned to hospital after another stroke. Her daughter Maria insisted that she be moved to the Columbia-Presbyterian Medical Center in New York for treatment, where she checked in under the name Mrs Rudi Sieber.

Marlene did not even see Rudi during her stop-over in LA. She never saw him again. He died in 1976 in the house in the Valley that he had shared with Tamara, one week after Marlene got out of hospital. Missing seeing him that one last time in LA, Dietrich said, was 'the greatest mistake in my life'. She had him buried in Hollywood Memorial Park Cemetery, near to Tamara. His headstone bore the one word 'Rudi'.

With Rudi dead, Marlene abandoned her career, though she was persuaded to appear in the disastrous *Just a Gigolo* with David Bowie in 1978, and she appeared in a film documentary about her life, directed by Maximilian Schell.

She died on 6 May 1992 in Paris, in her flat on Avenue Montaigne, not far from Jean Gabin's old apartment. Her coffin was draped with the French flag at a service held for her at the Eglise de la Madeleine. Then her coffin, draped with the American flag, was flown to Berlin where it was covered with the flag of the newly reunified German Republic and laid to rest.

8

PURE AS THE DRIVEN SLUSH

Not all the bisexual screen goddesses were European. Tallulah Bankhead was home-grown, although it can be argued that she was not one hundred per cent committed.

'I needed the publicity – I had to get a job,' she said. 'In the twenties and thirties, a lesbian was tops in desirability, especially with a girlfriend as a side dish.'

Bankhead may not have been in the same movie-star league as Garbo or Dietrich, partly because she preferred the stage, but for her breathtaking sex life in and around Hollywood – and anywhere else she went – Tallulah was a legend. She claimed to have had five thousand sexual partners, found fidelity impossible and specialized in taking her clothes off at parties.

'Why do you do that, Tallulah?' her lifelong friend Estelle Winwood once asked. 'You have such pretty frocks.'

In an uptight age, she was completely outspoken. A lady reporter in the 1930s asked: 'Miss Bankhead, what is your definition of love?'

'Do you mean fucking?' Tallulah replied.

At a society wedding, while the bride and groom were walking down the aisle, Tallulah is said to have remarked loudly: 'I've had both of them, dahling, and neither of them is any good.'

When sex researcher Alfred Kinsey asked her if she would tell him about her sex life, she said: 'Of course, dahling, if you will tell me about yours.'

Later she remarked that making love in the conventional fashion was uncomfortable, but of the other alternatives one gave her claustrophobia, the other lockjaw. A woman of noted and self-deprecating wit, she was all too aware of her shortcomings.

'I am,' she said, 'as pure as the driven slush.'

Tallulah Bankhead was a southern belle born in Huntsville, Alabama on 31 January 1902. Her mother died three weeks later due to complications arising from the birth. Her father was a lawyer who was elected to Congress in 1917 and went on to become Speaker of the House.

Tallulah was a lively and energetic child. There was one particular childhood story she loved to tell in later life. She was having a picnic in the woods with some other children one day when a rattlesnake bit her on the behind.

'Quick as a flash, Daddy snatched off my panties and sucked the blood from the wound,' she said. He had a cut on his gums and became quite ill. Ever after, in her passport, under the heading 'Distinguishing Marks' she would put 'snakebite'.

At the age of fifteen, she won a competition in *Pictureplay* magazine. The prize was a movie contract with a company in New York at a salary of $50 a week. She stayed at the Algonquin and quickly got to know members of the famous round table. When the movie contract failed to appear, her grandfather sent her an allowance of $50 a week. Her room cost $21 a week, so that should have been enough. But Tallulah hired a French maid at $25 a week and eked out her existence on the remaining $4 a week by crashing parties.

Soon she was appearing as a walk-on in a play called *The Squab Farm*, and she got a role in a movie called *Why Men Betray*. In 1918, Sam Goldwyn – who was still using his original name, Goldfish – signed her for his picture *Thirty-a-Week*, and she got a speaking part in a play called *39 East*.

During that period she met Estelle Winwood, an English actress with more than thirty years experience on the stage. She took the young Tallulah away on holiday to Atlantic City. On the train, they met actor John Barrymore. Tallulah fell for him instantly and, although he had a lover already lined up in New Jersey, Tallulah mooned about hoping to bump into him. Later, her devotion was rewarded. Back in New York, Barrymore invited Tallulah to visit him in his dressing-room. He offered her a part in his movie version of *Dr Jekyll and Mr Hyde* as he locked the dressing-room door with one hand and led her to the couch with the other. Tallulah, still young and naive, declined the part she was being offered – and lost the chance to be in the movie too. She remained obsessed with Barrymore though and went to see him thirteen times in *The Jest* on Broadway.

Soon after, she was seen kissing a girl at a party.

'I want to try everything once,' she said. She was already experimenting with marijuana and cocaine, though she did not drink at that point because she had promised her father not to touch alcohol if he let her go on the stage.

Although Tallulah never bedded John Barrymore, she had better luck with his sister Ethel. At a party, Tallulah was prompted into doing an impression of Ethel. Miss Barrymore was there and took exception. She slapped Tallulah's face. Later they became close friends. When Tallulah was living in London, Ethel Barrymore turned up at a party at Tallulah's flat in Farm Street, intending to stay only a few minutes. She stayed the night. More nights followed. It is not recorded whether Ethel offered Tallulah a movie part, but around that time Ethel turned down a proposal of marriage from

Winston Churchill.

At a party in New York, Tallulah met Lord Napier Alington. He had been invited by Jeffery Holmesdale, theatre critic for the *Morning World*. There had been a shortage of men at the party so Holmesdale called Alington, who was in bed.

'Don't bother to dress, come as you are,' said Holmesdale. Alington took him literally and turned up in his pyjamas clutching a bottle of gin.

A young aristocrat, Alington had been invited to America by Mrs Cornelius Vanderbilt to study banking. He had found it rather boring, so had moved into Greenwich Village with English music-hall actress Teddy Gerrard.

When he turned up at the party, Tallulah was smitten by his English accent and his air of recklessness. In confessional mood, she admitted that she was still, technically, a virgin. By technically, she meant that she had not made love to a man. An older actress had already initiated her in the delights of sapphic love.

Alington immediately volunteered to amend her sexual status and make her a woman of the world. After all, he was already in his pyjamas and dressed for the part. Tallulah said no, on that occasion. For a while they stepped out together in a reckless round of drunken parties. They danced till dawn with Noël Coward and walked barefoot in the snow. Then, suddenly, Alington disappeared back to England.

Tallulah knew Alington had his faults. He was a gambler, a womanizer and thoroughly irresponsible. He did not even write.

She went to a fortune-teller, who told her what she wanted to hear.

'Your future lies across the water,' the fortune-teller said. 'Go, if you have to swim.'

A few days later, the impresario Charles B. Cochran, who had seen Tallulah on Broadway, cabled from London. He had a part for her in a play by Gerald Du Maurier. A few days later, Cochran cabled again, saying Du Maurier had changed his plans. Tallulah borrowed $1,000 and set sail for England anyway.

This audacious strategy worked. When Du Maurier saw her in the flesh, he gave her the part. She was a sensation. Every night she packed them in. The newspapers noted that her fans were almost exclusively female. Unlike the other actresses, she attracted few stage-door Johnnies, but one important one turned up – Lord Napier Alington.

Tallulah found Alington infuriating and enchanting in equal measure. While she was pursuing him, she was being pursued herself by Sir Francis Laking – 'a witty young man of cloudy gender' – who took her on holiday to Venice. Alington suddenly disappeared completely. Tallulah mourned his loss by indulging in affairs with lots of men. Laking was fiercely jealous.

As Tallulah's fame on the English stage grew, stories circulated about her. One woman, who had formerly complained that her husband was a homosexual, accused Tallulah of stealing him from her. The Duke of Kent was an avid fan. She seems to have gone through half of Berks Peerage, but she did not confine her favours to the aristocracy. A taxi driver who drove her home one Friday night was invited in for the weekend. When the poor man left, exhausted, on Monday morning, she shouted down from her bedroom window: 'Dahling, you're as good as the King of England.'

Many of these stories she planted herself. She was great at PR. When a journalist came around, she would simply take him to bed and let him do all the probing he wanted there.

Tony Wilson, grandson of the Earl of Ribblesdale, proposed six times; she had a moving affair with Michael Wardell, editor of the *Evening Standard*; and she nearly married Count Anthony de Bosdari, but pulled out when she began to suspect that he was exploiting her celebrity to float a speculative business deal. Later she said that Alington was the only man she really loved.

SEX LIVES OF THE HOLLYWOOD GODDESSES

In the theatre, she was cast as prostitutes, fallen women and unfaithful wives.

'Don't think for a minute I enjoy doing sex plays,' she said in an interview. 'But when you are climbing, you've got to take what God offers.'

She was fêted by Augustus John, Winston Churchill, Lloyd George and the then prime minister Ramsey MacDonald. MacDonald invited her to lunch at Number Ten. Afterwards, he brought his straitlaced sister to visit Tallulah in her dressing-room. Tallulah immediately introduced her to a doctor who was also visiting, and said: 'You must remember his name, dahling, he's absolutely wonderful at abortions.'

She once asked T.E. Lawrence to visit her, telling him that she loved brave men. Asked what she would do if he turned up, she said: 'He's not that brave.'

Playing a seduction scene in the play *Scotch Mist* with Godfrey Teale, Tallulah put on such a compelling performance in rehearsal that Teale's wife, who was in the auditorium, began to cry. Tallulah turned to director Basil Dean and said: 'All right, Basil? Good thing I had my drawers on, isn't it?'

She made a habit of sleeping with her leading men, then sending them home to their wives. Leslie Howard, who played opposite her in *The Cardboard Lover*, said that his wife was suspicious and he had to be ever vigilant.

She had an affair with Wimbledon tennis champion Bill Tilden and went to Paris with him when he was playing in the Davis Cup. While the crowd were looking left, she would look right; and while they looked right, she would look left, just in case Alington was there somewhere. Meanwhile, Sir Francis Laking drank himself to death at the age of twenty-six for love of Tallulah.

On another trip to Paris, Tallulah did bump into Alington. He told her that he was booked on the midnight train to Geneva, where he was supposed to be taking a cure for his tuberculosis. When midnight came, he could not go.

For five nights running, he missed the train to stay with Tallulah. On the sixth night, he boarded the train, but leapt off when it started, saying that he could not bear her distress. On the seventh night, he boarded the train again – and got off again. This time the excuse was that the train was bound to Genoa, not Geneva.

He finally left on the eighth night, but not before making Tallulah promise to spend two weeks with him at Evian-les-Bains on Lake Geneva, where he was taking the cure. When she turned up, as arranged, he was nowhere to be found. She waited impatiently for forty-eight hours, then a Belgian turned up with all sorts of unbelievable excuses, but he promised that Alington would be back the next day. Somewhat placated, she accepted the Belgian's invitation to visit the casino, only to find Alington there playing *chemin de fer*.

Tallulah tried to blast Alington there and then but within a few minutes they were drinking and laughing together. They spent the remainder of the two weeks together. Tallulah remembered it as a magic time. When she left, she cried the whole night.

Back in England, Tallulah continued her wicked ways. While she was dining with Gerald Du Maurier at the Savoy Grill one day, a young woman stormed up to their table and slapped Tallulah across the face for sleeping with her husband. The restaurant fell silent. Everyone knew Tallulah's reputation. She had smashed up restaurants before and everyone expected all hell to break loose. Instead, she turned to Sir Gerald, who was renowned as the master of the understatement, and said coolly: 'As I was saying, dahling...'

In 1931, Tallulah signed a contract with Paramount Pictures and headed back to the States. Her first stop was Astoria, Long Island, where Paramount still had a studio. There, she filmed *Tarnished Lady* with George Cukor. The director of her next two movies, *My Sin* and *The Cheat*, was George Abbott, who said she flirted with him outrageously.

When he visited her to discuss the script, she got him to help her pour a huge can of milk into her bathtub. She stripped off and told him that she loved only cads. He fled.

On the set, she would sit on his lap between shots and whisper in his ear as if they were lovers although privately there was nothing between them.

'She was not,' Abbott said, 'what a lady would call a lady.'

Then it was on to Hollywood. On the train she met Joan Crawford and her new husband Douglas Fairbanks Jnr. Tallulah said to Crawford: 'Dahling, you're divine. I've had an affair with your husband. You'll be next.'

Crawford was somewhat intimidated and all she could muster as a reply was: 'I'm sorry, Miss Bankhead, but I just love men.'

By the time they reached Los Angeles, they were firm friends.

Tallulah was determined to maintain her reputation for being outrageous but she had some stiff competition in Hollywood. Carole Lombard liked to unbutton a man's pants while he was taking a screen test to see if he could handle it. Tallulah's tactics were hardly more subtle. When a man she had not met entered a restaurant or party, she would say: 'I've slept with every man here, and now I am going to sleep with you.'

Tallulah used this tactic on Gary Cooper, though she complained he never said a word all evening. A friend pointed out that he might not have said 'yup' but certainly did not say 'nope'. Tallulah was even credited for thawing Garbo out at a party.

Tallulah kept a kinkajou monkey which she always put on Joan Crawford's shoulder at parties.

'It would curl its tail around my neck and promptly do large bits of things down my back,' Crawford said. She ended up throwing away a lot of expensive dresses.

At a certain time in the evening at a party, Tallulah

would strip.

'She would get drunk and later on, for no reason what-soever, she started to take her clothes off,' recalled actress Tamara Geva. 'Then she'd laugh like a loon. It just made me embarrassed for her.'

Tallulah lived for a time in the Garden of Alla with her then lover and drinking companion Robert Benchley. At a party there, Tallulah and Tarzan – former Olympic swimming champion Johnny Weissmuller – leapt fully clothed from the highest diving board at five in the morning. Tallulah was wearing a heavy beaded dress and sank to the bottom like a stone. Realizing the danger, she shed her clothes and emerged naked, shouting to the sleeping residents: 'Everyone's been dying to see my body. Now they can.'

There were quite a few takers.

Tallulah's antics did not find favour with the studios who were now having trouble with the Hays Office's morality clauses. She had indiscreet encounters with grips and other employees, rather than confining her favours to the management like the other stars. When Paramount lent her out to MGM, she found herself hauled into Louis B. Mayer's office for a dressing down about the way she was behaving.

Tallulah asked him to be more specific.

'Your sex life,' said Mayer.

Again Tallulah asked him to be more specific.

'With women.'

Once more she asked him to be more specific.

'I hear you've been hibernating with them,' said Mayer.

'You mean fucking,' said Tallulah. Then she reeled off a list of names of MGM actresses she had been sleeping with and, for good measure, she added a list of the studio's top actors to whom she had extended similar privileges. If the full extent of Tallulah's conquests ever reached the ears of the Hays Office, they would have closed the studio down. Mayer wished he had never asked. Tallulah turned and left him sweating behind his big round desk.

In 1933, Tallulah was rehearsing *Jezebel* in New York, when she went into hospital for a hysterectomy. After five hours on the operating table, she emerged from hospital weighing less than eighty pounds.

'Don't think this has taught me a lesson,' she told the doctors as she tottered home.

She spent Christmas in Huntsville with her father and tried to moderate her behaviour so as not to shock the old man. Nevertheless she got drunk and when her friend Glenn Anders put her to bed, he told her to be a good girl, so Santa Claus would put something nice in her stocking. Anders was treated to a ribald exposition of what, exactly, Tallulah would do to Father Christmas if she laid hands on him.

A rich publisher named George asked her to marry him. She was having a wild affair with another man at the time, who recalled that, when they were getting up to the most kinky things, she would suddenly say: 'Please stop now. I'm engaged to George.'

In 1935, when the young Burgess Meredith became Broadway's newest star, Tallulah invited him to a party. When she opened the door, she grabbed him in her arms and kissed him passionately. There was no question in his mind that they would be making love by the end of the night. Later, he was treated to the sight of Tallulah walking naked around the party. None of her friends took any notice, but Meredith's eyes almost popped out of his head.

Despite all this, Tallulah's heart still belonged to Alington. She was thirty-five and went back to England to give him one last chance to marry her. Cecil Beaton recorded the scene in his diaries: 'Tallulah danced frenziedly, throwing herself about in a mad apache dance with Napier Alington. After he left, she wept and bemoaned the fact that he had never married her, then she threw off all her clothes, performing what she called her 'Chinese classical dances'.'

Beaton made his excuses and left.

Tallulah was in the Café de Paris when Alington turned

up with his latest conquest. He tried to ignore her, so Tallulah walked up to him and said in front of his lady friend: 'What's the matter? Don't you recognize me with my clothes on?'

Her hopes of becoming Lady Alington dashed, Tallulah returned to the US to redouble her efforts to make it big in the movies. David O. Selznick was casting *Gone with the Wind* and the search for Scarlett O'Hara was on. Being a southerner, Tallulah considered herself perfect for the part. After all she had a scarlet reputation. One of the major backers of the project was Jock Whitney, who was one of Tallulah's current lovers. He was not a man Selznick could afford to offend.

George Cukor was to direct and he arranged a test. Tallulah was playing on Broadway and had to fly out to the Coast on Saturday night to shoot the test in Hollywood on the Sunday. On the way, her plane was caught in a thunderstorm. The loss of Alington had been causing her sleepless nights; she was drinking heavily and taking sleeping pills. Despite make-up and Cukor's careful lighting, she did not quite look like the fresh-faced eighteen-year-old that Scarlett is at the beginning of the picture. Selznick was less than impressed.

But Tallulah had a great many influential connections in Alabama. They held town meetings, got up petitions and ran letter-writing campaigns. Even the State Governor was on her side. The State of Alabama was of one mind, he told the studio boss, Tallulah Bankhead must play Scarlett O'Hara. Selznick very nearly gave in. Then Tallulah put a foot wrong.

In 1936, Tallulah and another lover, playwright Edward Barry Roberts, went to see the Dorothy L. Sayers thriller *Busman's Holiday* at the Westport County Playhouse. On to the stage strode John Barrymore lookalike John Emery, who was playing Lord Peter Wimsey. During the first act, a kerosene lamp on stage set fire to some drapes. Emery put the fire out with his bare hands, before making a gracefully reassuring speech to the audience. Then the action resumed.

Tallulah was lovestruck. After the show, she swept into Emery's dressing-room and invited him to stay the weekend at the house she was renting with Roberts in Connecticut. He accepted. Back at the house, Roberts packed his things. When Tallulah saw him with his bag in his hand, she said: 'Eddie, you always were tactful.'

'Yes,' said Roberts. 'I know when I'm licked.'

Emery came for the weekend 'and she never let him out,' said Emery's third wife Tamara Geva.

He stayed for six weeks.

'Why the dickens don't you marry him?' said Estelle Winwood. 'You said you would try anything once.'

So she did. But the marriage ruined her chances of playing Scarlett O'Hara. It immediately lost her the support of the influential Jock Whitney. It also lost her the backing of Hollywood's homosexual lobby who had been rooting for her. Even the bisexual Cukor cooled.

Other would-be Scarletts moved in. Norma Shearer slept with Selznick to get a test. Miriam Hopkins went to work on Selznick's brother, the agent Myron, while Loretta Young displayed her charms for Cukor.

All three spent a lot of time interviewing young hopefuls. Evelyn Keyes recalled being chased around Selznick's desk before landing a small part in the movie.

Selznick had long lusted after Joan Fontaine and lured her into his office. When he showed her his couch, Fontaine asked: 'Scarlett?'

Selznick said no, Melanie – Scarlett's sister in the picture. Fontaine shook her head. On the way to the door, she suggested he try her sister Olivia de Havilland. She got the part.

A hat model named Edith Marriner found herself in Selznick's office. She tested twice. Although she failed the casting, she stayed on in Hollywood, changed her name and built a career as Susan Hayward.

Other young hopefuls took extreme measures to impress. One girl had herself delivered in a packing case. When the case was opened, she popped out half undressed. Security was tightened at the studio, so another girl had herself delivered to Selznick's home on Christmas morning. Friends and family were standing around the tree when the young woman burst out of the box stark naked, shouting: 'Merry Christmas, Mr Selznick.'

Cukor went to Georgia where he was besieged in his hotel room. Girls turned up at the studio from all over the country carrying notes announcing that they were the new Scarlett and had been discovered by some roving talent scout that Selznick had never heard of. These phoneys avoided arrest because the girls were too shamefaced to testify against them. However, a few were prosecuted for statutory rape.

Eventually, when the nationwide publicity had reached fever pitch, Selznick revealed the Scarlett he had had up his sleeve all along – his brother Myron's client, Vivien Leigh. Everyone agreed that she could not be bettered and she was a good ten years younger than Tallulah.

Tallulah and Emery were married at her father's house in Alabama. On the way back to New York, a reporter asked Tallulah if she planned to retire. She said: 'If I wanted to retire, you idiot, would I marry an actor?'

In fact, she planned a stage partnership and they walked straight into a production of *Antony and Cleopatra*. It bombed. The critics said that Tallulah was 'less the Queen of the Nile, more the Queen of the Swannee', but Emery got good reviews. It was a less than auspicious beginning to their married life. They had the misfortune to open at the same time as Orson Welles's production of *Julius Caesar*, which was rapturously received and played on a bare stage. Tallulah went to see it. How much did the production cost, she asked.

'Eight thousand dollars,' said Orson.

'Eight thousand dollars!' said Tallulah. 'That's less than one of my breastplates.'

During the early days of their marriage, Tallulah would stick to Emery like glue. They kept open house.

Joan Crawford and Douglas Fairbanks would often turn up. Tallulah, playing the good little wifey, would make sure that Emery got a Planter's Punch every day for his breakfast, explaining that it was full of fruit, nourishment and vitamins. They fought, flinging things and throwing punches, but they both enjoyed it.

Tallulah made a lifelong friend in Otto Preminger when she helped get his family out of Vienna. The US immigration quota for Austria was full, so Tallulah persuaded her father to introduce a bill in the House to extend the quota due to the likelihood of a forthcoming war. She also teamed up with homosexual playwright Tennessee Williams, with whom she shared a passion for alcohol and barbiturates. According to Williams, they belonged to the same church.

'You and I are the only two constantly high Episcopalians I know,' he said.

However, in June 1940, after Dunkirk, she swore to keep off the booze until the British returned to the continent. She was nearly as good as her word, slipping off the wagon just twice in four years. It would have been perfectly understandable if one of those times had been when she heard that Alington, then a fighter pilot, had been killed during the Battle of Britain.

Although she gave up the booze, she kept taking cocaine and took to drinking spirits of ammonia as if it were bourbon. One of her favourite tricks at that time was to stand on her head at parties to show everyone in the room that she had no underwear on.

When Danny Kaye's wife, the lyric writer Sylvia Fine, commented that this behaviour was distasteful, Tallulah said: 'How would you know? You come from Brooklyn.'

Emery stood as much of this behaviour as he could. The marriage had already damaged his career. Before Tallulah had grabbed him, he had led another famous Hollywood star to believe that he would marry her. Jilted, she had barred his way into pictures.

He left Tallulah for her arch-rival, the actress Tamara Geva. Tallulah was furious and, at first, refused him a divorce. When she did eventually divorce him, it was on the grounds of cruelty.

One of Tallulah's friends pointed out that there was a particular irony in Emery's choice of a new mate. Tallulah had married Emery because he had looked like a second-rate John Barrymore. Emery had married Tamara Geva because she looked like a second-rate Tallulah Bankhead. But later, when Tallulah was asked why she had married Emery, she said: 'Because I loved him.'

And why had she divorced him?

'Because I loved him.'

Somehow the curse of Tallulah hung over Emery for the rest of his life. He became accident prone and his career suffered. He stayed with Tamara Geva for twenty years. Then he married Joan Bennett, who said: 'John never had a bad word to say about Tallulah. They were friends until the end.'

To fill the hole in her life left by the divorce, Tallulah bought a lion cub she called Winston Churchill. As it grew older it would stalk around the house and chew the furniture. Seeing this, Tallulah would yell: 'Has no one fed the fucking lion?' Eventually, she donated it to the Bronx Zoo.

One evening, a young man named Cleveland Amory turned up at her house in upstate New York with a letter of introduction from Katherine Hepburn and heard what sounded like an orgy going on inside. After the butler had taken his note to Tallulah, he heard her shout: 'Goddamnit, I can't see every last damn one of Kate Hepburn's friends.'

The sounds of the party continued and Amory was passed back a note which read: 'It doesn't seem to be a good time.'

Then Tallulah bawled: 'What does he look like?'

The butler stepped aside so she could see. Amory was invited in and soon became a fixture.

Another denizen of Tallulah's home around that time

was a young actress named Jacqueline Susanne, who went on to write *Valley of the Dolls*. She drew considerable inspiration from Tallulah's stories.

Always eager to do her bit for the British war effort, Tallulah Bankhead took the lead in Alfred Hitchcock's *Lifeboat* for $75,000. She had another great wartime movie triumph in *A Royal Scandal*, in which she played Catherine the Great. It was Ernst Lubitsch's project but when he had a heart attack, Otto Preminger took over. Preminger hired Tallulah. While Lubitsch was convalescing, he heard that Garbo wanted the part. Preminger insisted that now Tallulah had been hired for the part, she would play it. Garbo could go hang. Everyone agreed that Tallulah was great in the role. But in Hollywood Lubitsch and others branded her as the woman who had prevented Garbo returning to the movies.

In the 1950s, Tallulah turned to the radio. She wrote and starred in her own show which was full of innuendo and straightforward smut.

She took a considerable risk when she charged her housekeeper with theft. In court, the housekeeper tried to blacken her accuser's name by detailing her drug and sexual habits. Tallulah carried off her courtroom performance with typical aplomb, wooing the jury, like an audience, on to her side.

Tallulah continued to work on the stage and continued to find young men, but she increasingly surrounded herself with young homosexuals who she called her 'caddies'. In 1964, she returned to England to make one last movie, a horror film called *Die! Die! My Darling!* When Columbia could not get completion insurance on her, she put up her own salary.

She died in New York City in 1968. Her last coherent word was 'bourbon'.

9

THE BARE-ASSED CONTESSA

Ava Gardner was born in 1922 in Brogden, North Carolina. She was a country child who loved the great outdoors and spent hours roaming through the tobacco fields usually bare-foot. The thought of becoming a movie star never occurred to her. When she was eighteen, Ava went to visit her older sister, Bappie, who had married a photographer and moved to New York. Her brother-in-law took some pictures of her and put them in the window of his Manhattan studio. They were spotted by an MGM talent scout, who sent her to Hollywood. Bappie went too.

'She can't act. She can't talk,' said Louis B. Mayer when he saw Ava's screen test. 'She's terrific.'

He signed her to a seven-year contract at $50 a week. After all, Ava Gardner had everything Mayer wanted in a woman – alabaster skin, a tiny waist, high firm breasts and prominent nipples.

She was given acting lessons and a diction coach to try to rid her of her southern drawl. After four months in Hollywood, Ava was on a sound stage when she was spotted by Carmen Miranda, or so she thought. In fact, it was Mickey Rooney in drag. He could not take his eyes off her.

Although he was only two years older than Ava – and

four inches shorter– Mickey Rooney was already a big star in Hollywood. He called her every day for two weeks, asking for a date. She refused. MGM's publicity department thought it might be a good idea for her to be seen out with a big movie star – and it never did Rooney any harm to be seen with a pretty girl. Ava had been brought up strictly though, and insisted that Bappie came along as chaperone.

Rooney quickly discovered that Ava had been taught that even kissing outside marriage was next to prostitution. So he proposed. Ava accepted provided they waited to get married until she was nineteen.

Rooney took Ava to meet his mother. Ma peered over the top of *Racing Form* when he told her that he was going to get married and said to Ava: 'I guess he ain't been in your pants yet.'

Mayer was against the marriage, but after a tearful session with Rooney gave his permission. The couple were married quietly outside Los Angeles on 10 January 1942. Even with the wedding band on her finger, Ava was not really ready for sex. Rooney, on the other hand, was experienced with women. However, he confessed to being awkward with Ava at first, but gradually Ava shed her shyness and became warm and willing. Years later he admitted to being proud to have taken Ava's virginity.

The next day, however, he went off to play golf. Later Ava said that, on her honeymoon, she saw more of the MGM publicity man sent to accompany them than she did of her husband. She never forgave him.

Back in Hollywood, Ava found that she had to compete, not just with the golf course, but also with the racetrack, poker games and drinking binges with his cronies. Ava told friends that she and her husband were sexually compatible, but otherwise they had no life together.

After Ava had appendicitis brought on, she said, by worrying about whether he would come home or not, he began to be more attentive. He took her to parties, but when she began to mingle and dance with other men, he would fly into a jealous rage.

He used his influence to get her better parts, and later, when she became a star, she admitted that she owed everything to Rooney.

'He didn't understand marriage,' she said, 'but he sure as hell understood show business.'

They wanted to separate in the autumn of 1942, less than nine months after getting married. Worried about the bad publicity this might engender, Mayer persuaded them to give it one more try. They moved into a cottage in Bel Air, and Ava was rewarded with a leading role in *Ghosts on the Loose*. But Rooney had not changed and their rows grew violent. She threw things at him when he turned up drunk, and slashed the furniture and curtains with a knife.

Rooney thought a baby might help save their marriage. Ava told him straight: 'If I ever get pregnant, I'll kill you.'

She began to go to nightclubs with Lana Turner, who had recently been divorced from band leader Artie Shaw. When Rooney threw a jealous tantrum, she threw him out.

Mayer was getting worried about the situation and sent Rooney to Connecticut to film *A Yank at Eton*. Rooney was still in love with Ava and from the other side of the country, bombarded her with expensive gifts. On his return to California, he tried to force his way into her apartment when she was entertaining and had to be restrained.

Ava told MGM's publicity department that if Rooney persisted in this sort of behaviour, she would go to the press. Mayer took Rooney aside and persuaded him to leave her alone. In 1943, they divorced. She was awarded $25,000 and a car. Mayer had warned her that if she asked for any more she would never work for MGM – or any other studio – again.

As a young Hollywood starlet whose career was taking off, Ava was expected to go out on the nightclub circuit. She was seen with British heart-throb Peter Lawford, Turkish actor Turhan Bey and Latino star Fernando Lamas, but when she got a juicy part in *Three Men in White,* it was Rooney she turned to for advice. He appeared on the set when she was shooting. They were seen holding hands in a restaurant afterwards and the press speculated about a reconciliation. The movie was an enormous success.

When Rooney was drafted, Ava told him that she would wait for him. He wrote every day and she replied to each letter, at first. Gradually her letters became few and far between until there were none at all. She phoned and asked him not to write any more. He told her he loved her. She said goodbye. He cried and set about getting drunk.

Ava began an affair with lawyer Greg Bautzer, who had also slept with Lana Turner and Joan Crawford. She had flings with actor John Carroll and singer Billy Daniels. Then she went on a blind date with Howard Hughes. At the time Lana Turner was seeing Hughes and was convinced that she would marry him.

Hughes had had his share of Hollywood screen goddesses – Ida Lupino, Billie Dove, Olivia De Havilland, Constance Bennett, Carole Lombard, Ginger Rogers, Bette Davis, Susan Hayward. He liked newly divorced women.

He kept women in houses all over Hollywood, to be at his beck and call any time. Ava refused to live in the house he rented for her and stayed, instead, with her sister Bappie. She could not escape Hughes that easily, however. Eventually she did move into the house Hughes had rented. One of his Mormon bodyguards was assigned to watch her twenty-four hours a day. She soon learned how to give him the slip though. One night at the Mocambo, she met a Mexican bullfighter – the first of many – and took him back to the house. He was just leaving in the morning, when Hughes arrived. Ava and Hughes had a monumental row. He slapped her so hard he dislocated her jaw. She knocked him cold with a brass ornament.

Despite such fights, their stormy relationship continued

for two years. She was impressed by the way he would fly her down to Mexico at a moment's notice in his private plane, book an entire restaurant just for the two of them or send her hundreds of flowers on a whim.

Hughes, however, was a dangerous man to cross. One time he was having the Cadillac he had given her for her birthday mended when they had a minor row. When she got it back, she drove just two miles before the engine fell out. Hughes himself, she was told, had had it fixed.

Years later, she admitted that she had not been in love with Hughes, but what woman could resist a guy who turns up with a tray of diamonds and asks her to pick one?

In 1945, Ava met bandleader Artie Shaw at the Mocambo. The ex-husband of Lana Turner, Shaw had also had affairs with Judy Garland and Betty Grable. When he married Turner, Garland wept and Grable had her first abortion.

Ava was immediately smitten. After a couple of dates, she moved into his house on Bedford Drive. The studio were appalled. Their stars were not meant to co-habit. Mayer only kept her on because she had been married to Mickey Rooney and the MGM publicity department sweated blood to keep Ava's domestic arrangements out of the papers.

Shaw was a martinet and when he discovered that Ava had only read one book, *Gone with the Wind*, he set about educating her. When she confided to him her worries about the small parts she was getting, he put her in analysis.

'It really messed me up,' she said.

She enrolled at UCLA and struggled to live up to the standards Shaw set. The dinner-party conversation of his intellectual friends went over her head. She preferred gossiping about who was sleeping with whom and dishing the dirt on the latest crop of juicy divorces. She was more at home with the movie magazines than Hemingway or Steinbeck. She liked nothing better than to kick off her shoes and walk barefoot through the house, even if guests were present.

'It's uncivilized,' Shaw would bellow. 'You are not in the tobacco fields now.'

Ava would run from the room in tears.

Witnessing such scenes, friends assumed that the relationship was coming to an end. Instead, they got married. The gossip columnists were already hinting about their cohabitation and Mayer told them that they must either marry or separate. They both knew it was a bad move, but Ava was hopelessly in love with Shaw and Shaw, like Rooney, was hopelessly addicted to Ava's body.

Despite her marriage, the studio was still not pleased with Ava and began contracting her out. Ironically this got her better parts. At Universal she played opposite Burt Lancaster in *The Killers*, which was based on a Hemingway short story. She met Hemingway and it was rumoured that they were lovers.

Ava's career began to blossom which meant spending long hours at the studio during the day. As a bandleader, Shaw worked at night so they saw little of each other and no longer shared the same bed. On 8 July 1946, Ava moved out of Shaw's house.

Hughes – who it was rumoured she was still seeing – had had a plane crash and Ava rushed to his bedside. She found Lana Turner already there. As Hughes slowly recuperated, the two women had lots of time to swap notes about Artie Shaw. Lana said that life with Artie was a college education. Ava agreed; she left before she flunked out.

Ava filed for divorce on the grounds of mental cruelty. She asked for no alimony nor for any of Shaw's property. When Shaw put his house up for sale, the purchasers noticed that a waffle iron was missing from the inventory.

'Ava took it when she left,' Shaw explained.

The joke went around town that a single waffle iron was Ava's settlement.

Two days after the divorce was granted, Shaw married Kathleen Windsor, the bestselling author of *Forever Amber*.

When Ava heard the news, she cursed. Once, in Chicago with Shaw, she had bought a copy of *Forever Amber*. Shaw had grabbed it from her hand and thrown it across the room.

'I'm in charge of your education,' he had said. 'You're not going to read rubbish like this.'

Shaw admitted to his new bride that he had never read her bestseller – it was too long, he said. The marriage lasted two years.

When Hughes got out of hospital, he and Ava resumed their torrid affair. He proposed marriage, but then he proposed to lots of women. He offered Elizabeth Taylor $1 million to marry him. She preferred Michael Wilding. Gene Tierney, Terry Moore and numerous unknown girls had been offered marriage by Hughes. Usually it was a ploy to get them into bed. If they accepted, Hughes would go through with it and buy himself out of trouble later. Ava was not taken in and while Hughes was out of town on business, she played the field.

A friend noted that Ava was not the same after she left Artie. 'She no longer trusted men. It was as if she wanted to get back at them. Make love and run. She was wild. She preferred fast flings. This was so unlike the Ava who came to Hollywood with a dream – to meet a nice guy and live happily ever after.'

She slept with English actor David Niven, who considered Hollywood his own personal 'playpen', and the director John Houston. The affair continued during Houston's four-year marriage to Evelyn Keyes and got Ava roles in *Night of the Iguana* and *The Bible*. Meanwhile, she renewed her affairs with Fernando Lamas and Peter Lawford, and started a fresh one with singer Mel Torme. While Torme was having an affair with her, he saw her out on the arm of Peter Lawford. At two-thirty that night he got a phone call from her asking him to come over. When he arrived, Lawford answered the door, explaining that he was just leaving. Torme went in and took over.

Ava had certainly lost her shyness. She had an affair with Clark Gable during the filming of *The Hucksters*. Actor Howard Duff dropped Yvonne DeCarlo to begin a long-term affair with Ava, even though she was seeing Ciro's band-leader Jerry Wald, mobster Johnny Stompanato, Peter Lawford and Howard Hughes on the side.

In *One Touch of Venus*, Ava played a statue of a goddess brought to life by a kiss. She posed nude for the sculptor, but the director insisted that she cover up. In the movie, she wore a sheer Grecian gown, with nothing on underneath it. The most popular job at that time at Universal was operating the wind machine.

During the shooting of *One Touch of Venus*, Ava began an affair with her co-star Robert Walker, who was still carry-ing a torch for his ex-wife Jennifer Jones. Nevertheless, Walker fell in love with Ava. He became obsessive. She had to hide out in other people's flats and called in Howard Duff to protect her. She was only free of him when he died in a drunken stupor after doctors tried to revive him with a shot of sodium amytal.

Ava also began seeing Frank Sinatra on the quiet. He was under contract to MGM and was married with two kids at the time. So far Mayer had managed to hush up his affairs with Lana Turner and Marilyn Maxwell.

In *The Bribe*, Ava co-starred with Robert Taylor, who was married to Barbara Stanwyck. The marriage was failing because of Taylor's bouts of impotence. Ava cured him of that. She would be seen on the set massaging his crotch with her toe. He would take her back to his mother's house to make love to her. When his mother complained about this arrangement, he pointed out that he was merely safeguarding his career.

'Would you rather I went to a motel and got pho-tographed?' he asked.

MGM at last began to get behind Ava. They gave her $1,250 a week, Norma Shearer's old dressing-room and promoted her as 'Hollywood's Glamour Girl of 1948'. She also had an abortion that year. The studio hushed it up.

The studio floated the possibility of a forthcoming engagement between Ava and Howard Duff. They could hardly publicize her other affairs. Jane Russell says that Ava was Howard Hughes's girl in 1948, but it was Frank Sinatra who was making the big play for her.

During a drunken spree, they shot up the town of Indio, California, not far from Palm Springs. Shop windows and street lights was smashed, a bullet grazed a man's stomach and the pair were arrested. Sinatra's veteran press agent, George Evans, bailed them out and paid for the damages. The charges were dropped and the whole thing was hushed up.

In *My Forbidden Past*, Ava was cast opposite Robert Mitchum and she was determined to seduce him. She put her whole heart into their love scenes. Their kisses were long, lingering and full of passion. Mitchum, however, had a problem. Recently he had been busted for possession of marijuana. The police had caught him and a buddy with two actresses smoking a joint. His wife had stood by him and so had Howard Hughes. Hughes had bought out Mitchum's contract, given him money to buy a house and cast him in *My Forbidden Past*, opposite Ava, when no one else in town would touch him. Mitchum knew that Ava was one of Hughes's girlfriends. So he called Hughes and asked whether he should go to bed with her.

'If you don't, everyone will think you are a pansy,' Hughes replied. This was hardly helpful. Whether Ava got her man or not, nobody knows. He was certainly taken with her and called her affectionately 'Honest Ava' because she did not pad her bust. In her memoirs, she says that she did not pursue him. She was too busy with Sinatra.

When they first met, there was instant hostility between Ava and Sinatra. She found him pushy and arrogant. He found her elusive. She would never spend more than one or two evenings with him before disappearing.

Sinatra had dated lots of women during his four years in Hollywood, but he remained a family man. His wife Nancy told showbusiness columnist Hedda Hopper that Frank wanted his freedom without divorce. After a two-week split over his affair with Lana Turner in 1946, Nancy had taken him back.

In January 1950, Ava was due to go to Spain to film *Pandora and the Flying Dutchman.* Sinatra persuaded her to stop off with him in New York on the way. They stayed at a suite in the Hampshire House and turned up together at the première of *Gentleman Prefer Blondes.* George Evans was working overtime to keep the lid on things and managed to plant the story that they had merely 'run in to each other' at the première. But on 12 December, Ava accompanied Sinatra as his date to his birthday party at the Copacabana.

Ava dropped Howard Duff and Sinatra asked his wife for a divorce. It was a mistake, he admitted later, but he was so much in love he did not care. His wife took it stoically.

'Frank's left home before and he'll do it again,' Nancy said. 'But I am not calling this a marital break-up.'

Nancy was a good Catholic girl and there would be no divorce.

Then things got out of hand. The shooting of *Pandora and the Flying Dutchman* was postponed until March and Ava returned to LA. Evans, who for years had managed to keep Sinatra's affairs out of the headlines and his marriage to Nancy on the rails, collapsed and died at the age of forty-eight. Mayer got wind of what was happening between his two stars and forbade Ava to leave Los Angeles. This was a red rag to a bull. She flew with Sinatra to Houston where he had a two-week engagement. A press photographer spotted them in a cosy little Italian restaurant. Next day their affair was on front pages around the world.

On Valentine's day, Nancy changed the locks on the Sinatras' Toluca Lake home. Showbiz columnists were calling Ava a jezebel and a home-wrecker. Her postbag was even more blunt. Mayer was beside himself. He could not punish Ava, she was too big for that, but he terminated Sinatra's contract. Sinatra said good riddance. He was tired of playing sailor roles anyway. Besides, he told the press, he did not see why they were making all this fuss over 'a few dates with Ava'.

Ava flew with Sinatra to New York, where he was going to open at the Copacabana. Although they booked into separate suites in the Hampshire House, the press had a field day. Sinatra's career was on the slide and he was under tremendous pressure from his family and friends to return home. Ava helped him nurse his nerves in the dressing-room and sat out in the audience to lend her support.

Things did not go well. His voice was weak and the critics panned the show. He sang 'Nancy with the Laughing Face'. Many in the audience thought this was a joke. Ava fumed. Sinatra explained that it was his lucky song and he had sung it for years.

'Either that song goes or I do,' she said.

He dropped the song.

Seeking to stir things up, Artie Shaw invited Ava and Frank to Bop City, where he was performing, and to dinner in his apartment. Sinatra hated Shaw and refused point blank. Ava went anyway. When Sinatra got back to the Hampshire House after his own show at the Copacabana, he expected to find Ava there waiting for him. He called Artie Shaw's, got Ava on the phone and said goodbye. Then she heard two shots.

At the Hampshire House, David Selznick heard them too.

'I thought the son-of-a-bitch had shot himself,' he said later.

Head of Columbia Records Manie Sachs and actor Tom Drake came running. They found Sinatra gun in hand and two bullet holes in the mattress. They took the gun and quickly switched the mattress for the one in Sachs's room before the police arrived.

Ava had to fight her way through the crowds to get into the hotel. She found Sinatra sitting up in bed, reading a book. She blurted out her story to the police. Sinatra denied everything.

The next day MGM insisted that she fly to Spain immediately. If not, they would invoke the morality clause and terminate her contract. After Sinatra's bogus suicide attempt, she was glad to go.

During the filming of *Pandora and the Flying Dutchman*, Ava took a fancy to Mario Cabre, a real-life bullfighter who played the matador in the film. He was the dark slim-hipped Latin type she never could resist. He spoke little English but he wrote love poetry for her and serenaded her on a gypsy guitar.

Although to her this was just a casual affair, MGM seized on it as an opportunity to undo some of the damage that had been done by her relationship with Sinatra. Pictures of the two of them appeared in the papers. Sinatra grew terribly jealous. On the phone, Ava reassured him there was nothing to the stories in the press, but later admitted that, after a drunken night in Spain, she had woken up one morning to find Cabre beside her in bed. Sinatra responded by being seen around town with an old flame, Marilyn Maxwell. Phone calls between New York and the Costa Brava grew heated.

Then Sinatra's voice gave out. He had to cancel the remaining shows at the Copacabana and, against his doctor's advice, flew to Spain, carrying with him a $10,000 diamond necklace. With no movie contract, a dearth of hit records, no club bookings and raw vocal cords, it was a gift he could barely afford.

Heavy rain had stopped shooting and, getting wind of Sinatra's imminent arrival, MGM packed Cabre off to Italy where he told journalists of his deep and enduring love for Ava and read some of his love poetry aloud at a press conference. MGM's publicity people housed Sinatra and Ava in

Jean Harlow

Joan Crawford

Greta Garbo

Marlene Dietrich

Lana Turner

Rita Hayworth

separate villas and chaperoned them every minute. This did not stop them rowing.

'If I hear that Spanish runt has been hanging around you again, I'll kill him and you,' Sinatra threatened over a crowded dinner table.

Ava pointed out that she and 'the Spanish runt' were supposed to be making a movie together. Besides, he had been seen out with Marilyn Maxwell.

'But we are old friends,' protested Sinatra.

'Well Mario and I are new friends,' said Ava.

Sinatra cut short his trip and arrived back in Los Angeles in time to read in the newspapers about Ava's passionate reunion with Cabre at a bullfighting festival at Tossa del Mar. According to the papers, Cabre had bared his chest to show her the scars he had sustained in the ring the day before. He had been thinking of her and had lost his concentration, he had explained.

There were plenty of pressmen on hand to witness Cabre and Ava kissing goodbye at the airport. Ava explained on the phone that she had kissed a lot of people. Sinatra did not buy it but, nevertheless, went ahead with a property settlement, pledging a third of his dwindling income to his wife and kids.

Ava flew to London to complete the filming. Sinatra flew there too. He was opening at the London Palladium. She was in the front row for his triumphant British début. As a couple, they were invited everywhere. Despite a few grumblings by clergymen, they were even presented to the Queen at a Royal Première.

Back in Los Angeles, things were different. Nancy was still refusing to give Sinatra a divorce and the studio were desperate to protect the reputation of what was now their hottest property. Ava was forbidden to see Sinatra without other people being present. She took no notice and took off with Sinatra for New York where they went to the Joe Louis–Ezzard Charles title fight. Nevertheless, Ava was given the plum part of the mulatto Julie in *Show Boat*.

Dinah Shore, who was plainly more suitable, wanted to play the part. When she asked producer Arthur Freed why she had not got it, he said: 'Because you are not a whore. Ava is.'

Despite Sinatra's triumph in London, his career was in trouble. His promised TV and radio series were cancelled. Ava used her influence to get Hughes to use two Sinatra songs in RKO's *Double Dynamite*. Sinatra accepted a measly $25,000 to make *Meet Danny Wilson*, a film freely based on his own life. On the set, he got visits from his kids, priest, psychiatrists. He lost his voice and fell out with his co-star, Shelley Winters. She quit the picture and only returned after a call from Nancy Sinatra telling her that Frank would not get the $25,000 until the movie was completed and the bank was about to foreclose the mortgage on her house.

Sinatra spent a lot of time at home for the sake of his kids. Ava thought a clean break would be better for all concerned – especially as Sinatra was accusing her of sleeping with Artie Shaw.

In her next picture, *Lone Star*, Ava played opposite Clark Gable, who had just separated from his fourth wife, Lady Sylvia Ashley. They poured out their troubles to one another. When the movie was finished, Ava told Sinatra that she was going to Mexico for a vacation. Sinatra feared this would be the end and started begging his wife for a divorce. The public's sympathy was slowly turning against Nancy, but she hung on.

Sinatra took off to Mexico with Ava. They took so much luggage that it was rumoured that Sinatra was planning a Mexican divorce, a quick marriage and a Latin American honeymoon. Everywhere they went they were pursued by reporters. Ava, who was confident that her career was on the rise, took it all in her stride. Sinatra, who feared he was all washed up, did not. There were ugly scenes. The police had to be called when Sinatra threatened to shoot a photographer. Back in Los Angeles, Sinatra almost ran over a reporter when he and Ava tried to make a high-speed exit from the airport.

MGM had had enough. Ava must either marry Sinatra or give him up. Sinatra still had friends. He was offered singing engagements in Reno and Las Vegas, which would bring in badly needed cash and establish his residency in Nevada prior to a divorce. He also tried to patch it up with the press. But on 1 September 1951, he was back in the headlines again. The story was that he had overdosed on sleeping pills after a vicious row with Ava.

Sinatra denied everything and Ava flew to his side. MGM grew impatient. Their lawyers took over the divorce proceedings to prevent any further delay and the studio set a date for the wedding – 19 September, the day after Sinatra's six-week Nevada residency qualification period was over. But Ava and Frank jumped the gun. On 17 September, they turned up together at the première of *Show Boat*. MGM were livid, but disaster turned to triumph. The crowds outside Hollywood's Egyptian Theater cheered the couple and the movie itself was a major success.

Nancy contested Frank's Nevada divorce. She insisted on a Californian divorce and seized Sinatra's Palm Springs house against back alimony. Ava collapsed under the strain and was rushed to hospital. It was rumoured she had an abortion.

On 31 October, Nancy got her Californian divorce on the grounds of mental cruelty and Ava and Frank set about making their wedding plans. Even though the studio had handled Ava's private marriage to Mickey Rooney so discreetly, Sinatra no longer trusted them. He applied for a marriage licence in Pennsylvania. They would marry in the Philadelphia home of CBS founder Isaac Levy.

Ava and Frank spent the weekend before the wedding in New York. On the Saturday night, they went to the Sugar Hill Club in Harlem with James Mason and his wife. Sinatra flirted openly with a woman on the next table. Ava flew into a jealous rage. She told Sinatra that the wedding was off and flung her six-carat diamond engagement ring across the room.

The real cause of the row was not Frank's flirting. It was a letter that Ava had received from a woman who purported to be a prostitute and claimed to have had an affair with Sinatra.

Back at the Hampshire House, the row continued. Sinatra threw a very expensive gold bracelet that Howard Hughes had given Ava out of the window. He contended that Hughes was responsible for the letter. Once before, Hughes had had Sinatra followed and had told Ava of a chorus girl Frank was then seeing.

James Mason interceded and the row was eventually smoothed over when Sinatra's mother Dolly invited them over to Hoboken for some home-made Italian cooking. Dolly and Ava hit it off right away. They both loved Frank and wanted to see him on top again. That Wednesday, the wedding went ahead as planned.

However, the very public row in New York had not gone unnoticed. The press were on the couple's trail again. They got wind of the marriage licence and turned up outside Levy's house. Sinatra, true to form, started threatening reporters and photographers, but the wedding went ahead without a hitch and the happy couple headed for Florida for their honeymoon. Once their luggage caught them up, they moved on to the Hotel Nacional in Havana.

When the newlyweds moved into Sinatra's Palm Springs home, the MGM publicity machine blitzed the fan magazines with Ava's redecoration plans, the recipes Dolly Sinatra had sent her, and the secrets of the couple's happiness. Despite MGM's best efforts, the Hollywood gossip columnists were soon calling them the 'Battling Sinatras'. In fact, they thrived on their tempestuous relationship because they had a special way of making it up. Visitors recalled that after one of their terrible rows, the smell of Ava's perfume would come wafting down the stairs. Frank would smile and follow his nose. After half-an-hour upstairs, they would come down arm in arm, smiling. Before long, though, the rowing would start again.

Sinatra's career was plummeting and Ava took time to be with him whenever he needed her. This led to her suspension by the studio, but she was such a big star, they took her back. In May 1952, she planted her hands and feet in wet cement outside Grauman's Chinese Theater. Soon after she was rushed to hospital with a suspected miscarriage – which is Hollywood speak for another abortion.

There were problems in the relationship, too. Ava became possessive. She kept Sinatra from seeing his children. When he spent too much time talking to a male friend one night in a restaurant and she felt ignored, she drove to the airport and jumped on the next plane to Italy. Another evening, she spotted Sinatra's old flame Marilyn Maxwell sitting at the front at a concert. Sinatra was singing 'All Of Me' and Ava thought he was directing it at Maxwell. She stormed out and posted her wedding ring back to him.

Soon she was seen doing the round of Hollywood parties, while he was stuck at an engagement in St Louis. It would be ten days before he could get back to Los Angeles. He read details of her gallivanting each morning in the press. The wait was torture.

'That's what happens when you get hung up on a chick,' he told Sammy Davis Jnr.

In the meantime, Sinatra lost Ava's wedding ring. He had to have a duplicate made, which he slipped on her finger when he returned to LA and the two of them took off to Tijuana to watch bullfighting.

They carried on doing some fighting of their own. After a row in LA, Sinatra announced that he would be in Palm Springs with Lana Turner if Ava wanted him. Lana Turner was staying in their Palm Springs home at the time. Ava set off after him, determined to catch them in the act. There are several versions of what happened next, but the confrontation ended with the police being called to the house which had been wrecked by the feuding couple. Ava stormed out.

Sinatra had to make a grovelling apology in the press to get her back. The reconciliation took place at an election rally for the Democratic presidential candidate Adlai Stevenson. Ava came on stage in a strapless black silk gown and said: 'Ladies and gentlemen, I can't do anything myself, but I can introduce a wonderful, wonderful man. I'm a great fan myself. My husband, Frank Sinatra.'

Sinatra tagged along when Ava went to Uganda to make *Mogambo* with Clark Gable. Sinatra wanted to play Angelo Maggio in *From Here to Eternity* and Ava used all her influence to get him a screen test. He had to fly back to Los Angeles for it and she took the opportunity to fly to London where she checked into the Chelsea Hospital for Women for another abortion. In her autobiography, Ava says: 'I think Frank, in his heart, knew what I was going to do.'

She woke up after the operation to find Sinatra sitting beside the bed with tears in his eyes.

Sinatra went to Hawaii to film *From Here to Eternity* and Ava flew to London to film *Knights of the Round Table* with Robert Taylor. They were separated for four months and Ava suspected that he was seeing another woman. He flew to London and she accompanied him on a disastrous European tour. When they arrived back in London, they were the battling Sinatras again. One evening, they invited Stewart Granger and his wife Jean Simmons to the Ambassadors club where Sinatra was appearing. When the Grangers arrived at the flat the Sinatras were renting, Frank and Ava were not talking to each other. But at the club, Frank sang all his love songs to her. She cried.

'Goddamn son-of-a-bitch,' she said. 'How can you resist him?'

Sinatra headed back to the States alone. Ava took off for a short vacation in Spain where she met the famous matador Luis Miguel Dominguin.

'The first time I met Luis Miguel Dominguin,' she said, 'I knew without a doubt he was for me. He was tall and graceful with piercing, watchful dark eyes which he liked to move without turning his head.'

She never could resist a bullfighter.

Sinatra opened at the Sands in Las Vegas, while she attended the première of *Mogambo* in New York. Then she flew to Palm Springs. He was angry because he thought her place was with him. To show his displeasure, he got himself photographed at a party with two showgirls. Ava called her lawyer.

The gossip columnists began writing about Sinatra's escapades in Las Vegas. Ava complained that he seemed to want any other woman rather than her.

'Maybe if I had been willing to share Frank with other women, we could have been happier,' she wailed.

Sinatra denied he was seeing other women.

'If it took seventy-five years to get a divorce, there wouldn't be any other woman,' he lamented

Ava was sick of the marriage. She wanted to get away, out of the country. She twisted arms at the studio to get her the part of Maria Vargas in *The Barefoot Contessa* – over the heads of Elizabeth Taylor and Rita Hayworth – who was filming in Rome. It was the perfect role for her as it practically told the story of her life, tracing the career of a movie star who liked to go barefoot as she moved from lover to lover.

While Ava was away, Sinatra's health deteriorated. Friends feared a breakdown, or suicide. He called Ava regularly, but she was adamant. They needed a clean break. In the end, it did him good.

'It was Ava who taught him how to sing a torch song,' said bandleader Nelson Riddle. 'She was the greatest love of his life and he lost her.'

In Rome, Ava began seeing the young Italian comedian Walter Chiari. At Christmas, she had a week off filming and planned to go to Spain to see Luis Miguel Dominguin, but Sinatra phoned to say that he would meet her in Madrid.

They spent Christmas there together, but when he came down with a cold Ava got a chance to slip out to meet her bull-fighter.

Sinatra flew back to Rome with Ava for the New Year. They spent a few days alone together before Sinatra headed back to the US. As soon as he flew out, Dominguin flew in.

'I'll never figure you broads out,' said Ava's co-star on *The Barefoot Contessa*, Humphrey Bogart. 'Half the world's female population would throw themselves at Frank's feet, and here you are flouncing around with guys who wear capes and little ballerina slippers.'

But Dominguin was everything that Sinatra was not. He was the son of an aristocratic family, while Sinatra was the son of Italian immigrants. His friends were Hemingway, Picasso and Stravinsky. Sinatra hung out with gangsters. He was fearless in the bullring. Sinatra surrounded himself with bodyguards.

Sinatra accepted it was all over. He created a small shrine to Ava in his Hollywood home. He would sit up at night with a bottle of cognac, starring at her photograph and a statue of her that had been made for *The Barefoot Contessa*.

'We could have worked it out,' he told friends. In his grief, he began dating Judy Garland and Elizabeth Taylor.

Ava flew to Lake Tahoe to establish Nevada residency prior to a divorce. Dominguin followed but when he went back to Madrid, Howard Hughes moved back into Ava's bed.

She planned a tour of South America to publicize *The Barefoot Contessa*. The dates were to coincide with Dominguin's bullfighting tour, but her tour was a disorganized disaster. She cancelled it halfway through and flew to New York. Dominguin followed and proposed. She refused and he flew back to Madrid and out of her life.

Hughes was desperate to marry Ava and she humoured him. After all, he made life so easy. She told *Look* magazine: 'You're in Palm Springs and you want to go shopping in Mexico City. All you need do is to call and within minutes there's a chauffeur outside waiting to take you to the airport.'

There was a downside. Ava was back in the same old trap with Hughes. He surrounded her with spies while he disappeared from sight. One day, in frustration, she took off on a drinking spree with a journalist. In a bar in Mexicali, a man asked if she was Ava Gardner. The journalist said no, she just looked like Ava Gardner.

'You're lucky to look like her,' said the man, 'but I hope you don't have her bad morals.'

She was shocked. Her morals were above reproach. She blamed the journalist for the man's remark.

'Everywhere I go it's the same,' she complained, 'thanks to the lousy things newspapermen like you write about me.'

That evening she tried to get the journalist into bed.

Sammy Davis Jnr, a close friend of Sinatra's, called up and asked Ava whether she would pose for the cover of *Ebony* magazine with him. Some of the pictures fell into the hands of the Hollywood scandal sheet *Confidential*, who used them to imply that there was an affair going on between Ava and Sammy Davis Jnr. It also said she had some other 'bronze boyfriends'. Ava was advised that suing would simply draw the story to the attention of the rest of the press. In disgust, she quit Hollywood and moved to Spain.

She filmed *Bhowani Junction* in Pakistan with Stewart Granger whom she had always wanted to bed. He was happily married and gave her a wide berth. During the picture, her name was linked with that of British actor Bill Travers but generally it was conceded that she was 'amazingly chaste'. She made up for that by stopping off in Rome on her way home to Spain and renewing her affair with Walter Chiari.

Sinatra turned up in Spain to film *The Pride and the Passion* with twenty-four-year-old singer Peggy Connelly in tow. Even though he was seen dining alone with Ava on several occasions, there was no reconciliation. He even left Spain seven weeks early, promising to finish the scenes in Los Angeles.

Pursued by the House Un-American Activities Committee, Artie Shaw moved to the Costa Brava with his eighth wife, Evelyn Keyes. They had cocktails with Ava and Chiari and talked over old times. Ava and Evelyn had another beau in common – they had both dated John Houston in the 1940s.

Ava went to Mexico City to film Ernest Hemingway's *The Sun Also Rises*. She had Robert Evans fired from the part of the young matador in the movie and replaced with the real thing, Mexico's top bullfighter Alfredo Leal. She spent a lot of time with the scriptwriter Peter Viertel, but would disappear with her matador on her day off. When Walter Chiari turned up in Mexico City, he was so confused about what was going on that he thought she was having an affair with her co-star Tyrone Power.

While in Mexico City, Ava filed for divorce on the grounds of desertion. In fact, it was Sinatra's affair with the newly widowed Lauren Bacall that precipitated the final split. Ava went back to Spain where she began drinking heavily. One day, she tried her hand at bullfighting and was gored in the cheek. The wound healed completely and, with a touch of make-up, the scar was undetectable, though no one could convince her of that.

During the filming of *The Naked Maja* in Rome, Ava pursued her co-star Tony Franciosa, according to his then wife Shelley Winters. Winters put out the tale that there had been a fight and she had pulled Ava's hair out so that she would be no use in the movies. Ava called Sinatra and begged him to come to Rome. Later, when she heard about his latest affair with Lady Adele Beatty, she refused to take his calls.

During the filming of *On the Beach* in Australia, Ava was seen with tennis champion Tony Trabert. She called Chiari who flew to Melbourne at his own expense, but she practically ignored him when he turned up. When he arranged a show to defray his expenses, she accused him of trying to profit from their relationship and refused to come and see him. He was then seen around town with the dancer Dawn Keller and told the press that his affair with Ava was over.

Sinatra turned up in Australia but he was on a tour and could only spare her half-an-hour. When the filming of *On the Beach* was over, she pursued him back to the States, following him from city to city when he toured there. The situation was now reversed. He was back at the top of his form, while her contract with MGM had not been renewed. Now it was Ava who was washed up.

Back in Spain, she had a number of affairs with young Spaniards and USAF officers who were stationed near her home. Cast as a prostitute in *The Angel Wore Red*, she tried to get Sinatra a role as a priest in the picture, but he turned it down due to 'prior commitments'.

After that, for three years, Ava did not work. She went on binges in Spain and Madrid was full of stories about her wild antics. In the US, she was occasionally seen in the company of Sinatra.

In 1962, Ava appeared in *55 Days at Peking*, then in *Seven Days in May*. Former lover John Houston signed her for *The Night of the Iguana*, whose cast was a tangled web of lovers. Houston's ex-wife Evelyn Keyes was married to Ava's ex-husband Artie Shaw. Deborah Kerr's second husband, Peter Viertel, was one of Ava's former lovers. Richard Burton brought Elizabeth Taylor with him when they were shooting in Mexico. She was still married to Eddie Fisher, while her ex-husband Michael Wilding was handling Burton's publicity. Just to round things off, both Burton and Gardner had a reputation for sleeping with their co-stars.

On the set, John Houston presented them all with little gold-plated Derringers and bullets inscribed with the names of the rest of the cast.

'If the competition gets too fierce,' he said, 'you can always use guns.'

Ava did indeed try to seduce Burton.

'Richard is the man I should have married,' she told Elizabeth Taylor. 'He's got a sense of humour and he's a real man.'

Taylor countered by making sure that, although she was not in the film, all eyes were on her. She wore sheer tops with no bra and modelled a collection of forty scanty bikinis. Ava had to content herself with a couple of beach boys. At the première six months later, Burton and Taylor turned up newly wed, but the critics agreed that Ava had run away with the picture.

Ava returned to Spain where she was seen in the company of a succession of young matadors. According to neighbours they would be seen entering and leaving her house at all hours.

Houston decided to use Ava again as Sarah opposite George C. Scott's Abraham in *The Bible*, which he was filming in Italy. After a fling with a production assistant, Ava began dating Scott. He was married at the time. Nevertheless, he became jealous and demanding and the affair became unruly. Eventually, she sought refuge in a villa Sinatra was renting outside Rome while he was filming *Von Ryan's Express*. Houston finished off her scenes early, but when she fled to London, Scott pursued her. He broke down the door of her suite at the Savoy and punched her. He was arrested and spent the night in jail, appearing at Bow Street Magistrates' court the following morning.

A similar incident occurred at a hotel in Hollywood. Sinatra hired two bodyguards for her and Scott dropped out of sight for a long time to sort himself out.

'That's what love did to the man,' said Houston.

Meanwhile, Sinatra married nineteen-year-old Mia Farrow.

'I always knew he would end up in bed with a boy,' said Ava.

Nevertheless, Sinatra supported Ava, who was now

broke, and Ava rushed to his bedside when he was ill.

She played the Austrian Queen Mother in Mayerling, principally because her old friend James Mason was in it, but on the set she found the young Omar Sharif more to her taste. John Houston got her to play Lillie Langtry in *The Life and Times of Judge Roy Bean*. While she was filming in Tucson, Arizona, George C. Scott was filming *Rage* nearby. Houston posted extra security but Ava delighted in eluding the guards and visiting Scott.

Ava moved to London where she was seen with actor Charles Gray, entertainer Bobby Short, MGM executive Paul Mills and the black singer Freddie Davis. Davis was thirty, Ava fifty-two, but she loved him. She even checked into a health farm and went on the wagon for his sake.

Howard Hughes resurfaced in her life, briefly, before he disappeared into total seclusion in 1976. Sinatra married Barbara Marx, who bore a distinct resemblance to Ava. He remained in touch with Ava until her death in 1990 and it has been estimated that he spent over $1 million on medical bills during her final illness.

10

THE SWEATER GIRL

The discovery of Lana Turner is the stuff of Hollywood legend. She was having a Coke in the drug store across the road from her school, Hollywood High, when she was approached by a well-dressed gentleman who asked if she wanted to be in the movies.

The man's name was Billy Wilkerson and he was known to like pretty young girls. Lana was fifteen. She had been in Los Angeles for a month and was not yet used to Wilkerson's tired old line which was just as well because this time, unusually, Wilkerson meant what he said. He handed her his business card. He was the publisher of the *Hollywood Reporter*.

Wilkerson took her to Zeppo Marx, the fourth Marx brother who had quit to become an agent. He got her her first part as an extra of the 1937 version of *A Star is Born*.

Around that time director Mervyn LeRoy was looking for someone special. He needed a young girl who looked both innocent and sexy for a part in *They Won't Forget* (1937). He had seen more then fifty girls before Lana sashayed into his office. He knew immediately that she had what he wanted and more.

'There was something smouldering underneath,' he said,

'and she had a fantastic figure.'

He put her in a tight skirt that emphasized the movement of her hips and a silk bra with no padding so that her breasts could move freely. The bra was blue which would not show under her blue sweater. To draw even more attention to her charms, when the movie came out, the studio publicity department dubbed her the 'sweater girl'. It was a name she never lived down.

LeRoy was so impressed by what he saw on the screen that he signed Lana himself. He groomed her for success and took her with him when he moved to MGM in 1938. She was immediately cast as the love interest in *Love Finds Andy Hardy*. When she complained to the producer Carey Wilson about her 'sweater girl' image, he responded by putting her in a bathing suit.

As Lana had not yet graduated from high school, she had to attend the 'little red schoolhouse' on MGM's lot with her co-star Mickey Rooney, who was delighted to find that she was as oversexed as he was. Years later, he discovered that he had got her pregnant and she had had an abortion.

For *Idiot's Delight*, she bleached her brown hair blonde and, at the age of seventeen, became queen of the Hollywood nightclubs. Every night she was seen with a different man. One actor complained that 'Lana comes on like a romantic teenager and then turns into a feverish, passionate tiger who can't get enough.' Mayer drew her attention to the morality clause in her contract.

Lana may have been young and wild, but she was not stupid. After her talk with Mayer, she was still seen around town – but with only one man. She made a bad choice, though. That one man was Hollywood attorney Greg Bautzer, who made a habit of sleeping with stars and starlets.

'I was seventeen, romantic and a virgin,' Lana wrote, somewhat disingenuously in her autobiography. 'My only experience up to now had been necking, with very little petting. I'd always fought off my eager young dates when they wanted to touch my breasts.'

Bautzer was far too sophisticated to wrestle in the backseat of a car. Lana felt honoured that, when they finally did make love, he did not take her to a motel, but back to his own home.

'Greg was loving and patient with me,' she wrote. 'The act itself hurt like hell, and I must confess I didn't enjoy it at all. I didn't even know what an orgasm was. But I loved being close to Greg... I was giving him all of me. Now he would know how much I loved and adored and worshipped him. Now I was truly his.'

She did, eventually, achieve orgasm. He bought her a diamond ring and let her believe that they were engaged. She was sadly disillusioned when Joan Crawford invited her over to her house to inform Lana that the affair was over. Bautzer belonged to her.

'It's me he truly loves,' Crawford said. 'But he hasn't figured out how to get rid of you yet.'

Lana was hurt but refused to show it. She confronted Bautzer, who denied everything, but soon it became obvious to Lana that everything Joan Crawford had said was true.

Lana leapt directly from the frying pan into the fire. She had met 'King of Swing' Artie Shaw when they were both in *Dancing Co-ed*. She had found him egotistical and insufferable. Later, however, when he turned up on the set of *Two Girls on Broadway* and asked for Lana's phone number, she gave it to him.

One evening, when Bautzer had stood her up, Artie called Lana and asked her out to dinner. Driving down Sunset Boulevard, they began to talk about settling down and having babies. They could marry in Nevada with no delay.

'Suppose I were to call up right now and charter a plane,' said Shaw. 'Would you come with me?'

'Yes,' she said.

They skipped dinner and flew to Las Vegas. A taxi took them to a justice of the peace, George E. Marshall, who married them in his bathrobe. Artie pulled a blue star sapphire ring off his own finger, put it on hers and kissed the bride. While they were celebrating with a cup of coffee in an all-night diner, Lana suddenly realized that her mother had no idea where she was. So she sent a telegram which read: 'Got married in Las Vegas. Call you later. Love, Lana.'

Lana's mother naturally assumed she had married her steady boyfriend and called Bautzer. He knew nothing about any marriage and rang around to try and find out what was going on, in the process, alerting the press.

When Lana and Shaw returned to his Summit Ridge Drive house for their wedding night, they found the place besieged by newspapermen. Lana had been taught by MGM to keep her cool with the press. Shaw went berserk. He screamed obscenities and there was nearly a fight.

When the newlyweds got inside the house, the pressmen began banging on the windows. A pane of glass was broken. Lana had the composure to call the studio. MGM's head of publicity, Howard Strickling, sent a team over to handle the situation.

Late at night, the happy couple crept out of the house and drove to the house of Artie's friend, Edgar Selwyn. He let them use his guest room. Lana was tired after all the excitement and just wanted to sleep, but Shaw would not take no for an answer. It was all over in about a minute. Then he turned his back on her. It was then she realized that she had got married just to get back at Greg Bautzer. Now she was married to a man she did not even know, let alone like.

Seventeen-year-old Judy Garland was not happy either. She had been dating Shaw and when she read the headlines over breakfast the next morning she burst into tears. Betty Grable, who was pregnant by Shaw, phoned Shaw's friend Phil Silvers and said: 'That son-of-a-bitch, who does he think he is?'

Even more unhappy was Louis B. Mayer. He did not want his hot young star married; nor did he want her pregnant.

He dragged Lana and Shaw into his office and insisted that they use condoms.

Mayer gave her just three days off for their honeymoon, much of which was taken up with press conferences arranged by the studio. It was only then Lana learned that her husband had been married twice before.

Shaw refused to allow Lana to wear make-up. He banned her mother from the house, threw her home-cooked spaghetti on the floor in front of guests and insisted that she clear it up. After five months, she could stand no more. She called Greg Bautzer who came and rescued her.

The studio sent her to Hawaii to recuperate, then to a hospital for 'nervous exhaustion'. In other words, she had an abortion. She divorced Shaw, but this did not stop her visiting him at his house and spending the night with him.

At the same time, she was seen on the town with Bautzer, drummer Buddy Rich, bandleader Tommy Dorsey, muscle-bound actor Victor Mature and singer Tony Martin. During the filming of *Ziegfeld Girl*, she began dating her co-star Jimmy Stewart.

Carole Lombard hit the roof when she heard that Lana was going to play opposite her husband Clark Gable. Gable made a habit of sleeping with his leading ladies and Lombard grew so paranoid over the rumours of an affair between them that she had to be banned from the set.

Lana admitted to flirting with Robert Taylor during the filming of *Johnny Eager*. Taylor expressed some disappointment that she was not as busty as her publicity shots. Her face was delicate and beautiful, though, and he had never seen lips like hers.

'Though I was not one to run after blondes, Lana was the exception,' he said. 'I couldn't take my eyes off her, and there were times during *Johnny Eager* I thought I'd explode.'

It was her voice that attracted him most. She sounded like a breathless child. She did not seem to know how to talk without being sexy, he complained. She only had to say 'good morning' and Taylor melted.

'She was the kind of woman a guy would risk five years in jail for,' he said.

Taylor wanted her desperately, even if it was only for one night. The problem was that he was married to Barbara Stanwyck at the time. He told her of his desire for Lana and asked her for a divorce, but after a short separation they attempted a reconciliation. Stanwyck never talked to Lana again.

Clark Gable was teamed with Lana Turner again on *Somewhere I'll Find Love*. This sent Carole Lombard into more paroxysms of jealousy. Things were very strained between Lombard and Gable when she was killed in a plane accident on 16 January 1942. Joan Crawford said that Gable was with her on the night of the crash, but it was Lana who Louis B. Mayer assigned to nurse him through his grief.

After Gable left for wartime service in the Air Force, Lana met a shadowy figure named Stephen Crane. Mayer warned her against him. He claimed to be in the tobacco business but, actually, he was a small-time gangster and a friend of Bugsy Siegel.

She fell head over heels in love with him. After just three weeks, they eloped to Las Vegas. This time, she asked the justice of the peace to tie the knot a little tighter than he had with Shaw.

Although Crane lounged around at home while Lana went out to work, things were happy enough between them for the first five months. Then when she discovered that she was pregnant, he broke the news that he only had an interim divorce decree from his previous wife. It would not be final for another two months. Lana had married him bigamously.

She threw Crane out of the house and had the locks changed. MGM organized an annulment and the judge awarded her sole custody of the unborn child. Crane was devastated. He begged Lana to marry him again, so that he could be a proper father to his own child. She rebuffed him.

He drove over a cliff near her home, but emerged unscathed. A few days later, he tried to overdose on sleeping pills and a friend took him to a hospital. She rushed to his bedside.

Slowly the pressure wore her down and on Valentine's day, they eloped again, this time to Tijuana, Mexico. The witness was a stranger they got off the street who probably did not even speak English. Mayer could hardly contain himself.

Crane was drafted, but Lana used her influence to get him assigned to the Special Services at nearby Fort MacArthur so he could get weekend and overnight passes. But when she gave birth to their daughter Cheryl, he was at a boxing match.

While Lana remained at home with the baby, he spent nights out at Ciro's or the Mocambo. Soon money was getting low, but Crane did not offer to chip in. The quickest way for Lana to pick up ready cash was to do radio shows. The networks paid $5,000 per appearance, so Lana went to New York. Crane wangled some leave and went with her. On the way back to Los Angeles, he wanted to show her Crawfordsville, Indiana, the town where he grew up. He took her to a rundown pool hall with a cigarette shop as a store front. This was the tobacco industry he was in. She could never see him in quite the same light after that.

During the shooting of *Marriage is a Private Affair*, she started having her own private affair with her co-star, John Hodiak. She was also seeing Turhan Bey. Crane caught them dancing together. In the ensuing row, Crane got two black eyes.

When Lana divorced Crane in April 1944, he began an acting career of his own at Columbia, where he got minor roles in three films. He had an affair with Rita Hayworth, but when he dated the girlfriend of Columbia boss Harry Cohn, Cohn tore up his contact and that was the end of his acting career.

Howard Hughes had a particular penchant for recently divorced women and moved in. He said that Lana Turner was so sure that he would marry her that she had her sheets mono-grammed with the letters 'HH', though Lana denied this.

Gossip linked her name with those of Rory Calhoun, Robert Hutton, Rex Harrison and Frank Sinatra. Peter Lawford claimed that he was engaged to Lana in 1944. She jilted him for Artie Shaw's friend, the musician Gene Krupa. She was also seen out with her old flame Greg Bautzer and her ex-husband Stephen Crane.

In *The Postman Always Rings Twice*, she played oppo-site John Garfield. On-screen, they exuded sexual chemistry. Director Tay Garnett said: 'John teased her about sex, which tends to make me believe nothing happened.'

This is maybe because Lana knew of his 'private habits'.

'He had a penchant for picking up young girls, some-times two at a time,' she said, 'and a reputation as a demon lover. He died young, in bed, which is understandable.'

Soon after, Lana met the love of her life, Tyrone Power. She had met him fleetingly at nightclubs and parties, and was attracted to him but he was married so she kept her distance. After he had separated from his wife, the French film actress Annabella, he invited Lana over for drinks. Soon she was deeply in love. Power was the one man she adored above all others – and the one man who would never be hers.

She believed that if Power had settled his divorce quickly, they would have married. Friends even talked of a secret engagement. Lana got pregnant, but Power insisted on an abortion. The studio covered for her by arranging a dis-creet vacation in South America. Power was on a publicity tour there at the time.

Their affair, Lana said, was not sexually passionate – 'What we shared was, to me, far more important than the physical side of love.'

In her autobiography, Lana confessed that she was not the greatest lover in bed. 'I wasn't frigid [but] if I didn't make love for weeks I was content'. Holding hands, cuddling and being close were more important to her than sex itself.

'Tyrone never pressured me,' she wrote. 'Later I heard rumours of a homosexual element to his nature, but I never saw it.'

They stayed together for two years, but Power never pushed his wife to give him a divorce. He never even hired a lawyer and asked his wife to hold off. If he was free, he knew he would be under immediate pressure from Lana.

Meanwhile, Lana risked all for Power. When he was filming *Captain from Castile* in Patzcuaro, Mexico, she took time of from filming *Green Dolphin Street* to fly down there to spend New Year's Eve with him. Bad weather closed in and she got stuck down in Patzcuaro. Mayer was incensed.

'Why does she have to chase a man all the way down to Mexico?' he said. 'Doesn't she get enough action up here?'

By the time she got back, she had missed almost two full days of filming. She rushed straight from the airport to the set. It was dark. Suddenly the lights came on and the cast and crew came out from behind the flats singing 'South of the Border'. Director Victor Saville had shot around her, saving her a fine and a severe reprimand from the studio. She was merely docked two days' pay.

When Power returned to Los Angeles, Lana pressed him about marriage. He said he could do nothing until his wife returned from filming *The Eternal Conflict* in France. When she did, Power found that he had to go off on another publicity tour, this time to Europe. Lana organized a farewell party at which friends thought they would announce their engagement. The theme of the party was Cupid and she decorated her house with hearts and arrows. Power was embarrassed and left early.

'She's suffocating me,' he complained

Lana was pregnant again. She had another abortion.

While Power was in Europe, Lana flew to New York where she was seen with Frank Sinatra. This confirmed what Power had long suspected – that Lana would never be satisfied with just one man. In Rome, Power bumped into Linda

Christian, an actress who Lana had had a row with on the set of *Green Dolphin Street*. They became lovers.

Lana phoned Power and arranged to meet him in New York. Instead, he flew to Los Angeles. She followed him there, but when she arrived at the airport he was not there waiting for her. When he turned up he was drunk. Back at her house, she asked him straight out whether there was another woman. He said yes.

'This doesn't have to be the end for us,' he added. 'You know I care for you, so we can be friends, can't we?'

'No,' said Lana. 'Please leave.'

As if to rub salt in Lana's wounds, Power's wife granted him a divorce the following month. That same day, he married Linda Christian in Rome.

Lana flew to New York where she had a brief fling with tycoon John Alden Talbot. His wife sued for divorce, naming Lana as co-respondent. Next she started dating Bob Topping, heir to the $140 million fortune of tin-plate king Daniel J. Reid. When Lana told him that she did not love him, he said confidently: 'You will.'

Topping separated from his wife, actress Arlene Judge, who told the newspapers that her marriage was just fine until Lana came along.

The night before she was due to fly back to Los Angeles, Lana was having dinner with Topping at the 21 Club when she noticed something sparkle in the bottom of her glass. She fished it out. It was a fifteen-carat marquise diamond ring.

'What's this for?' Lana said.

'I'm asking you to marry me,' said Topping.

'I will,' she said, slipping the ring on to her finger.

Topping flew back to the Coast with Lana. Mayer was furious. She was now involved in two divorce cases; she had turned down the part of Lady de Winter in *The Three Musketeers*; and she was five days late reporting for work. He suspended her without pay and threatened to sue her to recover the pre-production costs.

There were frenzied meetings. Lana explained that she had only turned down *The Three Musketeers* because the part was too small for her. A week later, she was back on a salary of $5,000 a week.

Topping got his divorce on Friday, 23 April 1948. He and Lana married the following Monday. Three times before, Lana had eloped. This time she wanted a proper wedding.

The venue was Billy Wilkerson's mansion on Sunset Boulevard, which Topping filled with flowers. A huge reception was organized. Don Loper created a wedding gown of champagne-coloured Alençon lace over champagne silk. Her bridal bouquet consisted of orchids flown in from Hawaii. The press, who were shepherded into the reception by MGM PR men, thought this was a little over the top, even for Hollywood.

The newlyweds sailed to Europe for their honeymoon. Britain, which was still recovering from the war, gave the extravagant couple a cold reception. After a glorious time in the South of France, they returned to Topping's home in Connecticut. Lana was already pregnant.

Topping laid on extravagant parties. Lana talked of retiring. Then she began to notice that he was drinking rather too much.

In January 1949, Lana was rushed to hospital. The baby was stillborn. Topping took her to the Caribbean to recover. When they got back to Connecticut, he discovered that he could no longer afford the upkeep of the estate there.

MGM wanted Lana back to film *A Life of Her Own* in the summer of 1949. She had gained over thirty pounds in weight and went on a crash diet. They decided to move to California and Lana bought a twenty-four roomed house on Mapleton Drive, using her own money. Topping continued to bombard her with jewels and furs and other gifts, but when she finally fell in love with him, it was too late. He was a hopeless alcoholic and financially ruined.

Lana's career was on the slide too. She had to stop

drinking to keep her weight down. The problem was that when she did not drink with him, Topping went out on his own. She grew suspicious and accused him of seeing another woman. He packed his bags and left. He said he was going fishing in Oregon. In fact, he went to Sun Valley with an ice-skating instructress. Lana sued for divorce. The studio put out the usual story of the two of them wanting to pursue separate careers.

Lana was deeply depressed and attempted suicide. She was saved by her agent, Ben Cole. In her next picture *The Merry Widow*, she wore heavy bracelets and gloves to cover the scars on her wrists. On that movie she did not look the least bit depressed. The reason was that she was already having an intense affair with her co-star, the Latin lover Fernando Lamas. He had the keys to her house and came and went as he pleased. Although she said publicly that she had no intention of getting married again, Lana considered him as a possible husband number four.

During the filming of *The Bad and the Beautiful*, there were persistent rumours that Lana was seeing her co-star Kirk Douglas, although she insisted that she was in love with Lamas. In her next picture, the aptly named *Latin Lovers*, she was scheduled to play opposite him, but they had fallen out by then. At a party at Marion Davies's Malibu beach-house, the current 'Tarzan', Lex Barker, asked her to dance. When they smooched a little too closely, Lamas shouted out: 'Why don't you take her out in the bushes?'

When Lana got home with Lamas, they had a fight. She showed her bruises to Benny Thau at the studio. Fernando Lamas was dropped from *Latin Lovers* and replaced by Ricardo Montalban.

Lana went to stay in the Sinatras' house in Palm Springs, prior to her divorce from Topping. She was there when the famous fight with Ava Gardner took place. After that, the two women took off together for a week of fun in Mexico.

Back in Hollywood, Lana had a fling with bullfighter

Luis Sallano, before heading back to Nevada for her divorce. Outside the courthouse, she told reporters that she would never marry again.

Topping took the opportunity to marry his ice-skating instructress. This depressed Lana deeply. It was Tyrone Power all over again.

Lana was offered a part in *Mogambo* with Clark Gable which she turned down, preferring to film *Flame and the Flesh* in Italy, where her latest beau, Lex Barker, was also filming. They married in Turin in 1953 and honeymooned in Capri. They married again when they returned to the US because Barker's divorce from his previous wife was not final when they had married in Italy.

In *The Prodigal*, Lana played opposite Edmund Purdom who was having an affair with Tyrone Power's wife, Linda Christian. In the movie, Lana walks through the Temple of Love in a costume that consists of a g-string and a handful of beads. It only just got past the censors and some of the publicity shots had to be airbrushed.

She filmed *The Sea Chase* with John Wayne in Hawaii. There were the standard rumours of an affair between the two stars, but both were very much in love with their spouses at the time. By the time they got back to Hollywood, it was different. Barker was seeing other women. Worse, he began to abuse Lana's teenaged daughter Cheryl. At first, he said he was just giving her lessons in love by exposing himself. Later, when Lana had another miscarriage, Barker raped her.

Richard Burton was famous for seducing his leading ladies. Lana played opposite him in *The Rains of Ranchipur*. By all accounts, she resisted his advances. Burton's role was that of an Indian doctor. He refused to play it as an Indian.

'Yet he spent a good deal of time in his dressing-room entertaining our dusky little extras,' said Lana. 'For someone who didn't want to play an Indian, he did seem to enjoy playing *with* them.'

More rumours surrounded Lana and Jeff Chandler, her

co-star in *The Lady Takes a Flyer*. Rumours about Barker were also circulating in Hollywood. They became so persistent that Lana could not dismiss them as baseless gossip and she began to be seen on the nightclub circuit again.

At home, the strain became intolerable. Despite Barker's threats, Cheryl spoke up about the abuse she had been suffering. Lana had her examined by a physician who confirmed what the child said.

That night, Barker was lying in bed when Lana came into the room with a gun. He thought she was going to kill him. Instead, she gave him twenty minutes to pack his bags and leave. He denied her daughter's accusations, but prudently left anyway. He went back to Italy to work, telling the press that Cheryl was responsible for the break-up of their marriage.

Lana went off to Palm Springs with twenty-two-year-old basketball star turned actor Michael Dante. When Cheryl joined them, Lana accused her thirteen-year-old daughter of flirting with Michael, smiling at him and wiggling her bottom.

'I saw you – and you've done it before,' she said. She accused Cheryl of flirting with Lex Barker.

Cheryl was mortified. On the way back to Los Angeles, she jumped out of the car in the sleazy downtown area, but was lucky enough to be picked up by a man who turned her into the nearest police station as a runaway.

During the filming of *Peyton Place*, Lana began to get calls from a mysterious John Steele. She did not know him and refused to take his calls. Then he began to deluge her with flowers, accompanied by his card and phone number. Eventually, she phoned him. He said he was a friend of Ava Gardner's but Lana refused to meet him.

More flowers arrived, along with records by her favourite artists. It was plain that John Steele had done his homework. She called him again and agreed to meet him for a drink. He was to call first and she gave him her home phone number. When she got home from work, she found him sitting in his black Lincoln Continental outside her house.

They had a drink. He talked about Ava. He said that they had dated, but they never had a romance. He left after Lana agreed to see him again.

Next time he phoned, he suggested a light lunch at her apartment. He turned up with her favourite dish from her favourite restaurant. A package was delivered. It contained a gold watch inset with diamonds. She refused to accept it. He said he could not take it back because it had been engraved with her name and a special leaf design.

Throughout the summer of 1957, Lana was seeing several men, but Steele was the most attentive. He bought her jewellery, always with the same leaf design on it. In the face of all these expensive gifts, she asked him: 'Do you happen to have a money tree?'

'No, just the leaves,' he replied.

He commissioned a full-length portrait of her by an artist she had never met. It showed her reclining, with her body barely covered by flimsy cloth. She never liked it; it embarrassed her.

Soon she was deeply in love. It was only then that she discovered that John Steele's real name was Johnny Stompanato. He was a gangster and a well-known womanizer. When she confronted him, he admitted that he was Johnny Stompanato. If he had told her his real name at first, he explained, she would not have gone out with him. She told him that she wanted to break it off.

'Just try and get rid of me now,' he said, laughing.

She tried going out with other men but Stompanato kept calling. One night, he broke into her apartment. She was in bed. He put a pillow over her face and, just when she thought she was going to suffocate, he pulled it away and tried to kiss her. She repelled him with a volley of obscenities and told him to get out or she would call the police. He knew that was the last thing she would do. She could not afford the scandal.

She knew that she could not get away and she found his consuming passion strangely exciting.

'Call it forbidden fruit,' she said later, 'but this attraction was very deep – maybe something sick within me – and my dangerous captivation went far beyond lovemaking.'

In fact, sex with Stompanato was nothing special but, such was her obsession, she began to buy *him* expensive gifts.

Her chance to escape came when she went to film *Another Time, Another Place* in England. Stompanato pleaded to be allowed go with her, but as she was co-producer of the film as well as the star, she would have little time for him. She would write.

Stompanato called every day and wrote long love letters. Soon Lana began to feel lonely in England and his pleas began to get to her. She sent him an airline ticket and he travelled to London on a passport in the name of John Steele.

Lana did not want to be seen out with Stompanato and hid him in a house she had rented in Hampstead. He was also banned from the set.

After the day's shooting, Lana would sometimes go to the pub with Sean Connery – *Another Time, Another Place* was one of his first films. Stompanato heard about this and flew into a jealous rage. He turned up on the set waving a gun. Connery decked him with one punch and security guards threw Stompanato out of the studio.

Stompanato got mad that Lana would not be seen in public with him. He wanted to be acknowledged as her lover. During a violent row at her Hampstead house, she threatened to call the police. He tried to strangle her. Her maid managed to beat him off, but Lana's larynx was bruised. She could not talk and filming had to be suspended for a few days. Eventually, Lana called Scotland Yard and had Stompanato deported. Two policemen accompanied him as far as the steps to the plane.

When the filming was over, Lana planned to take a long vacation in Acapulco. To catch her connection to Mexico, she had to stop over in Denmark. At Copenhagen airport, Stompanato was waiting and the press finally got pictures of them together.

In Acapulco, Lana insisted that Stompanato find a room of his own. It was January, high season, and all the hotel could provide was a closet with a sink and no lavatory. They were seen out together and word got back to Hollywood. As a form of escape, Lana began drinking heavily. When she refused to sleep with him, Stompanato kicked her bedroom door in and raped her with a gun to her head.

'I endured his lovemaking with no feeling whatsoever,' she said. 'The vodka I'd drunk took care of that.'

Back in Hollywood, she found she had been nominated for an Oscar for her role in *Peyton Place*. She had to go to the ceremony and he could not come. She could not be seen in public with a gangster. He accepted this, provided she did not go to the ball afterwards. Of course, she did. He was waiting for her when she got home. There was a terrible fight and Lana was beaten brutally. Cheryl overheard the whole thing. Stompanato threatened both mother and daughter. He had mob connections and he could make them disappear without anyone even knowing what had happened. Lana's mother called the police department, but they said they could not act unless Lana herself made a formal complaint. Lana could not afford to do that, or so she thought.

Eventually, during another bedroom row, Cheryl stabbed Stompanato to death, though Lana said she did it. Cheryl was arrested and held overnight. Attorney Jerry Geisler, who had successfully defended both Charlie Chaplin and Errol Flynn against charges of statutory rape, got her out, arguing that the slaying of a violent mobster by a fourteen-year-old girl was obviously a case of justifiable homicide.

Stompanato's apartment was burgled. A number of love letters went missing and were handed over to the *Los Angeles*

Herald Examiner by Stompanato's cohort, mob boss Mickey Cohen. Lana's simpering love letters made her a laughing stock, but also among the bundle were love letters from Cheryl. This opened the possibility that Cheryl's motive had not been to defend her mother but jealousy.

An inquest cleared Cheryl of murder, but the press bayed that the circumstances of the case proved Lana was an unfit mother. Cheryl was made a ward of court and went to live with her grandmother.

The case left Lana in dire financial straits and the publicity surrounding it made her a pariah at the box office. Producer Ross Hunter had a solution. He offered her the lead in *Imitation of Life*, which was about an actress who sacrifices her teenaged daughter and the man she loves for her career. Lana almost turned down the part because it was too close to home but Hunter argued that that was its strength. The movie was a smash at the box-office. Lana was nominated for an Oscar and, in the process, won back the public's sympathy.

During the filming of *Imitation of Life*, Lana met Fred May, a real-estate tycoon who bore a distinct resemblance to Tyrone Power. Soon she moved in with him in his ranch, which did not stop her having a number of discreet flings in Chicago during her publicity tour for the film.

Imitation of Life put Lana's career back on the road and in November 1960, she and May got married. May was a stable and understanding man.

'I wish I'd met him years ago,' Lana said.

However, his patience and sympathy made him boring. Lana thrived on drama. One evening she started a row and took off down the Pacific Coast Highway. She stopped at a bar and picked up the bartender. When May went looking for her, he spotted her car outside the bartender's home. While he beat on the front door, Lana escaped out of the back, wearing only a fur coat and dark glasses. They were divorced in October 1962, though continued to be friends.

While Lana was in the divorce courts, Harold Robbins published *Where Love Has Gone*, a thinly veiled retelling of the Stompanato murder case. To escape the publicity, Lana headed for Acapulco to film *Love Has Many Faces*. Mexico brought back too many unpleasant memories and she comforted herself with booze and beach boys.

She returned to Hollywood to play *Madame X*, the story of an adulterous wife turned prostitute. During the filming she met Robert Eaton. He was handsome, athletic and ten years younger than her.

'Speaking frankly, Bob introduced me at last to the real, fulfilling pleasure in sex,' she said. At forty-three, after five husbands and countless lovers, she finally discovered sexual passion. 'The way he made love was new to me – nothing crude or unusual, it was sensual, gentle, and sensitive. I felt adored, womanly, and beautiful.'

He could make her laugh and would keep her endlessly amused with stories of his bedroom conquests, but 'Bob always knew how to rekindle passion'.

They married in July 1965. She put him on an allowance of $2,500 a month.

'I was the perfect picture of a silly grown woman in love,' she said.

Eaton continued to live up to his reputation as a stud – with other women.

'As for me – well, I just looked the other way.'

That is, until she went on a USO trip to entertain the troops in Vietnam and Eaton started taking his conquests back to their Malibu house. The maid even kept the sheets smeared with lipstick as evidence.

'Infidelity was bad enough,' Lana said. 'I've never been able to stand that. But in my own bed!'

Lana told Eaton to pack his bags. He left. Lana vowed that she would never see him again and that she would never trust a man again, but before long, Eaton was back and she was giving it one more try.

Eaton introduced her to Harold Robbins, who she had
not forgiven for *Where Love Has Gone*, and she was persuaded to play the role of an adulterous wife in his TV series
The Survivors. While they were filming, Eaton got up to his
old tricks. Lana threw him out again and in April 1969 they
divorced.

Around that time, Lana went to a Los Angeles dis-
cothèque called *The Candy Store* where she spotted Eaton
standing at the bar with a striking brunette. So when a tall
man in white asked her to dance, she did not turn him down.

His name was Ronald Dante and he was a nightclub hyp-
notist. Two days later, he called and asked her out on a date.
He turned up on a motorcycle. She had never been on one
before, but climbed on behind him and held on tight.

Almost immediately, he asked her to marry him. She
refused. She missed him when he went to perform in a nightclub in Arizona. When he eventually called, he asked her to
marry him again and this time she said yes. They married in
Las Vegas in May 1969, five weeks after her divorce from
Eaton was finalized.

Dante had a gaunt face and bulging eyes, and Lana's
friends said that she must have been hypnotized to marry
him. In fact, an ex-wife had sued for an annulment in 1963,
claiming that Dante had hypnotized her into getting married
as part of a plan to swindle her out of her savings. The judge
annulled the marriage and gave her her money back.

Distressed at Dante's frequent out-of-town engagements,
Lana wrote him a cheque for $35,000 one Friday to invest in
a real-estate project that would keep him at home. The following day, they attended a benefit in San Francisco. After an
evening of heavy drinking, Dante went out to get some sand-
wiches and disappeared. When Lana returned home the next
day, Dante had left home, taking his clothes, his motorbike
and the $35,000 with him. Lana sued for divorce.

During her brief marriage to Dante, she had employed
one-time singer Taylor Pero as her secretary. He was in his

late twenties, divorced with a young daughter who was living with her mother, and he was frank about the fact that he was gay.

However, they began to be seen out more and more and in early 1970 he claimed they became lovers. They went on holiday to Hawaii together. He escorted her around the gay bars but soon she began to get jealous of his male friends.

'No one, man or woman, takes a lover from Lana Turner,' Pero said.

In the meantime, Lana was in an emotional turmoil over Cheryl, who moved in with a girlfriend and declared she, too, was gay. Lana blamed herself. She believed that her daughter's homosexuality was the result of her abuse at the hands of Lex Barker, which itself was caused by Lana's own neglect.

Pero became the mainstay in her life. In 1971, she appeared in her first stage play playing a forty-year-old divorcee in love with a man half her age, and found it did her no harm to be seen around with a handsome young man. She was then fifty. When asked if they were lovers, she laughed and said he was her secretary and nothing more. But they were rarely apart and, when he talked to other women at parties, she grew jealous. Few people who saw them together doubted they were lovers.

When they split in November 1979, she fell apart. Her weight dropped to under a hundred pounds. He was devastated, too, and said that he had wanted to marry Lana, but would not beg to get his job back. In 1982, she wrote her autobiography *Lana: The Lady, the Legend, the Truth*, saying that she had never been to bed with him and claiming that she had been celibate since 1969. Her later years were lived quietly as she disappeared into anonymity.

11

THE LOVE GODDESS

The silver screen's first technicolor love goddess, Rita
Hayworth, was born Margarita Carmen Cansino, in
Brooklyn, on 17 October 1918. She idolized her father,
Eduardo Cansino, a Spanish vaudeville dancer from Seville,
who enrolled her in dance classes at the age of four.

When Rita was nine, her family moved to California,
where her father hoped to break into the movies. He had a
brief career as a freelance choreographer before opening a
dance school of his own. Rita gave her first public performance at the Cathay Circle Theater in Los Angeles in 1931
when her brother's dance partner had twisted her ankle.

At the age of thirteen, Rita was already buxom and sul-
try looking.

'All of a sudden I wake up,' her father said. 'Jesus, she
had a figure. She ain't no baby anymore.'

Short of money, her father took her out of school and
made her his own dance partner. Although he was twenty-
two years older than her, people mistook them for brother
and sister. Together they worked the offshore floating casinos
during prohibition while her mother and the other children
stayed at home in Chula Vista. Rita and her father also worked
Tijuana, which prohibition had turned into 'Sin City'.

Prostitution was rife and the dancing girls were thought to be available for a price. Eduardo fiercely protected his young daughter from everyone – except himself. Years later she told her second husband, Orson Welles, that her father had repeatedly had sex with her.

Rita's mother knew what was going on. At home in Chula Vista, she would sleep with Rita to protect her from his incestuous advances. She would even neglect her other children to accompany her daughter to work. At the time, Rita and Eduardo were dancing at the Agua Caliente, a club owned by Joseph M. Schenck, co-founder of Twentieth Century Films with Darryl F. Zanuck who later became the patron of Marilyn Monroe.

Other girls Rita's age had dates with boys but her father would not allow it – except for one occasion when a respectable young boy who attended Loyola University was so persistent that Eduardo had to permit it. He arranged a table for them at the club, even bought them a bottle of champagne. He sat at the next table, scrutinizing their every move. The boy was so intimidated that he gave up and Rita had no more dates until she was married.

The Agua Caliente was full of movie people and her father encouraged Rita to attend private parties in the hope of securing a movie contract. At first, with her dark good looks, everyone thought that Rita was Mexican. She was so shy when she was not on stage, that they assumed she could not speak English. When Joe Schenck told Fox's production chief, Winfield Sheenan, that Rita was American, he arranged a test immediately. The results were awesome. Rita Cansino was billed as the new Dolores del Rio – a Mexican-born star of the silent era – and was given a sensuous dance sequence in *Dante's Inferno*, Spencer Tracy's last picture at Fox.

She was given a six-month contract and played dark-skinned beauties in *Under the Pampas Moon*, *Human Cargo* and *Charlie Chan in Egypt*. Then she was given the lead in

Hollywood's first technicolor film, *Ramona*. Rita was still only sixteen.

While her father prevented her seeing boys her own age, there were plenty of older men on the studio lot who offered to promote her career – in exchange for sexual favours. On the advice of Pinky Tomlin, who acted with her on *Paddy O'Day*, she turned them down. When Fox merged with Twentieth Century, Rita's patron, Winfield Sheenan, was sacked. King of the casting couch Darryl Zanuck took over. He called Rita to his office to 'assess' her. She proved less than co-operative and was kicked out.

Director Allan Dwan was miffed. He had already spotted Rita as a talent.

'The only reason I can think of why she was dropped was because she wouldn't play the game,' he said. 'A lot of the big guys didn't like girls who wouldn't come to their parties and if a girl said 'no' they could exercise their power by dropping her and getting somebody more congenial.'

Rita's career seemed to be over. Then self-styled 'oil man' Eddie Judson moved in. He was a thirty-nine-year-old salesman who had built a career on marrying rich women. After seeing Rita in *Ramona*, he was convinced that she was a hot property. He persuaded her father to let him intercede with the studios. In the meantime, she had to be seen in the Hollywood night-spots with him. He bought her clothes, groomed her and took her to the right places. Short of money as always, Eduardo had no choice but to go along with Judson's plans.

Although he had no contacts in the movie industry, Judson was a slick salesman. He quickly secured Rita a number of freelance parts in small-time movies and eventually, picked up a seven-year contact at Columbia for his protegée.

She came to the attention of studio boss Harry Cohn in a movie called *Girls Can Play*. He liked her, but thought the name Cansino was too Spanish. So Judson changed it to

Rita's mother's maiden name, Hayworth. Then she changed it again. Judson and his burgeoning starlet eloped to Yuma, Arizona, from where, the next morning, they despatched a telegram telling Rita's father and mother they were married. They were not best pleased. Rita's mother had struggled for years to keep her out of the hands of one old man, only to find that she had fallen into the hands of another. Eduardo had lost his buxom baby. Judson gained a lucrative asset.

'I married him for love,' she said of Judson later. 'He married me for an investment. From the beginning he took charge, and for five years he treated me as if I had no mind or soul of my own.'

Nevertheless, in later years, Rita acknowledged that she owed everything to Judson.

'I could never have made the grade in Hollywood without him. My whole career was his idea,' she said. 'After we got married, running my career was his only concern and he gave everything he had, and his efforts paid off.'

Although Judson enjoyed having a young wife, publicist Henry C. Rogers recalled: 'In Judson's life there could be only one ruling passion: the advancement of Rita's career.'

Initially, her career was still foundering. Judson thought long and hard about what was wrong. Eventually he decided that the Latin look that had got Rita into Hollywood in the first place was now *passé*. He dyed her hair auburn and signed her up for a painful course of electrolysis to raise her hairline.

Judson also sought to raise Rita's public profile. She quickly became known as 'the most co-operative woman in Hollywood'. There was no interview or photo opportunity she would turn down. Her rising profile impressed studio boss Harry Cohn who put her in a number of B movies. Judson made sure that Rita was 'co-operative' in other ways too.

'He tried to push her into having affairs with people if it was going to do some good,' said Roz Rogers, wife of publicist Henry. Judson did not seem to mind that his wife was sleeping with other men, just as long as he chose who and when.

'He would have sold her to the highest bidder,' said Henry Rogers.

'It's the saddest story in the world,' Orson Welles said later. 'She had the terrible thing with her father. And the continuation of that in one form or another. Her first husband was a pimp. Literally a pimp. So you see what she was. All her life was pain.'

Rita got her first important part in *Only Angels Have Wings*. How she got the role is part of Hollywood mythology. She bought a $500 outfit in three shades of grey that looked like molten silver had been poured over her body and went to the Trocadero where Howard Hawks and Harry Cohn were discussing the project. They cast her immediately.

The only problem was, once they were on the set, Hawks discovered that she could not act. He gave her lines to Cary Grant and told Rita just to stand there and show her figure off to the camera. In one noted scene, which she got high praise for, she had to act drunk. The only way to get a natural reaction out of her, Hawks found, was to have Cary Grant pour a pitcher full of iced water over her head.

Despite her lack of acting ability, the picture's female lead Jean Arthur knew what she was up against. The two women barely spoke during the shooting and Arthur refused to stand next to Rita for the publicity shots on the grounds that she was too pretty.

Hawks also spotted her potential. Cohn was paying a fortune to hire stars in from other studios. Hawks told him that if he wanted a home-grown star at Columbia, Rita's ego would have to be built up.

'The reason stars are good,' said Hawks, 'is that they walk through the door and they think 'Everybody wants to lay me'.'

Zanuck certainly wanted to lay Rita. Like everyone else

in Hollywood, Zanuck had heard that Judson was pimping his wife and hired her for his remake of *Blood and Sand* and turned her into an exotic, erotic *femme fatale*.

Cohn wanted to lay Rita too. Her contract was up for renewal so he invited Rita and her husband to spend a weekend on his yacht. At the last moment, Judson tactfully ducked out, giving Rita strict instructions to sleep with Cohn. When it came to it, Rita refused. This only inflamed the movie mogul's passion even more. He mooned over her like a jealous lover and followed every move she made. He even went so far as to bug her dressing-room.

'He had spies everywhere,' recalled her secretary, Shifra Haran. 'Miss Hayworth couldn't go to the toilet, he knew where she was.'

Cohn, of course, renewed her contract and the movie mogul's unrequited passion for Rita became the core of their tempestuous twenty-year working relationship at Columbia. He was insufferably rude to her. Even when she was a big star, she would have to punch a time clock at Columbia.

Actress Ann Miller said: 'He was really enamoured of Rita. Her whole life was running from him.'

But Rita was magnanimous about Cohn.

'I think if he could ever have been in love with anyone,' she said, 'he was secretly in love with me.'

In an effort to get into her pants, Cohn cast the *ingénue* in Columbia's most prestigious production at that time, *You'll Never Get Rich* with Fred Astaire. They worked perfectly together but her success did not make her husband happy. Her long hours at the studio made him paranoid. The studio was now promoting her as a love goddess. Although he had pushed her to sleep with other men, he was now jealous that she was taking lovers on her own account. Even her provocative publicity shots tormented him. Though she would return home from work exhausted, he would insist that they went out nightclubbing together. During his abundant free time, he began having affairs with other women.

Despite the fact that he still controlled her finances, after her defiance over Cohn, Judson felt that he was losing control over Rita. In an effort to re-assert himself, he began threatening her with physical violence – even telling her that he would mutilate her face, finishing her career in pictures. At other times, he would play on her pity saying that he was 'an old man on the decline'. Then he revealed that he had been married three times before and he knew how to make money out of the women he had divorced.

Indeed he did. In 1941, he cleared out their safety deposit boxes and hid her earnings in fake corporations and dummy bank accounts. He also threatened to blackmail her with a letter she had written, detailing the 'various intimacies with other men' he had forced her into. Its publication would have ended her career.

Nevertheless, on 24 February 1942, Rita sued Judson for divorce on the grounds of 'grievous mental and physical cruelty'. In the press, she tried to play down their marital difficulties so as not to antagonize Judson but he was going to fight the case anyway.

Terrified of the bad publicity a contested divorce would bring, Rita asked the court to seal all the papers surrounding the case. Her plea for secrecy was denied and an affidavit saying that her husband had told her that he had married her 'as an investment...for the purposes of exploiting her' got great play in the press.

From his suite in the Beverly Hills Hotel, Judson threatened to countersue on the grounds of adultery, even though he had forced his wife into other men's beds. This was more than the studio could stand. Cohn paid Judson $30,000 to withdraw his charges. In court, Rita surrendered everything she owned to Judson, except her car, and she agreed to pay him a further $12,000 in monthly $500 instalments.

Despite her penury, Rita was soon seen on the town with the most eligible bachelors in Hollywood – David Niven, Tony Martin, Errol Flynn, Howard Hughes and the Greek shipping magnate, Stavros Niarchos.

By the end of 1942, Rita's constant companion was Victor Mature. Mature was out of favour with the gossip columnists and the press took against the romance. The war intervened; Mature was called up into the Coast Guard service and posted to Connecticut. Cohn fumed when Rita travelled east to visit him. Together, they attended the New York première of *You Were Never Lovelier*, her last picture with Fred Astaire. At the premiere, Rita wore a big ring which he had given her. There was talk of engagement but back in Hollywood, Rita soon met the man she would call 'the great love of my life'.

Orson Welles was in trouble when Rita first met him. His first film *Citizen Kane* had brought the wrath of the all-powerful press baron William Randolph Hearst down on Hollywood. RKO found his second movie, *The Magnificent Ambersons*, too obscure and had wrested the cutting from him. His third film, *It's All True*, had been cancelled while he was away shooting in Brazil. His first marriage, to Chicago socialite Virginia Nicholson, had ended in divorce and Dolores Del Rio had just broken off their brief engagement. Enter Rita Hayworth.

'I saw that fabulous still in *Life* magazine where she's on her knees on a bed,' he said. 'She was in alluring repose, dressed in a satin-and-lace nightgown. That's when I decided.'

Welles was still in Rio at the time and told his associate Jackson Leighter that when he returned to Hollywood he would marry Rita Hayworth.

'He made a great point of it,' said Leighter. 'That was before he had even met her. In fact, the first thing he wanted to do when he got back was find her.'

When Welles returned to Hollywood to play the dashing Mr Rochester in *Jane Eyre*, he talked openly of his plans to marry Rita. The word spread. When Rita heard, she was not amused. Painfully aware of her own lack of schooling, she thought the erudite movie 'genius' was making fun of her. Nevertheless, she did turn up when Welles organized a party to meet her. He was shocked to find, not the love goddess that she portrayed in her films, but a sweet, shy, sensitive woman.

'There was a richness of texture about her that was very interesting and very unlike a movie star,' he said.

Rita concluded that Welles was only after one thing. After the party, she refused to take his calls. She was sick and tired of being chased around Hollywood. He persisted.

'I am like Casanova,' Welles said. 'Not as a sexual acrobat – because I'm not. But because I am willing to wait under the window until four-thirty in the morning. I'm that kind of romantic fellow, you see. I go the distance in the chase. It took me five weeks to get Rita to answer the phone, but once she did we were out that night.'

They met for dinner. It had to be discreet. She did not want the press to get wind of the fact she was seeing someone else in Mature's absence. In awe of Welles's intellect, Rita clammed up. Welles used an old mind-reading routine he had honed on showgirls to draw her out. He would try and guess what she was thinking. If he was right, it gave her a chance to elaborate. If he was wrong, she would have to correct him.

Soon she opened up like she had to no one before. She told him how much she hated being a movie star, but it was the only way she could make a living. One flop and she was finished, she thought. She told him how awful the men in her life had been to her and, he noticed, she was morbidly obsessed with Harry Cohn.

They spent the night together at his rented house on Woodrow Wilson Drive. Welles found her a revelation after Dolores Del Rio who had to be exquisitely coiffured and made up at all hours of the day and night. Alone in bed, Rita was a million miles away from her glamorous sex kitten image.

'She was much prettier without make-up,' he said.

'Her sexiness was womanly rather than girlish – a shy woman, but not a shy girl.'

Indeed, in bed she was confident and demanding. Sex was important to her.

'Miss Hayworth was someone who would only believe that someone loved her if they were making love to her,' said Shifra Haran. 'Her only security was knowing that someone would go to bed with her.'

Haran also noted that she was not into two-timing.

'When she was with one man I never knew her to play around with another man,' she said. 'During the time of the relationship, that was it. She did not cat around.'

Soon Rita moved in with Welles. Haran, who was his secretary at that time, was sent to move her things. Her instructions were precise. She was to give away all Rita's gaudier outfits, anything that Welles might find tasteless. She was to dispose of anything marked 'VM'. Although he did not know it yet, the affair with Mature was definitely over.

With Dolores Del Rio, Welles had acquired a taste for sexy underwear from the exclusive Juel Parks lingerie shop. Rita began running up enormous bills there. Though she would spend the day in an old pair of jeans and sweater, at night she would have to dress up in flimsy slips and gossamer nightgowns. Welles loved to watch her undress and she enjoyed it, too. When there was a new man in her life, she demanded his full attention – and stripping, she found, was one way she could get it.

Even though she had Welles captivated, Rita began to show signs of her deep insecurity. On the slightest pretext, she would accuse him of flirting with other women. This irritated him and he was determined to cure her of her irrational jealousy. In restaurants, he would suddenly stare across the room as if he had just seen the most beautiful woman. Anxiously, she would follow his gaze, only to find no one there.

Feeling guilty at having been rejected by the draft board

– he was rated 4F because of his asthma and bad feet –
Welles decided to put on a tent show called the Mercury
Wonder Show and tour army bases. This was the perfect
introduction for Rita to the Mercury Players, the company
Welles had brought with him from New York, whose
Shakespearian credentials intimidated her. The show was to
be full of illusions and magic tricks. Rita was a vaudevillian
at heart and Welles had inherited a love of magic from his
eccentric father.

Together they rehearsed a trick where GIs would write
numbers on a slate and Rita would add them up, sight unseen,
and announce the total from the stage. Welles also practised
sawing her in half.

The show was ruined for her when a court official turned
up. Judson was suing her for $10,000 as, on Welles's advice,
she had stopped paying his $500 a month. When Cohn heard
about the Mercury Wonder Show, he told her he would not
have her working on stage with her boyfriend at night when
she should be saving all her energies for her daytime job –
filming *Cover Girl* with Gene Kelly.

Rita was distraught. She told Welles that she would quit
the picture. He urged caution. Crossing Cohn could jeopar-
dize her whole career. Besides, he said, he could always get
someone else to do the show for her. She was mortified. It
was as if Welles had told her that their affair was over. His
words struck at her deepest insecurities.

Welles felt her distress. For the first time, he saw how
truly vulnerable she was. He felt protective towards her and,
there and then, proposed. Marlene Dietrich got to do the
magic act in the Mercury Wonder Show. Rita Hayworth got
married. This was not the outcome Cohn had planned.

After the end of filming *Cover Girl*, Rita travelled east
with Welles, where he planned to start a political career.
Unfortunately, he was struck down with hepatitis and Rita
was left to cope with a crowd of east coast intellectuals single-
handed.

Welles convalesced in Florida, where Rita nursed him and, although his illness drastically diminished their sex life, it seemed to Welles that, for the first time, Rita was just happy to be alone with him.

Rita reluctantly returned to Hollywood at Cohn's insistence. Welles came too. They rented a cosy new house on Fordyce Road. Once Welles was fit again they resumed a vigorous sex life and Rita became pregnant. Welles was not best pleased. He did not relish fatherhood and already had one estranged child. Yet he was delighted to see Rita so thrilled.

Welles volunteered to go on the road and campaign for the re-election of Franklin D. Roosevelt. Before he left, Rita had an anxiety attack. She had a premonition that she was going to lose him, she said. Welles told her not to be so silly. He would never betray her.

Once he was gone, friends from the studio turned up at the house to drink beer and swap the latest gossip. Those who were jealous of the maverick Welles said how awful it was that he had gone away and left her when she was pregnant. Anxiety overwhelmed her again. She took the long flight to New York and stayed with him on Long Island. Her anxieties were allayed but this was the very moment Welles chose to betray her.

One night he slipped out to the 21 Club in Manhattan. There, he saw the youthful Gloria Vanderbilt with her husband and a group of people. Orson joined them.

'Something happened when our eyes met,' Vanderbilt recalled. 'Later, under the table, he kept touching my knee and soon we were holding hands.'

At a party afterwards, Welles and the young heiress found themselves alone. They kissed and embraced. She knew that he had left his pregnant wife alone on Long Island and fought him off, but for the days and weeks that followed, she could not get him out of her mind.

Rita gave birth to a daughter, Rebecca, by Caesarean section on 15 December 1944. While she was convalescing,

Welles took off for Washington to attend the inauguration, travelling on to Baltimore and New York to give lectures on the evils of fascism. Rita was upset that he was taking so little interest in their newborn child. When Welles returned, he whisked Rita off to Mexico for a second honeymoon, leaving the baby behind with a nurse.

Back in Hollywood, Welles realized that he was not going to make it in politics and took a role in *Tomorrow Is Forever* with Claudette Colbert. His long hours at the studio prompted Rita to renew her jealous accusations. This time they were true. Welles embarked on a series of affairs, most notably with Judy Garland.

Welles made a habit of buying huge bunches of white flowers for Garland. One night, in the heat of the moment, he forgot to give them to her and left them on the backseat of the car. Rita naturally assumed they were for her. Miss Haran discreetly removed the card before Rita could find it.

These affairs meant little to Welles. He believed he had failed as a director and as a politician, and needed them as balm for his wounded ego.

'If you took the ego and vanity out of sex,' Welles said, 'the actual amount of sexual activity would be reduced drastically. I am thinking of men particularly, more than women. A man is to a great extent operating on other juices than the sexual ones when he's chasing around.'

Rita did not see it that way. Her girlfriends delighted in giving her a blow-by-blow account of his dirty dealings. In later life, Welles shuddered to think of how much pain he caused his wife during that period.

He even felt guilty at the time. His infidelity caused Rita to start drinking heavily. She would storm out of the house drunk and head for the car. Afraid she would kill herself, Welles would go with her, careering around LA at night. Still Welles spent more and more time at the home of Sam Spiegel with prostitutes who made no emotional demands on him.

The real tragedy was that they were complete opposites.

While Rita longed to quit the movies and have a normal home life, Welles lived for his work. One day when he was working with a group of writers in a New York hotel suite, the sound of Rita's weeping came issuing from the bedroom. Welles asked one of his colleagues to take her to the hair salon. When she had gone, he said callously, 'Now I can concentrate.'

Hours later, when she returned freshly coiffured, he was still immersed in his work. He did not even look up. She sat quietly on a chair, then she exploded. Only then did he look up. She ran into the bedroom. He followed. The writers packed up and left.

The only way out of the marriage for Rita was to go back to the work she hated. She took the lead as a temptress in *Gilda*, a role which many people believe secured her title as a love goddess. Welles went to Goldwyn to direct *The Stranger*. Because of his reputation for being difficult and unreliable, Rita was called on to indemnify his contract. He repaid her by having a series of affairs in his apartment on the Goldwyn lot, regularly staying there at night. Rita heard every detail of his activities through the studio grapevine at Columbia. Even so, she would often go over to Goldwyn to talk to him. People who saw them together believed that they were still very much in love.

Welles abandoned his political ambitions, largely because he was convinced that Rita would either have a breakdown or divorce him, which would have disqualified him from his ultimate goal – the presidency. The inevitable divorce did come finally. When he left for New York to talk to Cole Porter about making a Broadway musical of *Around the World in Eighty Days*, she went to see her lawyer.

The first Welles heard about the divorce was the public announcement Rita made in the press. Although he still adored her, he was relieved the marriage was all over. When he returned to Hollywood to do post-production work on *The Stranger*, he did not even bother to contact her. When the film was finished, he took a vacation alone in Mexico.

Rita spent that New Year's Eve at a party at Sam Spiegel's house. She shed a few tears with Shelley Winters. Later Ava Gardner found the emotionally drained Rita asleep and draped a coat over her. When she woke, everyone thought she would go home. Instead, she fixed her hair and her tear-stained face, and headed for the dance floor. Soon she was dancing with Tony Martin. When someone asked how she was getting home, she said that Tony was taking her. He did and for the next few weeks they were a hot item in the press. Rita suddenly broke it off. She told Martin that Welles was back on the scene. In fact, he was not. He was back in New York, working on his production of *Around The World In Eighty Days*. He had heard about the affair with Martin but had simply phoned to make a property settlement.

Everything was settled amicably, but Rita had not yet given up on the marriage. Welles's production of *Around The World In Eighty Days* had run into financial difficulties. Possibly at Rita's instigation, Harry Cohn helped him out, on the condition that Welles made a film for him. It was to be a small thriller Welles had written called *The Lady from Shanghai*.

Cohn reckoned that if he could cast Rita in a movie opposite her estranged husband he would have a publicity coup. Welles wanted a French actress called Barbara Laage for the part, but Rita started a campaign to win him round.

When Welles arrived back in Los Angeles, he found an invitation to dinner waiting for him at the check-in desk of the Bel-Air Hotel. It was from Rita. Over dinner, she persuaded him to give her the part in the movie – and to stay the night.

'You know,' she told Welles, 'the only happiness I've ever had in my life has been with you.'

'If this was happiness,' Welles said years later, 'imagine what the rest of her life had been.'

Welles moved back in with her. It was all part of

Rita's plan. Her new home in Brentwood had been made over by Columbia set designer Wilbur Menefee. He had been given specific instructions to have her bed in the master bedroom strengthened to accommodate Welles's increasing weight.

He worked overtime to turn *The Lady from Shanghai* from a low-budget thriller into a vehicle for Columbia's biggest star. To give the screenplay more psychological depth, he wrote in a lot of autobiographical references. The film begins with an attempted rape and ends with a symbolic personality disintegration in a hall of mirrors. Welles overlaid this with things he knew about Rita's relationship with her father and Judson, as well as the guilt he felt about his own mistreatment of her.

On the set, Rita was mesmerized by him. She did whatever he told her. As a publicity stunt he even had her trademark auburn mane shorn and bleached metallic blonde. Welles was going to show the world a Rita they had never seen before.

To record the transformation, Welles called in sixteen photographers. Cohn was furious about the hair.

'Oh my God,' he said. 'What has the bastard done now?'

Rita and Welles flew down to Mexico for location work. Although they worked together wonderfully well on the set, people began to notice that the spark of passion was missing in their personal life.

After the movie was over, Welles no longer lavished all his attention on Rita, as he had on the set. In fact, he was rarely home. A death threat to Rebecca from a crank in February 1947 briefly threw them back together again but by March, Welles had moved out to a beach-house in Santa Monica and Rita was in Palm Springs, one of the many actresses comforting David Niven after the tragic death of his young wife.

By the end of the month, Rita announced that she intended to divorce and the newspapers were full of speculation about a possible marriage to Niven.

During their reconciliation, Rita and Welles had planned to go to Europe to film. Even though they were divorcing, Rita decided to take the trip. Grudgingly, Cohn gave his permission. He could do nothing with Rita until her hair had grown back anyway.

In London, Rita accidentally bumped into David Niven which further fuelled the rumours that they were about to announce their engagement. Always the gentleman, Niven denied that he had had an affair with Rita in the first place.

Besides, Rita was seeing bandleader Teddy Shauffer. The brief but passionate affair ended in Paris, where she locked him out of her hotel room. He risked his life scaling the outside of the Hôtel Lancaster to reach her window, while a crowd of Frenchmen cheered him on from the pavement.

When she returned to Los Angeles in October, Rita finally filed for divorce. She heard nothing from Welles. He was busy filming his bare-set *Macbeth* at Republic and having an affair with Marilyn Monroe.

The very day that the Los Angeles Superior Court granted Rita her divorce, 10 November 1947, *Life* magazine ran a cover story on her under the headline 'The Love Goddess'. Rita saw this as a grotesque irony. Having just lost the great love of her life, Rita was convinced that she was a failure in love. Perversely, the label stuck.

Cashing in on the image, Harry Cohn immediately cast her as the wanton gypsy in *The Loves of Carmen*. Meanwhile, Mahmud Pahlavi, the Shah of Iran's brother, would often pick her up after work and take her dancing at the Mocambo. Howard Hughes would visit her house late at night. If Cohn spying on her was not bad enough, she now had Hughes on her case as well.

Before the shooting of *The Loves of Carmen* was over, Rita found she was pregnant. An abortion was hastily arranged, after which she headed to Europe with Shifra Haran, Welles's former secretary who Rita had now hired.

She hoped to run into Welles who was filming there, but he was already embroiled with an Italian actress. Nevertheless, when she caught up with him on the French Riviera she managed to lure him out for a night on the town in Cannes. A kiss in a restaurant led to headlines in America saying they were to remarry. Rita, too, believed that Welles was coming back to her. She waited for days in her room in the Hôtel du Cap, but he never called.

Meanwhile she was pursued by King Farouk and the Shah of Iran, but out in front of the pack was the greatest Casanova of them all, Prince Aly Khan. They met at a dinner party. The prince was immediately smitten. Rita was not. To her, Khan was just another married playboy.

She agreed to go out on a date with him, but when he turned up he was informed that she had accepted a luncheon engagement with Argentine millionaire Alberto Dodero. The prince would have to wait three hours.

When, at last, she was free, he whisked her off to his villa on the Côte d'Azur. She fended him off and, eventually, he had to leave for Ireland where one of his horses was running.

While he was away, he filled her hotel suite with roses every day. When he returned, he buzzed the hotel in his private plane. Soon Rita and Khan were seen everywhere together. He was romantic and attentive. Rita was happy as long as he toyed with her like a charming playboy. The moment she thought he suggested anything more serious, she took flight.

She hid out in the Hôtel La Réserve in Cannes where a mysterious gypsy woman turned up. She told Rita that she had already met the love of her life and, foolishly, spurned him. Only if she gave herself to him completely would she find true happiness.

Although it was pretty obvious that Aly Khan had sent the gypsy woman, Rita was taken in completely. She rushed back to Khan's villa, into the arms of her passionate prince.

In the International Sporting Club, they danced cheek to cheek. Soon she moved into his ten-bedroomed villa.

As always, Rita wanted just one man in her life to love her and love her completely but Aly Khan was not that kind of person. He did not want to be alone with Rita in the serenity of his villa. He liked to party and packed his place with house guests, some of whom seemed to stay indefinitely. This was the chic society of the Riviera. They looked down on Rita who spoke no French. She called Welles in Rome for help and he flew to Cannes. Sensing Rita was about to flee again, Khan whisked her off to Spain on a motoring holiday.

The trip was supposed to be discreet. Khan, after all, was married. As a direct descendant of the Prophet, Khan was also a religious leader. His father, the Aga Khan, had 15 million followers in Africa and Asia and had told Aly to curb his womanizing ways.

Khan was a demon driver. Heading south from Biarritz, he hit a horse-drawn cart. News of the accident alerted the press. By the time they reached Madrid they were mobbed by the paparazzi and Rita's adoring fans. A bullfight in Toledo turned into a real-life scene out of *Blood and Sand* when the matador presented Rita with the bull's ears as a tribute to her beauty. In Seville, her father's birthplace, she was mobbed by relatives.

Khan was used to attracting attention in his own right. To be with a consort who drew such adulation intensified his love. It had the opposite effect on Rita. With Aly, she realized, she could never have the peace and privacy she sought. After the holiday, she packed her bags and headed back to the States, leaving him heartbroken.

Back in Hollywood, Rita quashed the rumours about a reconciliation with Welles and denied any affair with Aly Khan. Khan, however, was not a man to give up easily. Realizing that filming commitments made it impossible for Rita to return to Europe, he flew to America and moved into the house directly across the street from her in Brentwood.

To protect her reputation, Rita issued a press statement saying that her old friend Prince Aly Khan was in town and they would be seen out together frequently. They weren't.

'They just stayed in her room and made love,' said Haran.

This was not at the gregarious Khan's bidding, but Rita's.

'I never saw the prince as a sex maniac,' said Haran. 'It was Miss Hayworth who was insatiable in her appetites.'

At last, Rita had what she wanted – absolute privacy with a man who was attentive to her every need. Her greatest need had always been in the bedroom, where the prince was reputedly a king. At an early age he had been sent to the brothels of Cairo to learnt the art of *imsak* – the indefinite postponement of ejaculation.

Even though they were discreet, Cohn gave Rita a tongue-lashing for involving herself with a married man. This upset Rita and she fled with Khan to Mexico City, where a sharp-eyed desk clerk alerted the press. Soon their hotel suite was under siege, with journalists even dressing as hotel staff to gain access.

Rita travelled to Cuba with him to be by his side when she should have been reporting for work in Hollywood. Columbia suspended her, and once the couple had closed up their Brentwood homes, they headed back to Europe. There was no peace for them there either. In Britain, the *Sunday Pictorial* declared in a headline that their affair was 'a very sordid business' and reported it in lurid detail. The *People's* banner headline read: 'This affair is an insult to all decent women'. The newspaper then refused to cover Rita's affair with her 'coloured prince...on the grounds of public decency'.

In the US, the American Federation of Women's Clubs was up in arms and threatened to boycott Rita's movies unless she mended her ways. Faced with this level of public condemnation, they had two choices – marry or split. There was another fly in the ointment. Rita was pregnant.

They were skiing in Gstaad when reporters caught up with them. After a hazardous car chase down icy roads, they managed to shake the newshounds and slipped over the French border. They headed for the Aga Khan's twenty-one-roomed villa outside Cannes to ask his permission to wed.

The Aga Khan was furious about the scandal his son had brought on the Ismaili sect. Nevertheless, once the old man, no mean womanizer himself, met Rita he gave his approval. He did not even demand that Rita become a Muslim, only that any offspring be brought up in the faith.

Aly Khan's divorce was rushed through the French courts. The date was set for the marriage. Meanwhile, Rita and Khan returned to his villa on the Côte d'Azur to find it, as usual, full of house guests, half of whom Khan did not even seem to know.

Despite the impending nuptials, Khan had not abandoned his wanton ways. He would slip out of the villa in the early hours of the morning for secret assignations with other women.

As the wedding day approached, Rita got cold feet. She cabled Welles in Rome. Again he flew to her rescue. He could not even get himself a seat on an aircraft this time and had to stand up on a cargo plane all the way to Antibes.

Rita awaited him in a hotel room with a bottle of champagne. When she closed the door behind him, she said: 'Here I am. Marry me.'

Welles stayed the night but next morning headed back to Rome.

'She was marrying the most promiscuous man in Europe,' he said. 'It was just the worst possible marriage. And she knew it.'

Marriage to Aly Khan, however, had one thing in its favour. Now she could tell Hollywood and Harry Cohn to get lost. Just to rub in the point, she personally invited Cohn to the wedding. He did not turn up.

The wedding itself was a disaster. They were denied permission to have a private ceremony. The local mayor, who would conduct the civil formalities, was a Communist who insisted that – alongside the princes, princesses, maharajahs, nabobs and emirs who had been invited – the local peasantry must be allowed to participate. Thousands of fans turned up. The press had a field day. Hundreds of extra policemen had to be bussed in from Nice to control the crowds. Ismaili devotees fell to their knees to kiss Rita's feet. The Imam of Paris declared her wedding to be the biggest Muslim marriage of the century. The Vatican declared the marriage to be invalid and informed Rita that any fruit of the union would be 'conceived in sin'.

As Welles predicted, it turned out to be the worst possible marriage. While she longed for privacy, Aly Khan loved to show his film-star wife off at international sporting events and occasions – to the point where Rita, who was heavily pregnant, risked being crushed in the crowd. The couple's image was so opulent that they were the constant target for thieves and kidnappers. Khan continued his womanizing ways. When she went to sleep at night, he would slip out to pursue other women, often very publicly. Their various houses were crammed full of house guests and Rita could never be sure which ones of the female freeloaders were her husband's current mistresses. She even gave birth in the middle of a media circus with guards on the doors of the delivery room to prevent journalists and photographers bursting in unexpectedly. After a protracted labour, Rita gave birth to a healthy five-and-a-half pound daughter, Princess Yasmin.

They went back to Gstaad where Rita enjoyed a brief period of family life. Soon Khan grew bored and they returned to the south of France where he would be surrounded by amusing guests. Rita could not stand them and withdrew to her room. She wanted to go back to America. He wanted to go horse racing. Violent rows ensued. These had the effect of turning him on and after a 'tender reconciliation', Rita would usually do what he wanted to do.

One night in Paris, he took her to see an adaptation of Marlowe's *Dr Faustus* featuring Orson Welles and Eartha Kitt. When Welles came on stage, he spotted Rita in the audience and could not take his eyes off her.

In the play, Eartha Kitt delivers the line: 'Dr John Faustus, who then is this Margarita with whom you are so in love?'

Welles directed his reply to his ex-wife.

'Margarita, Margarita,' he said. 'Ah yes, a girl that I have known.'

Rita laughed appreciatively. Khan was furious.

As part of his religious duties, Khan took Rita on a tour of the Ismaili communities in North Africa. In Cairo, she finally grew tired of his playboy ways. She walked out, flew back to Cannes where she collected the children and set sail back to the States. When Khan heard that she had gone, he realized there was nothing that could be done without creating further scandal.

In the US, the papers were thrilled that the Love Goddess was heading home and Cohn announced that he was delighted to welcome Princess Rita back to the Columbia fold. Her errant husband was seen at the Cannes Film Festival with a bevy of beautiful girls. Rita announced her divorce plans to the press and decamped to Nevada. Khan sent a conciliatory letter. When that had no effect, he began legal action in France to retrieve his daughter, Princess Yasmin.

While the lawyers thrashed out a property settlement, Rita filed for divorce. Aly Khan had been kept on a tight rein by his father and had spent a great deal of Rita's money. She was penniless and was forced to return to Columbia to work on *Affair in Trinidad*.

She began dating again.

'She seemed to drift in and out of relationships with men. It was a need,' said her long-time make-up man Bob Schiffer. Among them were her former lover Victor Mature, agent-producer Charles Feldman and singer Robert Savage. There followed a brief but intense affair with Kirk Douglas. He broke it off, explaining: 'I felt something deep within her that I couldn't help – loneliness, sadness – something that would pull me down. I had to get away.'

But during that period, the man Rita was closest to was Schiffer himself. They even ran away to Mexico together during the filming of *Salome* and Schiffer stuck by her through thick and thin.

'I went through all these romances with her,' he said – he was even around during her marriage to Welles who, out of jealousy, had tried to have Schiffer dismissed. 'I don't know how I did it because I was crazy about her myself.'

Cohn tried it on again. He turned up at her house demanding that she come with him on a family holiday to Palm Springs.

'I'm going to give you one last chance, Hayworth,' he said. 'You'll have your own bedroom where you can sleep alone, for a change.' The clear implication was that he was going to join her there. 'And don't give me that bullshit about being busy, because that prince of yours is fucking his brains out with some model in the Alps.'

'He's skiing,' she said.

'If you can fuck on skis, then he's skiing,' Cohn bellowed. 'So get your goddamn diaphragm and get your ass in the car.'

Rita made her excuses and Cohn went away complaining that she had done nothing but reject his offers of friendship.

'And don't think it's not going to affect the parts offered you,' he threatened.

The answer was still no.

At the behest of the ailing Aga Khan, Aly made one more

attempt at reconciliation. He phoned her and she consented to see him. But Aly could never change. He had just made headlines with a wild party he had had in Argentina. Now he was having an affair in France with actress Yvonne De Carlo. The French press had run a picture of them with the caption: 'Watch out, Rita – I've got your man.'

On his way to California, Khan stopped off for a few nights of passion in Saratoga Springs with De Carlo. When he arrived in Los Angeles, Rita gave him permission to stay the night, then changed her mind. The following day, Yasmin swallowed sleeping pills by accident. She was rushed to hospital to have her stomach pumped and survived undamaged. The incident worked to bring the family back together.

Rita agreed to join Khan in France when she had finished filming *Salome*, but when she turned up at his house in Neuilly it was full of house guests and Khan was nowhere to be seen. When he turned up, they slept together. After that she left word that she was indisposed and he returned to his womanizing.

When she first arrived in France she had made a press statement that the divorce was off. Then she announced that it was on again. She could no longer stand his playboy existence, besides she could no longer afford him. He spent too much and she had to work to support both of them.

She split from him very publicly and took the train to Spain for a holiday. In Madrid, she sought reassurance in the arms of a number of men. There was talk of an affair with Ava Gardner's beau, Luis Miguel Dominguin, Spain's number one bullfighter, but her principal lover was the dashing Count José-Maria Villapadierna, a close friend of Khan. They travelled around Spain together. When Catholic activists began demonstrating against her immoral conduct, he accompanied her back to Paris. She even delayed her return to America to spend more time with him.

Back in the US, she quickly obtained a Nevada divorce. Then she met thirty-five-year-old one-time crooner

Dick Haymes. He was an unpleasant character who was already on the slide and was known around Hollywood as 'Mr Evil'.

When she was filming *Miss Sadie Thompson*, he was on *Cruisin' Down the River* and they used to have a dry martini together at lunchtime. When she let it slip that she was going to New York for the première of *Salome*, he contrived to meet her on the train. He managed to wangle an invitation to the post-première party at the Stork Club and there, he made his move. The couple danced together all night and he escorted her back to her hotel. Everyone was shocked. Even by Hollywood's standards, Haymes had an abominable reputation.

Back in LA, Rita and Haymes were seen everywhere together. For him, she was the meal ticket he badly needed. Although he had once been popular, in a series of drunken sprees, he had blown $4 million, and he had a string of ex-wives and a handful of children to support. Being seen out with Columbia's biggest star could do no harm to a man who had a reputation as a loser. He was right. His association with Rita earned him a singing engagement at the Sands in Las Vegas. Haymes was convinced it would be the beginning of his long-awaited comeback.

To Rita, Haymes's broken marriages were a plus. They made him the perfect soul-mate. In fact, Aly Khan, now planning to marry Gene Tierney, another movie actress, was refusing to pay Rita child support – the same complaint that Haymes's ex-wives were making about him. Rita didn't see it that way.

She went to Hawaii for some location work taking Bob Schiffer with her. Haymes wangled an invitation to join her there.

Rita and Haymes spent two blissful weeks together in Hawaii. Cohn's spies soon reported his presence and Cohn was livid. Marrying a Muslim playboy was bad enough. Now his biggest star was involved with a notorious lowlife. He banned Haymes from the Columbia lot and, at Cohn's prompting, the Immigration and Naturalization Service (INS) began deportation proceedings against him.

Haymes, born in Argentina of American parents, had claimed to be a foreign national during the Second World War to dodge the draft. At that time, Hawaii was not a state. Technically, Haymes had left the country and could be denied residence back in the US.

Cohn's opposition made Haymes all the more attractive in Rita's eyes. To stop him being deported, she married him.

They honeymooned at the Sands in Las Vegas, which helped draw big crowds to his comeback concerts. He began a US tour, but could only draw an audience if Rita was with him. She dodged filming commitments to be by his side. The Internal Revenue Service were now after him; former wives demanded alimony; and the INS continued to hound him. Throughout all this, Rita stood by him. In return for her loyalty, Haymes, who grew violent when drunk, frequently gave her a smack in the face. Despite this abuse, the two of them were rarely seen out of each other's company.

When an anonymous death threat was made against Princess Yasmin, Aly Khan used this as an excuse to contest Rita's custody, hoping that her inappropriate choice of a stepfather would count against her. Fearing that Khan might try to take his daughter too, Welles stepped into the fray.

As Rita was constantly touring with Haymes, the children were left alone in the care of a housekeeper. The authorities took them into care. Rita contested this and what with that, the series of hearings in Haymes's deportation case, and the ex-wives chasing him for non-payment of alimony, for nearly a year they were rarely out of court. Consequently, Rita was making no films.

A judgement against Haymes in a Los Angeles court meant that he would go to jail if he set foot in California. Rita could not go to the studio as she would go nowhere without him, and they desperately needed money.

Haymes realized that this was the time to make a deal.

He contacted Harry Cohn. In a meeting in Las Vegas, Haymes established himself as Rita's manager and negotiated for her. Rita would return to work if the studio paid off his debts in California which had led to the judgement against him. They would lend their support in his deportation case, which was now on its way to the US Supreme Court. If he was deported, they must let her make the remaining films due under her contract in whatever country she chose. And he was to be allowed back on the Columbia lot.

Cohn did not like the deal, but he agreed. He figured that Rita had a couple more good pictures left in her. If she ran off after that, he would let her go. Besides, he had found someone he was grooming to replace her – Kim Novak.

Things had gone full circle. In Dick Haymes, Rita had a new Eddie Judson who took control of everything. Haymes spoke for her at press conferences, attended story meetings and went with her to fittings in wardrobe and to the hairdressers.

During the making of *Joseph and His Brethren*, Haymes was consulted on the casting. Cohn wanted Welles to play opposite Rita. Haymes vetoed this, without even telling her. He started growing a beard, secretly hoping to be offered the part himself. When Kerwin Matthews was picked for the part, he was furious. By this time, producer Jerry Wald had had enough of Haymes's interference and kicked him off the lot. Rita went with him, precipitating a fresh flurry of suits and countersuits.

Aly Khan redoubled his efforts to get custody of Yasmin. The pressure became unbearable. To earn money, Haymes began singing again. During an engagement at the Coconut Grove, they had a public row. Rita walked out for several days. When she returned, they had a stand-up fight in front of the customers. He slugged her in the eye. Before, she would have taken it, but now the clouds had lifted. The government had dropped his deportation case. She had no reason to stay with him. She packed her bags, picked up the children and walked out of his life forever.

Haymes was desperate. He thought he would be finished without her. But more people than ever turned up to his shows – just to see whether he could make it through the set without collapsing. Songs like 'Something's Got to Give' won him a standing ovation. In fact, he was singing better than he had in years.

Rita filed for divorce on the grounds of cruelty and sailed for Europe with the kids, so that Yasmin could see her father and visit the ailing Aga Khan. Her divorce was granted *in absentia*.

Aly Khan was now dating Bettina, the Jacques Fath mannequin who had modelled Rita's wedding gown. He, Rita and Bettina became good friends. In Paris, Rita found a new lover, Egyptian-born producer Raymond Hakim. Hakim's interest was professional as well as romantic. He wanted her to star in a movie about Isadora Duncan he was making. She was willing but first, she would have to clear up her position with Columbia. The day after Rita was granted a divorce from Haymes in Reno and the day before a hearing in a Paris court to validate her divorce from Khan, Rita and Hakim set sail for New York, leaving the children in France.

A hearing in a Los Angeles court initially blamed Haymes for the trouble between Rita and Columbia. Rita returned to her children in Europe, leaving Hakim in the US. Although she wired Hakim, urging him to join her in France, she was seen out dancing cheek to cheek with Aly Khan.

By the time Hakim arrived in Paris, the court in Los Angeles had found against her. She would have to make two more films for Columbia, then she could say goodbye to Harry Cohn forever. However, she refused to return to Los Angeles, so Columbia compromised and cast her as the love interest in *Fire Down Below* which was being shot in London and the West Indies.

Rita finally fulfilled her commitment to Columbia with *Pal Joey,* where Cohn cruelly cast her as the older woman in a love triangle with Frank Sinatra and her young replacement at Columbia Kim Novak. Of course, the filming was not complete without Cohn making one more crude attempt on Rita, but by this time she was seeing independent director Jim Hill. He was a bachelor friend of Bob Schiffer who had recently married. Hill gave her the privacy that she craved. Frequently they would hole up in his Los Angeles apartment with several cases of champagne and tins of beluga caviar.

Once more, Hill's interest in her was professional as well as romantic. He longed to direct her and cast her in a screen version of *Separate Tables* which his company was producing. Shortly before they started shooting, he asked her to marry him. She said yes. It was another disaster. She no longer wanted to be an actress but he kept urging her to take on new projects. They drank heavily and fought like cat and dog. At dinner parties they were known to fling crockery at one another. Once a gunshot was heard coming from their hotel room. When the police turned up, Rita and Hill were so drunk they could not remember where the gun had come from, who had fired it and why.

Rita also took up the cudgels again with Aly Khan, suing him for $18,000 in legal fees, but he had just been appointed Pakistani ambassador to the UN and claimed diplomatic immunity.

On 7 September 1961, she was granted a divorce by Santa Monica Superior Court Judge Orlando Rhodes, the same man who had married her to Orson Welles that very day eighteen years earlier. Unsurprisingly, Rita did not recognize him, but in fact, her memory was deteriorating. She swore off the booze. Only then was it discovered that she was suffering from Alzheimer's, the disease that was to dominate the remaining twenty-five years of her life.

12

AMAZING GRACE

Alfred Hitchcock dubbed Grace Kelly 'The Snow Princess' during the filming of *Dial M for Murder*. He did so ironically, because of her extraordinarily promiscuous behaviour on the set. Screenwriter Bryan Mawr recalled a few years later: 'That Grace! She went with everyone. Why she even had little Freddie [Frederick Knott] the writer.'

In Hollywood it was well known that Grace Kelly had 'slept her way to the top' – columnist Hedda Hopper called her a 'nymphomaniac' – but somehow Grace managed to retain her virginal image throughout her career. She was thought of as Miss High Society, the girl from the right side of the tracks in old Philadelphia who went on to marry a prince. The girl who had everything was also the girl who had everyone.

However, Grace was not quite the high society gal that the studios made her out to be. Her father, Jack Kelly, was a self-made millionaire and as the son of an Irish immigrant and a former bricklayer, did not qualify for polite society. In response, he took mistresses from among the wives of Philadelphia's socialites and groomed his daughter to marry a blue-blood, which he hoped would give him the prestige he required. Eager to please daddy, Grace cultivated a refined

English accent and behaved like a debutante.

The third of four children, Grace was largely overlooked as a child. At the age of eleven, her craving for attention led her to join an amateur theatrical society. By the time she was fourteen, she needed no theatrical help. She was tall with a clear complexion and her flirtatious manner attracted older boys.

She was barely fifteen when men started proposing to her. Jack Kelly took it as a mark of esteem that herds of eligible young men would flock to the house. There were so many of them, he could scarcely remember their names.

'You can take her out all you want,' he said. 'But don't think you are going to marry her.'

Her first love was Harper Davis, the son of a Buick salesman. Her father only discovered that the relationship was serious when Davis graduated from High School in 1944 and enlisted in the navy. He forced her to break it off.

'We never knew how much it meant to her at the time,' her mother said.

Years later, when she got engaged to Prince Rainier of Monaco, he asked her if she had ever been in love before. She said: 'Yes, I was in love with Harper Davis. He died.'

When Davis returned from wartime service in 1946, he was struck down by multiple sclerosis. By 1951, he was totally paralysed. Grace would spend hours at his bedside, though he could not move or speak. He died in 1953. When she flew back from Hollywood for his funeral, the studio made great play of the 'Philadelphia socialite' returning for the funeral of her childhood sweetheart.

Grace enrolled in the American Academy of Drama Arts in October 1947. Before she left Philadelphia for New York, she lost her virginity but not to her own true love.

'It happened very quickly,' she told another lover at the Academy. 'I went round to a friend's house to pick her up, and I found that she wasn't there. It was raining outside, and her husband told me she would be gone for the rest of the day.

I stayed talking to him, and somehow we fell into bed together, without understanding why.'

She did not repeat the experience with the man in question, though she stayed on friendly terms with the couple.

Grace's first sexual encounter was not as accidental as she made it seem. She explained later that she had not wanted to move to New York without knowing about sex, but none of the boys she knew could be trusted to keep a secret. When a friend commiserated, saying that it was a pity that her first sexual encounter had not been suffused with love and romance, she replied: 'It wasn't that bad.'

Despite this slip from the primrose path, Grace managed to maintain her virginal demeanour throughout drama school. However, she dated several boys at the Academy, including the best-looking guy in the class, Herbie Miller, who made a career in TV sitcoms under the name Mark Miller.

'We were turned on to each other from the first day at the Academy,' he said. 'We were two young, vital, horny kids and our relationship was very physical.'

There were plenty of others.

'There were these guys who would call for her,' said Miller. 'I would be thinking that I'm the only love in her life, and some stud would arrive at school. So I'd ask her, 'Who's that guy?' and she'd say, 'Just some guy I know. He's crazy about me.' She would laugh about it and brush it off, like she was just sort of doing the guy a favour. I never gave it too much thought. I was very naive, I suppose.'

She also had a month-long fling with Alexandre D'Arcy, a Hollywood leading man who at one time ranked alongside Gary Cooper, Cary Grant and Clark Gable. Once hailed as the 'new Valentino' and chum of Errol Flynn, D'Arcy had been born in Egypt of French parentage. Girls, he explained, were his hobby. He was twice Grace's age.

They met at a party on Park Avenue.

'She didn't dress as the sort of girl that would jump into bed with you,' he said. But he tried it on anyway. On the way home in a taxi, he touched her on the knee.

'She just jumped into my arms,' he said. 'I could not believe it. She was the very opposite of how she seemed.'

She went back to his apartment on 53rd Street and made love to him without a second thought.

'She was a very, very sexual girl,' he recalled, 'very warm indeed as far as sex was concerned. You would touch her once, and she would go through the ceiling. It was very obvious she was not a virgin. She was certainly experienced.'

Years later D'Arcy remembered the contrast between her demure appearance and her passionate nature.

'With sex, everything would come out,' he said. 'Maybe it was something she was hiding. She was like a different person.'

Grace continued seeing Herbie Miller – and any other young stud who turned up at the Academy. She split with D'Arcy when he had to leave New York for some film work in Paris.

In her second year, she was rescued from the class bully by her teacher Don Richardson. Grace was in tears. To calm her down, he took her to the Russian Tea Rooms, but found he only had a few cents in his pocket. So he took her to his attic apartment on 33rd Street.

'I got the fire going and went out to make some coffee,' he recalled.

When he came back, he found she had taken all her clothes off and was waiting for him in bed.

'I never saw anything more splendid,' he said. 'Her body was stunning. She was like something sculptured by Rodin. She had the most beautiful, delicate figure – small breasts, small hips – and her skin was almost translucent. She was the most beautiful girl that I had ever seen naked.'

The speed at which this happened took Richardson's breath away.

'We had no introduction to this,' he said. 'There was no flirtation. I could not believe it. Here was this fantastically beautiful creature lying next to me... I was lying there and discovering that I was in love, that this was not just getting laid...and she seemed to be madly in love with me. So that night was just sheer ecstasy.'

The next morning, though, he was full of remorse. He felt like a psychiatrist who had just slept with his patient. After all, he was her teacher. They decided that they must be discreet. At the Academy, Grace and Richardson pretended not to know each other any better than a pupil would a teacher. Grace also continued seeing Herbie Miller, though she kept that from Richardson, but most weekends, Grace would sneak downtown and make love to Richardson in his broken-down flat.

She liked to dance naked in the firelight to Hawaiian music. 'And if you don't think that was an incredible sight, you're crazy,' said Richardson. 'She was a very sexy girl.'

Despite their efforts, the affair was the talk of the Academy, but somehow Herbie Miller remained in blissful ignorance. Then 'I found out she was seeing this stud from Philadelphia, a real big handsome guy. I thought, where did this guy come from? And I got real pissed off. Very jealous. I had no idea about Richardson. We resolved the problem of this guy from Philadelphia, but we broke up over something else... It was very tragic for me.'

To make money, Grace would take on assignments modelling lingerie. At lunchtime, she would steal away to have hot soup at Richardson's apartment. Then they would jump into bed and make love. Afterwards, she would put her clothes back on and run back to model. She used to say that these lunchtime sessions were important for her modelling career. They put lights in her eyes.

When she modelled, she would often wear a 'Merry Widow' corset with a cinch to pull her waist in. In the flat, Richardson recalled: 'She would strip down to nothing but her Merry Widow and run around the place, cooking and cleaning and all that, with her buttocks only barely covered.

She was marvellously endowed in that department.'

He also marvelled how she would jump out of bed on Sunday mornings, run off to mass, run back and jump back into bed with him with her little gold crucifix around her neck.

She told Richardson the story of how she lost her virginity in Philadelphia and said that he was only the second man she had made love to. Richardson did not believe that – 'I mean, a girl who was as busy in bed as she was... I am not saying that she was a nymphomaniac. That was not Grace. She was happy in bed, but she always knew when she had had enough. We were young and after, say, four times, well that was just fine for her.'

However, Richardson did 'not think it was sex that she was doing it for. There was something else.'

Richardson was certainly a help to her at the Academy. Although he considered she had only minimal acting talent, he made sure she got good parts in the Academy's productions and lavished his directoral skills on her. Naturally, he picked her for the lead in the second year's graduation play *The Philadelphia Story*.

He knew she would never make it on the stage but when he took a photograph of her he realized that she had what it took to make a movie actress and took her to the William Morris Agency. He also accompanied her to audition for the part of Daisy Mae when Al Capp, creator of the syndicated cartoon strip Li'l Abner, was making a Broadway musical out of his Dogpatch characters. She emerged from Capp's office with her dress ripped, her lipstick smudged and her hair messed up. Capp had tried to rape her. When Richardson threatened to kill him, Grace said: 'The poor man only has one leg. Leave him alone.'

Later, Capp was arrested for another sexual assault.

Grace took Richardson home for the weekend to introduce him to her family. The family did not consider him husband material. He was not a Catholic and, worse, he was a married man, separated from his wife and currently in the throes of a messy divorce. And he was Jewish. In fact, part of Grace's great attraction for Richardson was that she was 'the ultimate shiksa'.

'To a Jewish boy, that kind of blonde, blue-eyed beauty was the forbidden thing,' he said.

Over dinner, Grace's brother made persistent anti-Semitic jokes. When they went to bed, her father stood at the bottom of the stairs to make sure they went into their separate rooms. Pointedly, he asked Richardson if he wanted to join the family at mass the next morning. Grace's mother had the temerity to go through his bags and found a packet of condoms. Richardson was thrown out of the house and Grace was lectured on immorality.

'I hope I'm pregnant,' she said defiantly through her sobs.

Grace was permitted to return to the Academy only for her graduation. But she seized the opportunity to go straight to Richardson's 33rd Street apartment and make love to him again. A few weeks later, Grace's father turned up on Richardson's doorstep. He tried to buy Richardson off with a Jaguar. When that failed, Richardson started receiving phone calls from Grace's brother who threatened to break every bone in his body. Richardson refused to be intimidated. The affair gradually went off the boil when he discovered Grace was seeing other men.

One of them was the Shah of Iran, who spent a week with her when he was visiting New York. He plied her with gold and jewels. When her mother read about this in the newspapers, she insisted that Grace give the jewellery back. Grace also received jewellery from Aly Khan, who had a passion for tall, slim women.

'She called me up and invited me to dinner,' said Richardson. 'Afterwards, when we were in bed together, she said: 'Do you want to see some lovely things?' Well, for me, the sight of her naked was the most lovely thing that I could think of. But she started to do a fashion show for me, coming out in all these expensive clothes. Gown after gown. I could not imagine where she got them from. And then she came out wearing nothing but a gold bracelet that had several emeralds around it.'

Richardson had known several girls who had been out with Aly Khan.

'On the first date, he would give them a cigarette case with one emerald on it. When he'd made love to them, he'd give them the bracelet. I was broken-hearted. I put my clothes on, and said that I was leaving.'

She asked him if it had anything to do with the bracelet. He said it had everything to do with it. On his way out, he dropped it in her fish tank. He left her, naked and beautiful, fishing around the tank for her bracelet.

She was also seeing Claudius Philippe, banqueting manager of the Waldorf Astoria who was on first-name terms with everyone from Gypsy Rose Lee to the Duke and Duchess of Windsor. He wooed her with champagne and the social connections he could make for her. She became deeply attached to him and spent most of her day hanging around his office. There was talk of marriage, but Philippe was forty and twice divorced. Grace's father put his foot down again. So Grace very obviously set her cap at Manie Sachs, the head of Columbia records who was a close friend of her father.

Those who knew her did not accuse her of using sex crudely to advance her career.

'Grace truly enjoyed sex,' said a male friend. 'She was very warm, loving, giving and emotional. There was nothing cheap or phoney about her passion. I had more respect for Grace than most girls who slept around and hated every minute of it.'

Nevertheless, word got around that she was available.

Although Grace was already attracting attention and made a number of small film appearances, she still longed to make it on the stage and in the summer of 1951 she took an engagement with the Elitch Gardens stock company in Denver, Colorado. There, she began an affair with actor Gene Lyons. She told her mother that she was in love. Her mother begged her not to do anything as drastic as getting married – especially not to someone in her own profession. Lyons was another divorcee, ten years older than her and Grace's mother did not consider him stable.

Lyons was in love with Grace too and told her that they would stimulate each other's careers and would be stars in the theatre together. But on 28 August 1951, she was asked to report to Hollywood to appear in the film that would make her name, *High Noon*.

Her co-star was Gary Cooper. He was a well-known womanizer and, although he was nearly fifty, he still lived up to the nickname Clara Bow had given him in the 1920s, Studs.

The movie began with Gary and Grace in a wedding scene. All Coop had to do was say 'I do', take Grace in his arms and kiss her. The scene was shot over and over again. Cooper kissed her at least fifty times.

Grace made no secret of the fact that she preferred older men. With Cooper she was star struck. Cooper was taken with her too and watched her intently during her close-ups. At the end of one take, she plopped herself down on his lap and planted a kiss on his cheek. He blushed under his make-up and wiped her lipstick off with a handkerchief. When she tried to kiss him again on the other cheek, he whispered: 'Not here.'

Cooper was planning a fishing trip with screenwriter Bob Slatzer, another of Marilyn Monroe's beaux. Grace asked whether she could come along. When Cooper tried to ignore her, she placed her hand on his knee and asked again. Cooper blushed once more and said that he did not think she would enjoy fishing.

Later, when Cooper was lunching with Slatzer, Grace blew a kiss in their direction.

'That was for you,' Cooper told Slatzer. 'Why don't you do something about it?'

'And compete with you?' Slatzer protested.

'I'm twice her age.'

Slatzer said he would not let that stop him.

'It hasn't, but I don't need it,' said Cooper.

He may not have needed it, but he got it anyway. Grace came over to the table and reminded Cooper that they had a love scene to do. There was an embarrassed silence.

'Coop, you're one lucky guy,' Slatzer said eventually.

'Isn't he?' said Grace.

Cooper chewed hard on his food, swallowed and said: 'Yep, guess I am.'

Cooper later told Slatzer that he was having an affair with Grace, not that it was not obvious.

'Just the way she looked at him, you could tell she was melting,' said Slatzer. 'She'd embarrass him sometimes by coming over and putting her arms around him and being obvious in front of other people.'

Grace's affair with her co-star was the first of many. Gore Vidal, then a scriptwriter in Hollywood, said: 'Grace almost always laid her leading man. She was famous for that in town.'

Cooper made a point of not being seen out with Grace. Nevertheless the affair made the gossip columns and Mrs Kelly was soon on her way to Hollywood to chaperone her wayward daughter.

High Noon's director Fred Zinnemann was also in love with Grace. His loving close-ups sent the film's other female star, the fiery Katy Jurado, into tantrums of jealousy. Grace also dated Slatzer. Slatzer had never known Cooper to ask a personal question, but on a fishing trip Coop said laconically: 'I guess I'd be kinda outta school if I asked you if you'd been to bed with her.'

'You would,' said Slatzer.

'I shouldn't ask a thing like that,' Cooper said. But he

could not help himself.

After *High Noon*, Cooper took a long time to get Grace out of his system.

'He was eaten up with the idea that she might have gone to bed with me,' Slatzer said.

Grace emerged unscathed. She flew back to New York and to Gene Lyons, but they were soon parted. She signed a seven-year contract with MGM and headed to Africa to film *Mogambo* with Ava Gardner and Clark Gable. From the moment she landed at Nairobi airport, she began flirting with Gable. He was unimpressed, but once they were out on the set and he found that Grace was the only available woman for hundreds of miles he succumbed. Donald Sinden, who played Grace's husband in the film, stumbled into Gable's darkened room to find the two of them in bed together.

Soon they were spending all their time together, like an old married couple. They would read together and she would follow him around, though he just watched when she went skinny-dipping in Lake Victoria. Like Carole Lombard before her, she called Gable 'Pa'. He was twenty-eight years older than her.

When they arrived in London to shoot the interiors in Boreham Wood, the press asked him about the affair. He denied any involvement.

'I hear you two made Africa hotter than it is,' said Hedda Hopper.

'Good god, no!' said Gable. 'I'm old enough to be her father.'

Although Gable got more involved with Grace than he intended to, he was old enough to handle it. She was not. She begged him to fly straight back to the US with her, but he wanted to stay in Europe. When Mrs Kelly turned up in London, Gable had had enough. He had a guard mounted at the top of the stairs at the Connaught to keep her out and did not return her phone calls.

When he drove her to Heathrow Airport, she burst into

tears. He hugged her and kissed her goodbye, but showed no emotion. A few weeks later he was seen doing the town in Paris with model Suzanne Dadolle, who he had started an affair with before he went to Africa.

In New York, Grace consoled herself with Gene Lyons, while seeing Don Richardson on the side. Her affair with Gene Lyons ended when she started shooting *The Way of the Eagle* for TV with leading French heart-throb Jean-Pierre Aumont.

At first, she resisted Aumont's blandishments. She declined his luncheon invitations and called him 'Mr Aumont' rather than Jean-Pierre in the studio. One day, they were filming a scene in a dancehall where there was some graffiti on the wall. Aumont pointed it out to her.

It read: 'Ladies, be kind to your gentlemen – after all, they are human beings too.'

Grace laughed and the ice was broken. It was the beginning of an intense affair.

'She showed me around New York,' he said, 'and gave me a tour of her favourite places, like Greenwich Village. For three months we never left each other...then life separated us.'

He had to go back to France and, after a phone call from Clark Gable saying he would not be in New York for the première of *Mogambo*, she was bound for Hollywood.

'I loved her,' Aumont said later, 'because she was so lovely.'

Aumont never understood why she was so stand-offish at first.

'The day that I can explain how women work is the day that I'll be sanctified,' he said.

Back in Hollywood, Grace attended the Academy Awards with Gable. They talked of marriage but Gable considered the age difference insurmountable. In the end, she concurred. She told a reporter: 'His false teeth turn me off.'

Alfred Hitchcock persuaded MGM to lend Grace to

Warners for *Dial M for Murder*. He had seen her in *Mogambo* and knew she was no 'Snow Princess' but rather a 'snow-covered volcano'.

'The whole cast seemed to fall in love with her,' said Grace's younger sister Lizanne, who was there as her chaperone. 'Everyone was sending flowers. At one point I said: 'This place looks like a funeral home.' I ran out of vases.'

Tony Dawson, who played the murderer in the movie, and Frederick Knott, who wrote the original play, fell for her. So did her forty-nine-year-old leading man, Ray Milland.

Milland had been more or less happily married for thirty years. Although he had had the odd peccadillo, he largely steered clear of actresses, which kept him out of the gossip columns, and his long-suffering wife Mal kept her eyes judiciously shut.

But she could not turn a blind eye to his affair with Grace. She simply made the affair too public. She was not in the wilds of Africa now, though, and the scandal sheet *Hollywood Confidential* got hold of the story.

When Milland told his wife that he had to go away on business, she had him followed. He was spotted getting on a plane with Grace. Milland and his wife separated.

During a long conversation, Milland told Grace's sister how much in love he was. The rumour got about that they were living together. Grace would answer the door at Milland's flat. When Joe Hyams of the *New York Herald Tribune* went there to interview Milland, the movie star answered the door dressed only in a towel and Hyams got the distinct impression that he was not alone.

Milland asked his wife for a divorce. She said yes – 'You go ahead and marry Grace Kelly. That's okay with me, because all the property is in my name.'

Milland had second thoughts. They patched it up but a bitterness remained. Ever after, Mal would refer to the period Milland and Grace were together as 'those agonizing days'. Mal's friend Skip Hathaway was caustic. She said: 'Grace

Kelly fucked everything in sight. She was worse than any woman I'd ever known. She knew how to lead a man on.'

Jimmy Stewart, recently married, may have spoilt Grace's perfect score with her leading men, while shooting *Rear Window*. Not that he was unaware of her charms.

'I am married but I'm not dead,' he told the press. He also refuted the idea that Grace was cold. 'Why Grace is anything but cold. She has those big warm eyes – and, well, if you have ever played a love scene with her, you'd know she's not cold...besides, Grace has that twinkle and a touch of larceny in her eyes.'

Stewart did make a habit of bringing her flowers. He said they were from his garden, but no one on the set believed him. When he heard that she was to marry Prince Rainier, he said: 'If she had married one of those phoney Hollywood characters, I'd have formed a committee of vigilantes.'

Throughout this period, Grace had also been seeing Bing Crosby. He was married, but his wife of twenty-two years, Dixie, was an alcoholic, incapacitated with cancer. Crosby pretty much came and went as he pleased. He lived next door to Alan Ladd and his wife. Crosby would use their pool for entertaining. He would often drop around there after dark with a girl. After a drink and a conversation, Alan and his wife would make their excuses and go to bed leaving the old crooner to have his way, even though they were close friends of Dixie's. One night, the Ladds caught Crosby and Grace cavorting on their couch. Ladd said that if they wanted to do that sort of thing they should go to a motel. Crosby was a well-known skinflint. Besides, going to a motel was a risky business and he could hardly afford to lose his nice guy image.

Grace was cast in *The Bridges at Toko-Ri* with William Holden who, at eleven years her senior, was her youngest co-star yet. Although he was married with children, Holden was a well-known womanizer and was on the rebound from Audrey Hepburn at the time. In the movie, they have a

Japanese-style bath together. *The Bridges at Toko-Ri* is the only movie in which Grace appeared in a swimsuit, or was shown in bed with a man. This was more than Holden could resist. An army friend of his said: 'Bill was absolutely crazy about her and they had quite a fling. I was hoping they would get married, because that's what Bill wanted and he was a wonderful guy.'

But Grace was still pining for Milland and to mend her broken heart she headed for New York where she met up with Jean-Pierre Aumont again. To placate her family, she would spend weekends in Philadelphia or at society parties on Long Island, where she would date wealthy businessmen.

One night, Aumont and Grace were out having dinner at Le Veau d'Or on East 66th Street when she was spotted by fashion designer Oleg Cassini who was seated nearby.

'I fell in love with her after I saw her in *Mogambo*' – which by coincidence, he had seen earlier that evening – 'she was all that I wanted: beautiful, clean-looking, ethereal enough, sexy enough...' On leaving the cinema, he had announced: 'I am going to meet that girl' – little knowing that he was about to do just that.

When his companion pointed out that Grace might already be in love, Cassini said: 'I don't care. That girl is going to be mine.'

Now, in the restaurant, he had the opportunity. An accomplished seducer, Cassini knew that Grace was not the sort of girl you simply called up for a date.

'A programme of action was needed,' he said, 'a plan – something outrageous, romantic, even silly – to pierce her reserve.'

It was to be 'the greatest, most exhilarating campaign of my life, using every bit of fantasy and energy I had'.

He knew Aumont slightly. In fact, they had long been rivals in love, first over Cassini's wife, then over actress Gene Tierney. Cassini approached their table and engaged Aumont in conversation. He pointedly ignored Grace and pretended not to know who she was when they were introduced.

'I sensed the direct frontal approach would not work,' he said. 'I wanted only to establish a bridgehead, to create an agreeable presence in her mind.'

The next day, he sent a dozen red roses to her Manhattan townhouse. He did that every day for ten days. Each bouquet had a card signed simply 'the Friendly Florist'.

On the tenth day, he called her.

'This,' he said, 'is the Friendly Florist.'

There was a pause, Cassini recalled, 'then that charming little laugh of hers and I knew I had won. As Napoleon said: 'A woman who laughs is a woman conquered.''

But it was still going to be a long, uphill struggle.

Grace consented to come out on a date, but she brought her sister with her. On the dancefloor of El Morocco, she said: 'I have two little surprises for you, Oleg.'

The first was that she was in love. When he asked who with, she said a handsome Englishman with the initials 'R.M.' (Actually, Ray Milland was Welsh.) Cassini said that was okay, because the man in question would never leave his wife. Besides, Grace would be engaged to him, Cassini, within a year.

The second surprise was that she was leaving for California the next day. Cassini said that he did not find the three thousand miles between New York and LA an insurmountable obstacle, either. He would send love notes to her every day and there would be regular phone calls – always light, delicate and amusing. A five-star general on the battlefield of love, Cassini knew that the best strategy was to keep a lady laughing.

Grace returned to Hollywood to film *The Country Girl* with William Holden and Bing Crosby. She quickly renewed her romantic attachment to Crosby. One night, Holden dropped around to Crosby's dressing-room. When Crosby answered the door with a drink in his hand, Holden could see

Grace inside.

'Hey, ol' Buddy,' Crosby said. 'Why don't we talk tomorrow? I'm kinda tied up for the night.'

Holden knew of Grace's earlier involvement with Crosby, but Crosby did not know that Holden was also one of Grace's lovers. When Grace told him about it, he invited Holden to his dressing-room for a gentlemanly chat.

'I don't mind telling you, Bill, I'm smitten with Grace,' he said. 'Daffy about her. And I was wondering if...'

'I felt the same way,' said Holden. 'What man wouldn't be overwhelmed by her? But look, Bing, I won't interfere.'

Crosby's wife had died and although being seen out with a widower was not going to attract the sort of scandal her affair with Milland had, on their public dates, Grace insisted they were accompanied by one of her sisters. Nevertheless, the newspapers dubbed the twenty-five-year-old actress and the fifty-year-old crooner 'Hollywood's newest romance'.

Before long, Crosby had fallen deeply in love with Grace. Working hard on his eligibility, Crosby took Grace and her mother to the movies, in the company of William Holden and his wife. They would spend hours in a restaurant called Scandia on Sunset Strip gazing into each other's eyes. He proposed. She turned him down. After that he sat in the Scandia alone, at the same table, nursing one drink all night, as if he thought she would walk in through the door any minute.

Publicly he took it well. He told a reporter: 'If I were fifteen or sixteen years younger, I'd fall willingly into the long line of limp males who are currently competing madly for her favours.'

Privately, he carried a torch for her for the rest of his life. Three years later, he married Kathryn Grant, a contemporary of Grace's. She was under no illusions. When Crosby died in 1977, Kathryn asked Grace to appear in a TV tribute to her dead husband. Her request was signed: 'Yours in love and jealousy'. When Grace refused, Kathryn wired her, explaining:

'I was jealous of you because Bing always loved you.' Grace agreed to appear on the programme and read a poem.

Grace invited Cassini out to the Coast but when he arrived in LA she had little time for him, as she had resumed her affair with Holden. This time she was serious. She even took him home to Philadelphia with her. Her father deeply disapproved of her having another affair with a married man and Holden's reception at the family home was 'cold and hostile'.

Confidential magazine got wind of the affair and reporters spotted his white Cadillac convertible parked outside her apartment one morning. The studio claimed that he was just picking her up for an early call. Holden claimed that the convertible was Mrs Holden's.

'Does anyone think I'm so dumb as to park my wife's car outside another woman's apartment all night?' he told Hedda Hopper.

'I don't understand all this publicity about Grace,' he went on. 'I like her but I don't think she's the *femme fatale* she's built up to be.'

'She's pretty *femme*,' said Hopper.

'But she's not fatale,' Holden responded.

Meanwhile, Holden's lawyers were demanding a retraction from *Confidential*. Grace's father took more direct action. He and his son went to *Confidential's* office and threatened to beat up the editor. The scandal sheet changed its tack. In the next issue it said: 'Hollywood wives stop biting your nails...this new Hollywood heatwave wasn't grabbing for a guy who already had a ball and chain.'

It went on to say that Grace had forsworn married men and implied that she was only bedding single men from now on.

'Behind that frigid exterior is a smouldering fire...and what the older fellows go for,' it said. 'She looks like a lady and has the manners of one. In the Hollywood of the chippies and the tramps, a lady is a rarity. That makes Grace Kelly the most dangerous dame in the movies today.'

Her sister agreed.

'Whatever quality she had,' she said, 'she should have bottled it and made a fortune. There was something about her that men just went ape over. It was amazing to see the big names just falling over themselves.'

Even though Grace ignored Cassini in LA he continued his campaign by being seen in Ciro's with Anita Ekberg, Pier Angeli and other beauties. He made sure his adventures made the gossip columns so that, even when she was out in the jungles of Columbia filming *Green Fire*, he would be in her thoughts.

It worked. When she went to France to film *To Catch a Thief* with Cary Grant, she sent him a postcard bearing the words: 'Those who love me shall follow me.'

He caught up with her on the Riviera. They had dinner together at the Carlton Hotel in Cannes and demolished two bottles of Dom Perignon. But, Cassini recalled: 'Our relationship was still distressingly platonic.'

Disappointed, Cassini went to bed alone that night, but resolved to give it one more try. The next day, he took her out on a picnic. On a swimming raft in the Mediterranean, over cold duck and a bottle of Montrachet '49, he poured out his heart. He told her of his devotion; his persistence had proved it.

'There is no need for artifice any longer,' he said.

'She said nothing,' Cassini recalled, 'but she was looking at me in such a way that I knew I had won.'

They went back to the hotel and went to bed.

'The actual mechanics of love,' Cassini said, 'were never as interesting to me as the events that led up to it. The art of seduction was always far more fascinating than the ultimate result.'

However, this moment of consummation was memorable. Cassini wrote in his memoirs: 'We seemed to float there, glowing, mesmerized by the intensity of our feelings.

217

She smelled of gardenias, at once exotic and very pure. There was a translucent, pearl-like quality to her; everything about her was clear and fresh and fine – her skin, her scent, her hair. I was enraptured, aware only of the transcendence of the moment.'

Back in the US, Cassini was introduced to Grace's mother at lunch.

'You're a charming escort,' she told him, 'but in my opinion, you are a poor risk for marriage.'

There had been too many women in his past, she pointed out. Cassini responded that attractive men – 'including your husband,' he added tactlessly – are popular with the opposite sex. 'Why am I being punished?'

Nevertheless, Grace suggested that Cassini spend the weekend with the family at their New Jersey beach-house. When he heard about it, Jack Kelly exploded, calling Cassini a 'worm', a 'wop' and a 'dago' – though Cassini was actually of Russian-Jewish descent – and threatened to kill him if he walked through the door.

When Cassini did turn up, Grace's father refused to speak to him. He was put in a room next to Grace's parents so his nocturnal movements could be easily monitored and Cassini said that having dinner with the Kelly family was 'like eating a chocolate éclair filled with razor blades'.

Cassini had no friends in the movie industry, either. Many of Grace's friends cold-shouldered him and Hedda Hopper wrote: 'With all the attractive men around town, I do not understand what Grace Kelly sees in Oleg Cassini. It must be his moustache.'

Cassini cabled Hopper saying: 'I'll shave off mine if you shave off yours.'

This opposition only forced Grace closer to Cassini. She considered herself engaged to him and even suggested that they get married right away.

'She told me to find a priest,' said Cassini.

Her family talked her out of it.

'Her family regarded her as a prize possession, a property, like a racehorse that must be handled, above all invested, wisely – not wastefully' Cassini said.

Grace remained committed to Cassini, but cracks began to appear. During the filming of *Tribute to a Bad Man*, there were rumours of an affair with her co-star Spencer Tracy.

Bing Crosby asked her out again. Grace phoned Cassini to ask his permission. He was not best pleased. But the affair was doomed when Frank Sinatra, freshly divorced from Ava Gardner, asked her out. Again she phoned Cassini and asked if he would mind.

'Yes, I would mind!' shouted Cassini, knowing of Sinatra's reputation as a lover. Besides, Cassini himself would be in Los Angeles that night. 'How the hell do you think it would look in the papers if you're photographed on Sinatra's arm going into Chasen's while I'm sitting in my room in the Beverly Hills Hotel? That's all Hedda will need to write tomorrow morning 'Cassini is out of the picture'. So no, you do not have my permission.'

She went anyway. She also began a discreet affair with David Niven. Years later, Prince Rainier asked Niven which of his Hollywood conquests had been best in bed. Niven replied without thinking: 'Grace.' Then, seeing the shocked expression on the Prince's face, he tried to recover the situation by saying: 'Er, Gracie...Gracie Fields.'

Cassini knew the affair was coming to a close and poured out his heart to Joe Kennedy, the future president's father. Kennedy offered to intercede with Grace for him, but instead he used the opportunity to pursue Grace himself.

At the 1955 Cannes Film Festival, Grace met up again with Jean-Pierre Aumont. Then she received an invitation to visit Prince Rainier in Monaco. She had accepted, but tried to wheedle out of it when she found she had a hairdresser's appointment that day.

'Grace,' said Aumont, 'you can't possibly do that. The man is a reigning prince. He has invited you and you have accepted.

You can't just say 'I'm going to the hairdressers.' It could be embarrassing for America if you cancelled the appointment.'

So Grace drove the fifty miles to Monaco to find that Prince Rainier was a good deal more attractive than she had expected. He graciously showed her around his palace and their gardens. It was not love at first sight, but Rainier was very taken with Grace. He was in the market for a princess. If he did not produce an heir, when he died, Monaco would be swallowed up by France.

Back in Cannes, Aumont asked her how things had gone.

'Oh fine,' she said. 'The Prince is charming.'

Two days later, Grace was photographed kissing and cuddling with Aumont. One picture showed Grace holding Aumont's hand and nibbling his fingers. *Time* magazine commented: 'Grace Kelly, commonly billed as the icy goddess, melted perceptibly in the company of French actor Jean-Pierre Aumont...had Aumont, who came and thawed, actually conquered Grace?'

Cassini's brother Igor, who was a syndicated columnist, said that it was all a put-up job, an attempt by Aumont to revive his flagging career.

Aumont told the press: 'I am deeply in love with Grace Kelly' – though he admitted that he did not think that she felt that way about him.

The Kellys were horrified. Grace immediately cabled her family denying any romance. Her mother cabled back: 'Shall I invite Mr Aumont to visit us in Philadelphia?'

'Mother,' Grace replied, 'that's entirely up to you.'

Rainier was upset too. Two years before at the Cannes Film Festival, his mistress Gisèle Pascal had had a fling with Gary Cooper. Grace received a curt note from the Prince's spiritual adviser Father Francis Tucker thanking her for showing the Prince 'what an American Catholic girl can be and for the very deep impression this has left on him'. No irony was intended.

Grace and Aumont left for Paris, pursued by the press.

There were rumours that they were going to get married.

Cornered, Aumont was asked whether he wanted to marry Grace. He replied: 'Who wouldn't? I adore her.'

Grace was confronted with the same question.

'A girl has to be asked first,' she said.

The reporter then said that some of Aumont's friends insisted that she had been asked.

'We live in terrible world,' she said. 'A man kisses your hand and it's screamed out from all the headlines. He can't even tell you he loves you without the whole world knowing about it.'

When the couple managed to give the press the slip, it was reported that they had eloped. When they were found together with Aumont's family at his weekend home in Rueil-Malmaison, the newspapers took this as confirmation that they were already married.

Eventually, Grace flew back to America alone. She told reporters that 'differences in our age or nationality present no obstacles in marriage between two people who love each other'. However, it would have been an obstacle to the Kelly family. A few days later, Grace issued a formal statement saying that she and Aumont were 'just good friends'. She began seeing Cassini again.

Aumont conceded that, with her based in Hollywood and him in France, it would not have worked out. Nevertheless, Aumont was one of the few people who received a telegram from Grace telling him that she was going to get engaged to Prince Rainier before the formal announcement. He married actress Pier Angeli's twin sister, Marisa Pavan, three weeks before Grace's wedding.

In 1953, Aristotle Onassis had bought the casino in Monte Carlo, but the economy of the principality was flagging and the casino and his other investments in Monaco were in trouble. He talked to Gardner Cowles, publisher of *Look* magazine about it. Cowles suggested that if Prince Rainier married a movie star it would help lure rich

Americans there. Cowles approached Marilyn Monroe. Monroe was game.

'Do you think that the Prince will want to marry you?' Cowles asked.

'Give me two days alone with him and of course he'll want to marry me,' Marilyn replied.

The Prince, however, had plans of his own. By chance, friends of the Kellys had been in Monaco. Unable to get tickets for the Red Cross Gala at the Sporting Club, they called the palace and used the magic words 'Grace Kelly'.

They were invited to the palace where Rainier told them that he planned to visit the US and would like to see Grace again. There was a flurry of phone calls between Monaco and Philadelphia. Rainier wanted to visit Grace on the set of *The Swan*, which she was filming in Asheville, North Carolina, but Aumont was visiting her there.

Instead, the Prince was to meet her in Philadelphia on Christmas Day. He turned up with Father Tucker, who told Grace's father that the Prince wanted to marry his daughter. Jack Kelly was not impressed. He did not know where Monaco was and thought the Prince was only after Grace for her money.

'I don't want any broken-down prince who's head of a country that nobody ever heard of marrying my daughter,' he bellowed.

Grace and Rainier spent the next three days together. When he proposed, she accepted.

'I don't want to be married to someone who feels inferior to my success or because I make more money than he does,' she explained. 'The Prince is not going to be 'Mr Kelly'.'

Grace called Oleg Cassini and asked him to meet her on the Staten Island ferry. In the middle of the bay, she told him that she was going to marry Prince Rainier.

'But you hardly know the man,' Cassini protested. 'Are you going to marry someone because he has a title and a few acres of real estate?'

'I will learn to love him,' she said.

Cassini took a long time to get over the loss of Grace. He only saw her one more time. He was jogging down the beach in Monaco.

'Hello, Oleg,' she said.

'Hello, Grace,' he replied as he jogged on by without losing a stride. He never married again.

Before Grace could marry her Prince, there was a matter of the marriage contract to sort out. The Prince demanded a dowry. Monaco was going through a political and financial crisis at the time. A figure of $2 million was mentioned. Jack Kelly went ballistic, but paid up. He'd come round to the idea; having his daughter married to royalty would at last give him one over the Philadelphia blue-bloods who had always looked down their noses at him.

Grace also had to submit to a fertility test. Rainier had brought his own doctor with him to examine her. Rainier had had to reject previous love Gisèle Pascal because she had failed the fertility test. When he had finally given her up, he told Father Tucker: 'Father, if you ever hear that my subjects think I do not love them, tell them what I have done today.'

Later, Gisèle married and gave birth to a child. Rainier was devastated. The fertility tests had been falsified as part of a plot by Father Tucker who did not consider Gisèle a suitable candidate for the role of princess.

Grace was terrified of the examination and phoned Don Richardson.

'She was frantic that the tests would reveal that she was not a virgin, because the Prince thought she was,' Richardson said. 'She told me she explained to the doctors that her hymen had been broken when she was playing hockey in high school.'

Far away from Hollywood gossip, it is just conceivable that Rainier was taken in by Grace's chaste screen image and may actually have believed that she was a virgin.

Their first public function together was a charity gala entitled 'Night in Monte Carlo' at the Waldorf Astoria in New York. A female admirer rushed up to Rainier and kissed him on the cheek. Grace ordered the Prince to wipe the woman's lipstick off his cheek. When Grace asked Rainier who the woman was, the Prince said he had no idea. The next day, the woman identified herself to the papers as Ecuadorian socialite Graciela Levi-Castillo.

'He knows who I am,' she said.

But the incident failed to spoil Grace's evening. She danced the night away with her Prince at the Harwyn Club and Grace was spotted nibbling Rainier's ear.

Grace made one more movie, *High Society* with Bing Crosby and Frank Sinatra. Rainier rented a villa in Los Angeles and visited the set every day, although he could not understand the private jokes that seemed to pass between his fiancée and her two male co-stars.

Generally, the reaction to the marriage was negative. It was considered that Grace was marrying beneath her station.

'She is too well bred to marry the silent partner in a gambling parlour,' wrote the *Chicago Tribune*. Many of her friends thought that Rainier was the ruler of Morocco and wondered how Grace would fare amongst camels and sand dunes. When they discovered that Monaco was actually a tiny Mediterranean principality, Dore Schary, head of MGM, complained that it was smaller than the studio's back lot. Most people who knew the real Grace thought that she would never get her prince up the aisle.

She almost didn't. Thrilled by the prospect of her daughter's marriage, Mrs Kelly began talking to the newspapers. She spilled the beans on her daughter's former love affairs, which ran as a scandalous ten-part series in newspapers across America. headlined 'My Daughter Grace Kelly: Her Life and Romances'. The myth of Grace's virginity was blown forever. Embarrassed, the Prince headed for home.

The studio were also in shock. The chaste image they had struggled for so long to preserve was being besmirched. It was too late to do anything about the stories running in the American papers but they managed to get their hands on the articles and edit them before they went out in Europe.

Grace still had four years to run on her contract. She wanted to make *Designing Woman* with Jimmy Stewart, but the Prince put his foot down.

'No more movies for Miss Kelly,' he announced as he travelled home.

MGM were now in a bind. Realizing that they could hardly sue a princess for breach of contract, they swapped *Designing Woman* for exclusive rights to film the royal wedding.

Grace did the rounds of Hollywood farewell parties 'chaperoned' by Frank Sinatra. Then with a party of six-five guests, she sailed for Monaco on board the *Constitution*. They were met in the Bay of Hercules by the royal yacht. Aristotle Onassis arranged for a plane to drop red and white carnations in the harbour when they docked.

Needless to say, the Kellys and Rainier's family, the Grimaldis, did not get on. There were rows, tears and fights. Jack Kelly could not find the bathroom in the Palace. The servants spoke no English and he could not ask them where it was. So he would take a limousine to a nearby hotel where a friend was staying to use his bathroom.

At the civil wedding, Grace was read the one hundred and forty-two titles she held as Princess of Monaco. That afternoon, she was awarded the Order of Charles. Grace hoped that this honour meant that she would share the Prince's bed that night. He said that was impossible and retired alone.

The following day, Grace was united with her Prince at St Nicholas's Cathedral in Monte Carlo. Only one of her former lovers – David Niven – turned up. Frank Sinatra had been invited, but reluctantly withdrew when he discovered that Ava Gardner would be there. Press speculation about a possible reconciliation between them would have detracted from Grace's day, he explained. Cary Grant sent his apologies. He was in Spain filming *The Pride and the Passion*.

'Bride is film star, groom is non-pro,' reported *Variety* in typical fashion.

After a reception at the Court of Honour, the happy couple sailed off together on the royal yacht.

Sadly, Grace was not a good sailor and was throwing up by the time they got out of port. Soon she had another reason to be sick. A few days into the honeymoon she became pregnant.

She spent her confinement alone in the Palace. Five months after she gave birth to a girl, she became pregnant again. Grace and Rainier had three children, two girls and a boy. Soon she was falling out with Rainier and she would spend long hours on trans-Atlantic calls pouring out her heart to her friends.

Grace returned to Philadelphia when her father fell ill. While she was away at what turned out to be his deathbed, the Prince was seen out and about with one of Grace's ladies-in-waiting. When Grace got back to Monaco, a well-meaning friend told her about Rainier's dalliances. She confronted the Prince. He denied everything. The lady-in-waiting was fired anyway.

To assuage her sense of isolation, Grace began inviting friends to visit. When Cary Grant turned up, pictures of Grace kissing him at the airport appeared in the papers. Rainier promptly banned screenings of *To Catch a Thief* which shows them in steamy love scenes together.

As a sop to his wife, Rainier gave his permission for her to appear in Hitchcock's *Marnie*, but the people of Monaco did not want their princess to be seen on-screen kissing other men and protested. The part was taken by Tippi Hedren.

In the 1970s, after his divorce from his third wife Dyan Cannon, Cary Grant began an affair with Grace. Somehow, she had overlooked him before. It lasted, on and off, for six or seven years.

After their first few years together, Grace did not share the same bed as her husband. In the early 1970s, they stopped sharing the same bedroom. Soon they stopped sharing the same country, with Rainier making a life for himself in Monaco and Grace living mostly in Paris. In 1979, there were rumours that she was having an affair with Hungarian documentary film-maker Robert Dornhelm, whom she saw a great deal of in France. He denied it, but said he would like to think that she did have affairs as they would have done her good.

This was disingenuous as Dornhelm knew that, at the very least, Grace was seeing other younger men. Per Mattson, a thirty-three year old Swedish actor who was considered for a part in a film about Raoul Wallenberg that Grace was planning with Dornhelm, was whisked away from a formal dinner in New York in 1982 by Grace. She took him up to her hotel room and he stayed there until five o'clock in the morning.

New York restaurateur and former model Jim McMullen spent a week in Monaco with her. They were also seen together at New York disco Studio 54.

As the years went by, Grace drank too much, ate too much and put on weight. Meanwhile the torch of sexual misadventure was passed to a new generation. Both her daughters, Caroline and Stephanie, became notorious.

On 13 September 1982, Princess Grace had a minor stroke while driving and was killed. Oleg Cassini made a brief statement to the press. Ray Milland was inconsolable. Most of the other men in Grace's life were already dead.

13

GOODBYE, NORMA JEAN

To many, Marilyn Monroe was the last – and, perhaps, the ultimate – Hollywood sex goddess. She captivated a generation and kept a president enthralled. After she died, the movies got smaller. Television took over as the western world's principal medium and no star would attain the status of a Hollywood screen goddess again.

Both privately and professionally, she used her body to entertain men.

'I like to make men happy – to see them smile,' she said. After all, 'nobody ever got cancer from sex.'

Hollywood gossip columnist Sheilah Graham had another take on her: 'Norma Jean Monroe went to bed with half of Hollywood, including Brando, Sinatra and members of the Kennedy family – JFK and Bobby. But strangely she was a sex symbol who didn't care too much for sex.'

Marilyn claimed that she had first had sex at the age of seven. Nothing more is known of the incident, though it was probably quite innocent as Marilyn said the boy concerned was younger than her.

She also said that she was molested at the age of nine by the boarder at a foster home she had been sent to. Later, she said that the husband of her guardian, Grace Goddard, had tried to force himself on her when he was drunk.

Marilyn also told of being raped by a policeman in her early teens. She told her maid, Lena Pepitone, that she had had a baby when she was a teenager but Grace Goddard had made her give the child up for adoption.

Marilyn Monroe's real name was Norma Jean Mortenson. She did not know who her father was. Her mother was sent to a state mental institution and, as an orphan to all intents and purposes, Marilyn was shuffled around a number of orphanages and foster homes. At fifteen, her breasts were fully developed and her figure began to attract a lot of attention in the street. She began dating Jim Dougherty, a worker in an aircraft factory who was two-timing her with a local beauty queen.

The Goddards were moving to West Virginia and were eager to get Norma Jean off their hands. They encouraged the courtship and on 19 June 1942, just three weeks after her sixteenth birthday, Norma Jean married Dougherty. He claimed she was a virgin on their wedding night.

She was not a good wife. She could not cook or make cocktails. But she was terrific in bed. Her appetite exhausted her husband, who switched to night shifts. He would find little love notes in his lunch box. These embarrassed him, but when he brought in a snapshot of his wife, his workmates were envious.

Norma Jean was less than satisfied. She knew little about sex and, although she was eager to learn, found it all strange. She knew there was definitely something missing. Once Jim was satisfied, she complained, he would fall asleep leaving her fitfully awake, feeling confused and discontent.

There were other strains in the marriage. Dougherty would stay out shooting pool with his friends, and he didn't like it when she turned other men's heads.

'She was just too beautiful,' Dougherty's sister recalled. 'She couldn't help it that men's wives looked at her and got so jealous they wanted to throw rocks.'

Going to the beach with Norma Jean caused problems for Dougherty 'because she wore a bikini that was two sizes too small'.

'Every guy on the beach is mentally raping you,' Dougherty complained.

After Pearl Harbor, Dougherty joined the merchant marine and was sent to Santa Catalina Island as a physical fitness instructor. Norma Jean went too and, as one of the few women on the base, attracted a lot of attention especially as she wore tight white blouses, short shorts and more 'skimpy bathing suits'. If her body was not already good enough, she took body-building lessons from an Olympic weightlifter.

One night, at a gala, Dougherty got only one dance with his wife in seven hours. He was left standing on the sidelines overhearing other men making lewd remarks about her. When he insisted that she come home with him, she said she would, but she was having so much fun she might slip out again and come back to the dance later. Dougherty said if she did she had better not come home again.

'I'll admit I was jealous,' he said.

Norma Jean got her own back for this. Soon after the dance, he came home early to find their apartment door locked. When he knocked, she called out: 'Is that you, Bill? Just a minute.'

When Dougherty responded, she yelled: 'Oh, sorry, I didn't think you were coming over so soon, Tommy.'

From inside, he heard whispering and the sounds of furniture being moved. Soon he was fuming. There was no backdoor to the apartment and he was convinced he had caught his wife *in flagrante*. She opened the door dressed in a towel. She had been taking a shower. The rest of the performance had been a cruel hoax.

Dougherty was posted to Australia. Norma Jean begged him not to go. When he explained he had no choice, she begged to be allowed to have his baby, so she could have a part of him with her. He said they would have children after the war.

While her husband was away, Norma Jean got a job inspecting and folding parachutes. The girls in the factory wore overalls and she was surprised by this.

'Putting a girl in overalls is like having her work in tights, particularly if a girl knows how to wear them,' she said. 'The men buzzed around me just as the high-school boys had done. Maybe it was my fault that the men in the factory tried to date me and buy me drinks. I did not feel like a married woman.'

However, she claimed that she remained faithful to Dougherty while he was overseas.

When he came home on his first leave, she drove him directly to a luxurious motel on Ventura Boulevard. She had bought a black net nightgown for the occasion. They spent the next few days in bed, having their meals brought in to them.

When Dougherty went back to the Pacific, Norma Jean went back to work, where she was spotted by the photographer David Conover who was taking pictures of women working in defence plants for *Yank* magazine. He used her for other assignments and her pictures came to the attention of the Blue Book Model Agency, who signed her up.

She posed for girlie magazines with names like *Peek*, *Parade*, *Sir* and *Swank* in a swimsuit or in shorts with a halter top. The pictures were respectable, but Norma Jean made every effort to show off her 36 inch bust.

She went on an assignment with thirty-two-year-old Hungarian photographer André de Dienes. He wanted her to pose nude for him. She refused. But she did go to bed with him. It happened one night when they could not find a motel with two separate rooms and the nineteen-year-old Norma Jean soon discovered new areas of sex unexplored by Jim Dougherty.

'In my dreams I had explored her body,' de Dienes wrote

later, 'reality far surpassed my imagination.'

For the rest of the trip, she was 'playful and provocative', eager to tease as well as satisfy.

When Dougherty came home on leave, he did not approve of his wife's new career, though he did not suspect she had been unfaithful to him. He did not think that being a professional model was an appropriate job for a married woman. Norma Jean also talked of her ambition to act. Dougherty told her that she would have to choose between 'a career in modelling and, maybe, the movies or home life with me'. She chose. He was back in China, halfway up the Yangtze River, when he got his divorce papers.

Scottish photographer William Burnside also found her co-operative.

'A kiss took two weeks to achieve,' he said, but the rest was easy. 'She did not like to be touched too soon. One could not even think of sexual conquest by force.'

She began posing topless, then naked, for artist Earl Morgan. Once she got over her initial shyness she would strip off for photographers, often before she was asked.

She worked as a stripper at a seedy joint on Sunset Boulevard and, short of cash, she fell into prostitution. It began when she was approached by a middle-aged man in a bar who offered her $15 to see her naked. A bit tipsy, she went back to his hotel room and stripped off. He wanted more and started to undress. She wanted to run out.

'Then I thought about it,' she said. 'It did not really bother me that much. So what was the difference?'

She insisted that the man wear a condom and sent him out to a drug store to buy some. He was surprised that she was still there when he got back. When it was all over, he gave her the $15 and she bought a new dress. She was not ashamed. In fact, she had rather enjoyed the experience. Clothed she was just another girl. Naked, she was someone special. There were more trips back to the bar, other takers and more pocket money.

She offered herself for quick sex with men in cars on side streets near Hollywood or Santa Monica Boulevard.

'She really did this for her meals,' said Lucille Ryman, a talent scout at MGM. 'It wasn't for cash. She told us without pride or shame that she made a deal – she did what she did, and her customers bought her breakfast or lunch.'

She told her drama teacher, Lee Strasberg, that she would be 'summoned if anyone needed a beautiful girl at a convention'.

One of her customers was in the movie business and suggested that she should try to break into the business, too.

'But I can't act,' she said.

He explained that this was not important.

'Do what you're doing now,' he said, 'but with important men who will do something for you.'

She followed his advice. Later, when she was asked how she broke into films, Norma Jean said: 'I met the right men and gave them what they wanted.'

In the meantime, she also dated regular guys. One was a young writer named Robert Slatzer. He met her when he was waiting to interview a minor celebrity in the lobby of Twentieth Century-Fox studios one day. He was reading a book of poetry when Marilyn came in carrying a big scrapbook.

'She caught her heel or something and the pictures fell all over the floor,' he said. 'I went to her rescue, and I'm glad to say there was only one place for her to sit down and wait – next to me. She said she was really interested in poetry, and I said I might be able to write a story about her. We ended up making a date for that same evening.'

He took her to Malibu where, after dinner, they walked on the beach. Marilyn suggested that they go for a swim. Slatzer said that he had not brought a swimming costume. Marilyn laughed, stripped off and ran into the surf naked.

'I was embarrassed,' he said, 'yet we made love on the beach that first night.'

When he drove her home, she asked him to leave her on the corner, rather than drop her at her front door so her aunt would not know what she was up to.

'We had an instant affection for each other,' Slatzer said. 'There was something magic about her, different from the other girls the talent men at the studios would fix you up with. I think I can say I loved her from the first time I saw her.'

They talked of marriage, but money was a problem. Besides, she was also seeing Tommy Zahn, the lieutenant in charge of the Los Angeles County lifeboat and a legendary figure on the beaches of California.

'She was in prime condition,' he said. 'I used to take her tandem surfing up at Malibu – two riders on the same surfboard. She was really good in the water, very robust, so healthy, a really fine attitude towards life.'

Her first break came when Howard Hughes saw her picture in a magazine while he was recuperating after a plane crash, and tracked her down. Ben Lyon, casting director at Twentieth Century-Fox, gave her a screen test and Darryl Zanuck said: 'Sign her.'

She was put under contract for $75 and her name was changed to Marilyn Monroe – Marilyn for Broadway beauty Marilyn Miller and Monroe was her grandmother's name.

Lyon sent her out on the rounds of the studio's executives at Twentieth Century-Fox. He gave her a sealed letter of introduction. After the executives had read it, they would all do the same thing – walk around the desk with their fly undone. It was some time before Marilyn realized that the letter said: 'This girl really likes giving head.'

Later she said of her early days in the film industry: 'I spent a great deal of time on my knees.'

'It was part of the job,' Marilyn explained. 'They weren't shooting all those sexy movies just to sell peanut butter. They wanted to sample the merchandise. If you didn't go along, there were twenty-five girls who would.'

It did her no good. Darryl Zanuck unexpectedly fired her. It was rumoured that the top brass had grown tired of her, but she had made one good contact.

During her time on the Twentieth Century lot she had been expected to make herself available for 'promotional parties'. These were all-night poker sessions. Contract actresses were supposed to work as hostesses. Seeking preferment, they vied with each other to see who could wear the shortest skirt or the most low-cut blouse. If a player pointed to his plate, a girl would bring him a sandwich. If he pointed to his glass, she would bring him a drink. If he pointed to his crotch, she would get on her knees under the table and perform a more intimate service for him. It was a point of honour among the players not to show any emotion during the girl's ministrations.

Marilyn was particularly adept at this. She had had lots of practice. Seventy-year-old Joe Schenck, one of the founders of Twentieth Century, found that she was so good she could give him a full erection. He moved her into the pool house at his home, so she would be on hand whenever there were stirrings.

'Sometimes it took hours,' she told a friend. 'I was relieved when he fell asleep.'

Marilyn had needs of her own and slept around a good deal. One of her lovers was Charlie Chaplin's twenty-one year old son, Charlie Jnr. He got her pregnant and she had an abortion. The affair ended when Charlie found her in bed with his brother Sydney.

Marilyn met journalist James Bacon at a party and took him back to Schenck's pool house to make love. They were just getting down to it when Schenck called. Bacon recalled that Marilyn got out of bed and 'with agonizing slowness' combed her hair and put on her make-up.

'Somehow I felt sorry for poor Joe, sitting up in his master bedroom counting the seconds,' Bacon said.

As Marilyn left, she said cheerily: 'Won't be long.'

Although her affair with Bacon lasted two years, 'I was under no illusion she was after me for me. She liked me, sure, but she was also after all the newspapers my syndicated column appeared in.'

Marilyn met minor matinée idol John Carroll at a drive-in restaurant. He took her home to meet his wife, Lucille Ryman. She got Marilyn a three-month contract at MGM. The Carrolls had an open marriage. Around that time their all-nude parties were exposed in *Confidential* magazine. Marilyn loved to go naked. Her earliest memories were of wanting to strip off in church.

'No sooner was I in the pew with the organ playing and everybody singing a hymn than the impulse would come to me to take off all my clothes,' she said. 'I wanted desperately to stand up naked for God and for everyone else to see me. I had to clench my teeth and sit on my hands to keep myself from undressing.'

She often used nudity to amuse male friends. Will Fowler, a friend of Bob Slatzer, remembered an evening in her apartment when she was stoned: 'She just took off all her clothes. She liked to show her body off to men. She used to do anything that men would ask her, just as a favour. It was her suggestion as much as ours, not even a sexual thing as far as that evening was concerned.'

The Carrolls invited Marilyn to stay in the spare room of their apartment and she and John became lovers. Marilyn wanted to marry him. Lucille said it was okay with her, but as she was the household's principal breadwinner, John thought better of it.

Her relationship with Schenck got Marilyn a contract at Columbia Pictures. Harry Cohn wanted to have sex with Marilyn simply because she was known around town as Schenck's mistress.

'Harry just told you to get into bed without saying hello,' Marilyn recalled.

Her reward was a small part in the musical *Ladies of the Chorus*. During her time at Columbia, she met director of music Fred Karger. He was ten years older than Marilyn, recently separated from his wife and living at home with his mother and his young son. Marilyn had been sent to him for voice coaching.

One morning, his sister blundered into his bedroom to find him in bed with Marilyn.

'Hi,' she said. 'Can I have some juice?'

Later, Fred's nephew and niece came in to find Marilyn nude, fixing her make-up in the mirror. She showed no embarrassment.

Marilyn fell in love with Karger and moved in. She wanted to get married, but he was never serious about her. He was embarrassed to be seen out with her because, he said, her low-cut dresses made her look like a trollop and he did not think that she would be a suitable stepmother for his young son.

Many of her friends said that Karger was the love of her life. She got pregnant by him several times but always had an abortion. For Christmas in 1948, she bought him a gold watch. It cost $500, which she could ill-afford. By the time she had finished paying for it, he was married to Jane Wyman. Marilyn was so upset by their wedding that she embarrassingly gatecrashed the reception.

Despite her devotion to Karger, she managed dressing-room flings with Milton Berle, Orson Welles and Howard Hughes.

At Columbia, Marilyn also met acting coach Natasha Lytess. She moved in with her and there were rumours of a lesbian relationship.

'When I started reading books I ran into the words 'frigid', 'rejected' and 'lesbian' and I wondered if I was all three of them,' Marilyn said. 'There was also the sinister fact that a well-made woman had always thrilled me to look at.'

Marilyn had a simple philosophy: 'No sex is wrong if

there is love in it.'

After a couple of months, she decided she was not a lesbian after all and moved out.

She appeared in *Love Happy* which the Marx Brothers were making at United Artists. Groucho immediately tried to seduce her.

'She's Mae West, Theda Bara and Bo Peep rolled into one,' he said.

Although she only had a single afternoon's work on the picture, Marilyn was sent off on a promotional tour. In New York, she posed for some publicity shots in *Photoplay* magazine's dream house, and she met up with André de Dienes again, doing some modelling for him on the beach. At El Morocco, she met thirty-eight year old millionaire dress manufacturer Henry Rosenfeld. They became lovers and life-long friends.

'Marilyn thought sex got you closer,' he said. 'She told me that she hardly ever had an orgasm, but she was very unselfish. She tried above all to please the opposite sex.'

Back in Los Angeles, Marilyn was broke again. She posed in a swimsuit, holding a beach ball, for a Pabst beer poster. It caught the eye of a Chicago calendar manufacturer, who asked if the model would pose nude. She said she would be delighted.

'I am only comfortable when I'm naked,' she told reporter Earl Wilson later.

On 27 May 1949, photographer Tom Kelley spread out a red velvet curtain on the floor and put one of Marilyn's favourite records, Artie Shaw's 'Begin the Beguine', on the record player. Marilyn stripped off and posed effortlessly while Kelley stood on a ladder above her and clicked away.

Of the dozen of shots, only two survive – 'A New Wrinkle' which shows Marilyn in a naked profile stretched out across the rumpled drape and 'Golden Dreams' which shows her full-breasted with her legs crossed for decency's sake. Kelley got $500 for publication rights; Marilyn got $50.

At a party in Palm Springs, John Carroll introduced her to Johnny Hyde, whose work as an agent at William Morris had made him a wealthy man. He was balding and short – he came up to her nipple line. Over lunch, she complained about her lovers and her career. No one thought she was good enough to marry, or had what it took to make it in the movies. He disagreed. Already seriously ill with a heart condition, he had less than eighteen months to live. He devoted that time to her.

He paid for cosmetic surgery to have two tiny blemishes removed from Marilyn's nose and chin. He bought her gowns and took her to all the right restaurants and clubs to be seen in. Soon he was deeply in love with her. He left his wife of twenty years standing and bought a house in Beverly Hills. Marilyn moved in with him.

Hyde had her hair dyed platinum blonde. He had her hairline raised and teeth fixed. Natasha Lytess was furious. She thought he was turning her into a Hollywood freak rather than a serious actress. But he got her a part in a serious film, John Houston's *The Asphalt Jungle*.

Told that the part required a busty blonde, Marilyn turned up to the audition with her bust padded.

'I reached into her sweater,' Houston said, 'pulled out the falsies and said, 'You've got the part, Marilyn.''

It was a foregone conclusion. Houston boarded his horses at the Carrolls' ranch and was well behind on his payments. Lucille Ryman told him they would sell his stallions to collect the money due if he did not give Marilyn the part.

Marilyn was also extremely grateful to Hyde.

'I had plenty of friends and acquaintances – you know what I mean, acquaintances?' Marilyn said. 'But not one of those big shots ever did a damn thing for me, not one, except Johnny.'

He got her a part in the academy-award winning *All About Eve* – a week's work guaranteed and a seven-year option. She played opposite George Sanders who immediately fell in love with her. He proposed, but when his wife Zsa Zsa Gabor found out about the affair, she forbade him to see Marilyn off the lot. On the set they were inseparable.

Hyde also used his influence to get her roles in *Right Cross* and *Hometown Story*, but Marilyn's gratitude did not extend to fidelity. She was still seeing Karger and told him: 'Hyde's so sweet. I love him dearly. But I don't feel the way he does.'

She met *Look* photographer Milton Greene at a party. He was eager to take her picture. Marilyn said she had a busy schedule but she would be happy to pose for him all night. Hyde was on vacation in Palm Springs and Marilyn went back to what Greene referred to as his 'West Coast house' – the Chateau Marmont Hotel on Sunset Boulevard. Greene returned to New York without taking a single picture of Marilyn. When he reached his studio on Lexington Avenue, a telegram was waiting for him. It read:

'Milton Greene, I love you dearly
And not for your 'house' and hospitality merely.
It's that I think you are superb –
And that, my dear, is not just a blurb.
    Love, Marilyn'

In bed with Bacon, she mocked the ailing Hyde's sexual ability. The Hollywood gossip was that Marilyn's sexual appetite was killing the poor man. He was so ill that he could not walk to his car and had to be carried. In bed, Marilyn would make him feel young and virile again. Hyde begged her to marry him. Even though he was loaded and dying, she refused.

'I don't love you, Johnny,' she said. 'It wouldn't be fair.'

Marilyn was having a costume fitting for *As Young As You Feel* at Fox when Hyde had the first of a fatal series of heart attacks and was rushed to hospital. When he died, his family took possession of his home, seized the jewellery and expensive gown he had given Marilyn and threw her out of the house.

They did not want her at the funeral, but Marilyn turned up defiantly in black and threw herself sobbing on to the coffin. She blamed herself for Hyde's death. If she had married him, it would have saved his life, he had told her.

'He was the only person who ever really cared about me,' she said years later.

Even though she had refused to marry him, Hyde had told his lawyers that he wanted to leave her a third of his estate, but he had not had time to draw up a new will. She got nothing.

All alone in the world again, Marilyn swallowed thirty Nembutal capsules in a forlorn suicide attempt. Natasha Lytess found her sprawled across the bed in a coma and called a doctor. Just twenty-five years old, it was, by her own account, her third suicide attempt.

Marilyn was terrified that, without Hyde's help, Twentieth Century-Fox would not pick up her seven-year option as Darryl Zanuck did not like her. So she went back to Joe Schenck. He had a private word with Fox president Spyros Skouras and, in January 1951, Marilyn signed a contract for $500 a week, rising to $1,500 in seven years. She waved it at her room-mate Shelley Winters in triumph.

She turned up to the dinner announcing Twentieth Century-Fox's new discoveries wearing a dress so tight that everyone held their breath, hoping it would burst. Long-established actresses sized her up as a threat, especially when she was seen dining out with Skouras. He was soon seen going in and out of her new apartment at the Beverly Carlton.

Marilyn worked on the press. She was seen around town in outfits slashed to the waist. Ted Strauss, a feature writer for *Collier's* magazine, took her to dinner at Romanoff's.

'She was in something red, semi-dressed or semi-undressed, with a cleavage almost to her navel,' he recalled. 'We came in down a sort of Ziegfeld Follies' staircase, and everything stopped. Everyone there looked.'

On other occasions, when journalists wanted private interviews, she would happily answer their questions in the nude. Her lack of coverage earned her plenty of coverage. Every magazine raved about her and US troops in Germany voted her 'Miss Cheesecake of 1951'.

Marilyn took out additional insurance by dating Howard Hughes. An anonymous car would whisk her off to a deserted airfield where he would be waiting in the cockpit of his plane ready to fly her off to some unknown destination. When she came back, her face would be scratched and she would complain about Hughes's five o'clock shadow. He had no reason to complain though. Marilyn amply fulfilled his expectations. As usual, he had bodyguards watching her place and was greatly amused to hear that Peter Lawford had been turned away.

Hughes stood by her when news of her nude calendar work hit the press. So, surprisingly, did Zanuck. Despite the morality clause in her contract, Marilyn thought she should admit to posing in the nude and Zanuck agreed with her. Marilyn told the press that she had been a penniless actress and she had posed nude to get money to eat, pay the rent and recover a repossessed car. She had been advised to deny that she had posed nude, but she said she would rather be honest about it. This candid approach won the sympathy of women. Men were won over when Hugh Hefner paid $500 for the calendar shots and published them as *Playboy* magazine's first centrefold.

Zanuck completed the PR triumph with a press release saying that Marilyn was an orphan and her mother had been confined to a state mental institution. Marilyn was now sexy and vulnerable. When the scandal first broke, the reporter did not even know her name. She was just 'the babe with the big tits'. Now everybody knew her and loved her.

Marilyn met New York Yankee baseball star Joe DiMaggio on a blind date. She offered him a lift home.

They made love in the backseat of her car. Later, when she was asked what they did after they had left the restaurant where they had met, Marilyn said: 'We did not discuss baseball.'

Although DiMaggio had been divorced from his wife, actress Dorothy Arnold, for almost ten years, he was still attempting a reconciliation. His backseat romp with Marilyn changed all that. They saw each other every night until he went back to New York on business.

DiMaggio had proposed to her on the first night, but she was not ready for marriage. One Sunday morning, Marilyn had said to Shelley Winters: 'Wouldn't it be nice to be like men and just get notches on your belt, sleep with the most attractive men and not get emotionally involved.'

So they sat down and each produced a list of their 'Most Wanted'. According to Winters, Marilyn's list included Albert Einstein, Eli Wallach, Arthur Miller, Elia Kazan, Ernest Hemingway, Jean Renoir, Yves Montand, Lee Strasberg, Zero Mostel, Charles Laughton, John Houston, Harry Belafonte, Dean Jagger, Nick Ray, Charles Boyer, Charles Bickford and Clifford Odets.

When she died, a photograph of Albert Einstein was found among her effects. It was inscribed: 'To Marilyn, with respect and love' and signed: 'Albert Einstein'. However, it seems that the father of relativity was not the lucky recipient of Marilyn's favours. The picture was sent to her as a joke by Eli Wallach, who said he did not sleep with her either.

The first on her list to get lucky was director Elia Kazan. He was a sympathetic listener – something he called 'the real art of seduction'. Photographer Jean Howard spotted her waiting for Kazan by the pool of agent Charlie Feldman's house. Later Alain Bennett sat with Marilyn while Kazan went to the Academy Awards when *A Streetcar Named Desire* was up for an Oscar. Agent Milt Ebbins recalled having a business meeting with Kazan in a suite in the Beverly Hills Hotel when Marilyn walked out of the bedroom wearing

Kazan's pyjamas.

Normally, they made love in her apartment or at Charlie Feldman's house. It was Marilyn's first uncomplicated affair. There was no possibility of marriage as Kazan had a wife and two children.

'Marilyn simply wasn't a wife – anyone could see that,' he wrote. He considered her 'a delightful companion' and, later, 'a simple, decent-hearted kid whom Hollywood brought down'.

The affair continued for about a year. It ended when Marilyn told him she thought she was pregnant.

'It scared the hell out of me,' he said. 'Like any other louse, I decided to call a halt to my carrying on.'

There were other men, too. Greek actor Nico Minardos complained that she was a 'lousy lay'. She was mixed up and wanted to get married.

'I was never going to let myself become 'Mr Monroe',' he said.

Spyros Skouras continued his nocturnal visits and, in an effort to free herself from dumb blonde parts, she even tried to seduce Darryl Zanuck.

'I would have done anything he wanted,' she said. 'I tried but he wasn't interested. He was the only guy who wasn't and I never knew why.'

Journalist Rupert Allan was writing an article about Marilyn for *Look* magazine when he spotted a photograph beside her bed which showed two men. One was Elia Kazan. The other was playwright Arthur Miller.

Marilyn had met Miller on the set of *As Young As You Feel*. She was crying and he tried to comfort her. They met again at a party. Miller was a close friend of Kazan and the three of them would frequently be seen together. Kazan soon complained: 'She was so obsessed with Arthur that she couldn't talk about anything else.'

The press was obsessed with something else – Marilyn's affair with Joe DiMaggio. She visited him in New York and he took her on a whirlwind tour of Manhattan's night spots.

Meanwhile, she was continuing her affair with Bob Slatzer. They met in a hotel at Niagara Falls for a weekend of booze and sex. He recalled that she was flaunting her nudity even more than she had done in California, appearing naked at the window and giggling when crowds in the streets below gathered to look up at her.

When a picture of Marilyn, DiMaggio and his father appeared in the press, DiMaggio's ex-wife tried to prevent him seeing his son. She told a court that the boy should not be exposed to people with immoral reputations, such as Marilyn. The judge found against her and said she should never have divorced the baseball star in the first place.

Marilyn continued to two-time DiMaggio with Slatzer. One evening, Marilyn made a mess of the arrangements. Slatzer was sitting outside her house waiting for her when DiMaggio turned up. Sometime later Marilyn turned up and let them both in. Slatzer poured them a drink and DiMaggio noticed that he knew his way around the place. There was a row. DiMaggio told Slatzer to leave. Slatzer refused. Marilyn threw them both out.

'About an hour later, she called and apologized,' said Slatzer. 'She said she'd got her schedules mixed up.'

Slatzer's relationship with Marilyn was getting some press coverage at the time.

'He's been wooing her with gifts of the world's greatest books,' said one piece. He admitted giving her *The Rubáiát of Omar Khayyám*. It is hard to imagine DiMaggio wooing her with Arabian love poetry.

One night, Marilyn said: 'I'm tired of sleeping around.'

On a drunken spree, she drove down to Tijuana with Slatzer and they got married. They consummated the marriage in the Rosarita Beach Hotel.

'Next morning, I awoke to find her sitting up in bed,' said Slatzer. 'She was crying but wouldn't say why.'

Even on their brief honeymoon, Marilyn could not get

away from DiMaggio. He was commentating on the World Series on the radio. Slatzer was a baseball fan and, in spite of Marilyn's pleading, insisted on having the game on.

The marriage did not last long. Back in Los Angeles the following day, Zanuck called them into his office. He explained to Slatzer that Fox had $2 million invested in Marilyn. The studio needed her to marry Prince Charming, not some lousy scriptwriter. What had been done had better be undone. Marilyn caved in under the pressure. The next day, they drove back down to Tijuana and bribed the lawyer who had married them to burn the marriage certificate and remove any trace of the marriage.

The particular Prince Charming the studio had in mind was Mr Squeaky-Clean All-American Baseball Star Joe DiMaggio. There was a problem. Marilyn was beginning to find him tiresome.

It was true that he was the perfect escort to be seen around town with, but he hated the revealing dresses she wore. Her sexy wiggle made him cringe. He threatened to beat up anyone who approached her for an autograph and he detested Hollywood parties and premières. Instead, Marilyn and Joe would spend quiet nights at home together. She put up with this for a while because DiMaggio was in love with her and he was a satisfying lover.

DiMaggio certainly would not have been pleased with the gold lamé gown she wore to receive her *Photoplay* Gold Medal for 'Fastest-Rising Star of 1952'. It was paper-thin and handstitched around her nude curves. Master of ceremonies Jerry Lewis stood up in an attempt to dive down her cleavage.

'How Marilyn flaunted her rear end,' said columnist Sheilah Graham. 'You could see every crevice.'

When DiMaggio was out of town, Marilyn made up for lost time. She was still seeing Bob Slatzer. She began affairs with Edward G. Robinson's nineteen-year-old son Eddie Jnr and his friend Andrew James. Then there was a fling with

Elizabeth Taylor's first husband, Nicky Hilton.

While his wife was out of town, Marilyn had an affair with Billy Travilla, who designed the dresses for *Gentlemen Prefer Blondes*.

'My introduction was the sight of her in a black bathing suit,' he recalled. 'She opened the sliding doors of my fitting room, and the strap fell off, and her breast was exposed...of course, she did it on purpose.'

When Travilla turned up at her place for a date carrying a bunch of flowers, another guy with a bunch of flowers was waiting at her door. Marilyn explained to the other guy that her date for the evening was Travilla, then took both the bunches of flowers and put in them in the toilet.

They went to Tiffany's on Eight Street. When Travilla went to the men's room, he passed the office and saw Marilyn's nude calendar.

'Oh Billy,' she said. 'Where is it? I want to see it.'

Billie Holiday was using the office as a dressing-room. When she found out that Marilyn had not just dropped by to say hello but to ogle her own nude picture, Lady Day screwed up the calendar and threw it in Marilyn's face. Later, Travilla got another calendar which Marilyn signed for him.

DiMaggio refused to take her to the première of *Gentlemen Prefer Blondes*, even though he was staying at her apartment. Instead, she went with Betty Grable. The word got around that he was ashamed to be seen in public with her.

Behind closed doors, things were different. She loved to cook for him and learnt to make his favourite Italian spaghetti sauce. They spent time away from Hollywood in his modest home in San Francisco and went fishing together. Here, Marilyn began to believe, was a man who would make a loving husband and a good father to the kids she longed to have.

While she was filming *River of No Return* with Robert Mitchum in Canada, she pretended to hurt her leg. DiMaggio flew to be by her side. With shooting halted, the two of them disappeared for the weekend.

When a film came along with Frank Sinatra, whose reputation for bedding his leading ladies was legendary, DiMaggio put his foot down. Marilyn refused the picture and was put on suspension.

Over Christmas 1953, they got to talk.

'Joe and I decided that since we could not give each other up, marriage was the only solution,' she said.

They did not set a date and, on 14 January 1954, when DiMaggio took her to City Hall in San Francisco, Marilyn said: 'What are we doing here?'

Despite her confusion, she went through with the marriage. As a wedding gift, she gave him a nude picture of herself, one from the calendar set that was considered too risqué for publication.

After the ceremony, at DiMaggio's insistence, they skipped the reception he'd planned. They spent their wedding night in a $4 room in the Clifton Motel in Pasa Robles. To this day, the room bears a plaque saying: 'Joe and Marilyn Slept Here'.

They headed on to the mountains near Palm Springs where they spent two idyllic weeks alone together in a friend's cabin. The place did not even have a TV. They spent their time walking in the snow and in bed. Of all her lovers, Marilyn said, DiMaggio 'was the greatest. If our marriage was only sex it would last forever.'

The honeymoon continued in Tokyo where DiMaggio was to open the Japanese baseball season. In the Far East, Marilyn brought her teasing exploits to new heights when a US Army officer asked her to fly over to Korea to entertain the troops. DiMaggio did not approve, but let her go. In whirling snow and sub-zero temperatures, Marilyn performed for the men of the First Marine Division in a tight low-cut purple dress with no underwear. When he saw the newsreels, DiMaggio was appalled. Marilyn caught pneumonia.

Before they had even got back to California, their marriage was in trouble.

'He threatened to divorce me on our honeymoon,' she lamented.

Back in San Francisco, DiMaggio grew sullen. She would walk around the house with very little on in front of female friends. He would watch the sports on TV, and was in no hurry to get to bed.

While she cooked and cleaned and ironed, he spent his time at the restaurant he had bought on Fisherman's Wharf. He asked her to come down there with him to bring in custom but she did not want to be used.

Marilyn went back to work on *There's No Business Like Show Business*. DiMaggio disapproved of her costume and the suggestive choreography of her 'Heat Wave' number. She grew nervous, fluffed her lines and cried all the time. Zanuck stepped in and barred DiMaggio from the lot.

At home, DiMaggio began to become abusive. He tried to stop Marilyn from seeing her acting coach Natasha Lytess, jealous they might be having a lesbian affair. She admitted at this time to having sex with a young homosexual 'to make him feel good'.

During the shooting of *The Seven Year Itch*, Marilyn wanted to do her love scenes naked, but the other actors could not handle it. DiMaggio followed her to New York, where they filmed the exteriors. By chance he was present when she did the famous scene where her dress is blown up by the hot air from the subway. He turned away in disgust, while others said he sobbed. Afterwards, the cast overheard a furious row in Marilyn's room. Later, Milton Greene's wife Amy saw Marilyn undressed.

'Her back was black and blue,' she said. 'I couldn't believe it.'

It was not all DiMaggio's fault Amy maintained: 'Marilyn could be a smartass, and when she drank champagne she would goad him. They weren't intellectuals, they couldn't discuss their pain, so they lashed out at each other.'

On 4 October 1954, Marilyn told *Itch* director Billy Wilder: 'Joe and I are getting divorced.'

When Marilyn got married, a Twentieth Century-Fox executive boasted: 'We haven't lost a star; we've gained a centre fielder.' Now they moved into action to minimize the damage. Zanuck hired the best lawyers. The Twentieth Century-Fox publicity department cited 'a conflict of careers'. The divorce papers talked of 'mental cruelty'.

'Really, deep down, I didn't want to marry him,' she told actress Maureen Stapleton.

DiMaggio was not finished yet. Marilyn was staying at her friend Sheila Stewart's apartment with voice coach Harry Shaefer. Some said that DiMaggio suspected, rightly, that they were having an affair – though Bob Slatzer said he believed DiMaggio had evidence that Marilyn was having a lesbian affair with Stewart.

DiMaggio and Frank Sinatra made a daring raid on the apartment. With flashguns blazing, they hoped to catch Marilyn in the act – either to countersue on the grounds of adultery or to blackmail Marilyn into coming back. The whole thing went horribly wrong when they broke down the door of the wrong apartment. The screams of fifty-year-old Florence Kotz sent them fleeing into the night, while Stewart, Shaefer and Marilyn overheard the commotion from the apartment above. After what became known famously as 'The Wrong Door Raid', DiMaggio settled out of court for $7,500.

There has been some speculation that Sinatra deliberately took DiMaggio to the wrong flat. They fell out afterwards and Sinatra rubbed salt in the wounds by dating Marilyn.

Marilyn got her divorce and had another abortion. She was down but not out. She had already told Sidney Skolsky of the New York Post that she was going to marry Arthur Miller.

In time, she managed to patch it up with DiMaggio and

they became good friends and saw each other often.

'I never loved any guy more,' she said, 'but he resented my career and refused to compromise.'

Marilyn resented her career, too. She desperately wanted to get out of the dumb-blonde roles Zanuck assigned her and into some serious acting. Unable to afford another suspension, she went into hiding, first at Frank Sinatra's until he got tired of her walking around nude in front of his friends. Then she headed to New York with Milton Greene. Her aim was to study method acting at the legendary Actors' Studio with Lee Strasberg – and to pursue Arthur Miller.

Miller's marriage was already on the rocks when she arrived in New York, but while she was at the Actors' Studio, she had an affair with Marlon Brando to fill in the time until Miller announced his divorce. Marilyn also used her time in New York to renegotiate her contract with Twentieth Century-Fox and secure herself a part in *The Prince and the Showgirl*, the film version of Terence Rattigan's *The Sleeping Princess*, which Sir Laurence Olivier was going to direct.

On stage, Olivier had played opposite his wife Vivien Leigh, but for the film version, he decided to give his wife's part to Marilyn. They had met at the apartment she was subletting on Sutton Place. He was so captivated by her at their first meeting that he could not remember a word they said.

'But one thing was clear to me,' he recalled. 'I was going to fall most shatteringly in love with Marilyn. She was so adorable, so witty and more physically attractive than anyone I could imagine.'

Soon he was wondering whether it had all been a terrible mistake. At the press conference called to announce that she would be going to England to make the movie, Marilyn turned up with a cleavage the depth of the Grand Canyon. Then suddenly – pop – one of her shoulder straps broke and the world's greatest living actor was trampled underfoot by a stampede of flash-popping newspapermen.

While Marilyn was in Nevada filming *Bus Stop*, Miller was there too, ending his fifteen-year marriage. Neither of them talked publicly about their affair, but the press constantly linked their names. This new notoriety brought him to the attention of the House Un-American Activities Committee which subpoenaed him. Despite the damaging publicity, Marilyn said she would stand by him.

Back East, he introduced her to his parents as 'the girl I want to marry'.

'At last, I have a mother and father,' she gushed, sobbing.

Miller announced their wedding plans in the most public possible way. Already facing a citation for contempt of Congress for refusing to reveal the names of friends he knew to be Communists, he was asked by the Committee why he had applied for a passport. He said that he wanted to go to England to be 'with the woman who will then be my wife'.

Marilyn said later that he had never even asked her to marry him. But that did not matter. One way to win the favour of the House Un-American Activities Committee, it seemed, was to announce a very American activity with an all-American girl.

Marilyn responded in true style by announcing that she was converting to Judaism and learning to cook borscht, chopped liver and matzoh balls. They were married in a brief civil ceremony in White Plains, New York, on 29 June 1956. Two days later, they were wed in the Jewish faith by Rabbi Robert Goldburg in front of Miller's family.

Miller was ten years her senior and the most distinguished playwright of his generation. Like all her husbands and long-term lovers before, she called him 'Pa'. They honeymooned in England, where Marilyn filmed *The Prince and the Showgirl*. She almost drove Olivier insane with her newly acquired method acting. When Miller flew back to New York because his daughter was sick, Marilyn fell apart. She stopped working completely until he came back.

While Miller was in England, he oversaw a production of his play *A View from the Bridge* in London. At the première, Marilyn turned up in a dress that was so low cut that no one bothered to look at the play at all.

Back in the US, Marilyn enjoyed playing housewife to Miller and mum to his kids. When his collected plays were published later that year, he dedicated them to her.

'I don't think I ever saw two people so dizzy with love for each other,' said a friend.

Marilyn thought that the marriage was going to last forever and in June 1957 she became pregnant. But it was a tubular pregnancy and had to be aborted. This left her deeply depressed. She overdosed on sleeping tablets twice, but Miller found her in time on both occasions. As a form of therapy, he began writing the screenplay of *The Misfits* for her.

By this time, Marilyn was famous all over the world. When the Soviet premier Nikita Khrushchev toured America, he wanted to be introduced to Marilyn. He took her hand, squeezed it hard and said: 'You're a very pretty girl.'

'He looked at me the way a man looks on a woman,' she told the press.

In private, she said he had too many warts.

'Who would want to be a Communist with a president like that?'

Marilyn was soon to investigate the alternative. She already had another president under her belt. During the filming of *Bus Stop*, she met President Sukarno of Indonesia – a Muslim and a well-known womanizer – at a party.

'He kept looking down my dress,' she said. 'You'd think with five wives he'd have enough.'

But the two of them struck erotic sparks off each other and they made love that night.

When the proposal for *Some Like It Hot* arrived, Marilyn turned it down but Miller suggested she took it. Work might be just the therapy she needed. During the filming, she was more exasperating than ever. She was hours late every day. She never knew her lines and needed vast numbers of retakes. Once she was sitting in her dressing-room reading Thomas Paine's *The Rights of Man*, when the assistant director called her on to the set. Not normally known for foul language, her response was: 'Go fuck yourself.'

Tony Curtis got so annoyed that, when asked what it was like kissing Marilyn, he replied, famously: 'It's like kissing Hitler.'

However, close examination of the film shows that she has her mouth open during their kissing scenes. Were Curtis's famous words, perhaps, directed at Miller?

During shooting, she became pregnant again but, on 17 December 1958, she miscarried. She blamed Miller for making her do the film.

She was offered *Let's Make Love*, but her reputation for being difficult was now so widespread that no one wanted to co-star with her.

'What's wrong with me?' she asked Miller. 'I can't have a baby and I can't find anyone who wants to work with me.'

Then Yves Montand turned up. Miller had met him in Paris and when he arrived on Broadway with a one-man show, Miller invited Montand and his wife, actress Simone Signoret, to dinner.

Montand had never seen a Monroe movie, but when he saw her in person he was immediately smitten. She was too. He had long been on her 'Most Wanted' list and he reminded her of Joe DiMaggio whose picture she still kept in her closet. She did not think he was very well suited to his wife. Although Montand and Signoret were the same age, her heavy build made her look considerably older.

'Simone's too old for him,' she confided to a friend. 'She's Arthur's type.'

Montand spoke little English, but Signoret translated for them. Quickly, Marilyn decided that Montand would be the perfect co-star in *Let's Make Love*. The studio did not agree. She prevailed.

The two couples moved into adjoining bungalows at the Beverly Hills Hotel. Marilyn and Montand went off to the studio each day. Signoret and Miller stayed home.

Signoret won an Oscar for *Room at the Top*. She was swamped with offers and headed back to Europe. Miller, knowing that Marilyn fancied Montand, bowed to the inevitable and absented himself, leaving the lovers alone.

Montand did not know how to handle the situation. Marilyn was already all over him on the set. If he gave in, she would dominate the picture. If he refused and put her back up, the filming would turn into a nightmare. He did not have to wait long to make up his mind. One evening, Marilyn knocked on the door of his bungalow. She was wearing a mink, with nothing on under it. The affair began.

'What else could I do?' he complained to a friend.

The affair soon became common knowledge around Hollywood. Marilyn and Montand would turn up at parties with a third person in tow. No one was fooled. When Montand left early on one occasion, Marilyn was seen running after his car.

There were rumours that Marilyn had asked Miller to write a part in *The Misfits* for Montand. It was also said that, when Miller returned to Los Angeles, he went looking for his pipe and found Montand in bed with his wife. Most people blamed Miller for the situation. If he had wanted to keep his marriage together, he would never have left his wife alone with the romantic Frenchman, they said – though, in fact, Montand was originally Italian.

Marilyn and Miller returned to New York discussing divorce, although Montand had given her no reason to think that he would leave his wife for her. The fact was he had had dozens of girls in Hollywood, but Signoret knew he would always come home.

On his way back to Paris, Montand had to change planes

at Idlewild Airport (now JFK). Marilyn turned up with champagne and whisked him off to a room in the nearby International Hotel. Five hours later, he was on his way again, to France.

He told the press that Marilyn was an enchanting child. If he were not married and she were not married, well... As it was, 'nothing will break up my marriage'.

In private, he said that Marilyn was on drugs and dangerously unstable.

Signoret was wonderfully understanding. She told reporters: 'If Marilyn is in love with my husband, it proves she has good taste. I am in love with him too.'

In her memoirs, she said: 'Marilyn never knew how thoroughly I understood.'

She stayed with her husband until her death in 1985.

Marilyn was left with Montand in celluloid. She watched *Let's Make Love* over and over, and at the end, where she marries Montand, she cried.

Her marriage finally fell apart over the filming of *The Misfits*. Marilyn wanted to shoot in colour; Miller insisted on making it in black and white. Marilyn complained that Miller had not asked for enough money. Gable got $750,000. They were splitting $500,000. Miller constantly reworked her dialogue without discussing it with her.

'It's not your movie, it's ours,' she was heard shouting as she beat on the locked door of his study. 'You lied.'

Marilyn had always wanted to play a love scene with Clark Gable. When she was little, her mother had given her a picture of him to pass off as her missing father. At fifty-nine, Gable felt a little old for fooling around. Besides, he was freshly married to Kay Spreckels who became pregnant with their first child during filming. He even passed up trips to Reno where director John Houston and the crew went crazy with drink, gambling and girls.

Marilyn had to be content horsing around with Gable's stand-in, Lew Smith. However, there was one scene where

Gable's iron resolve faltered. In it, he walks into the bedroom to find a naked Marilyn draped only in a bedsheet.

'I was so thrilled when he kissed me, we had to do the scene over several times,' she said. 'Then the sheet dropped and he put his hand on my breast. I got goose bumps all over.'

At night, Marilyn dreamed of having sex with Gable. She dreamt that they were kissing and cuddling. Gable was an obsession.

'Whenever he was near me, I wanted him to kiss me and kiss me and kiss me,' she said. 'We did a lot of kissing, touching and feeling. I never tried harder to seduce a man.'

His wife caught them, but Marilyn did not care. She also tried to seduce Montgomery Clift, the other star of *The Misfits*, but he was in worse shape that she was. He was rattling with booze and pills, and, it was rumoured, he was gay. Marilyn said he was oblivious to her advances.

Fortunately, Marilyn and Miller had moved into separate suites. Their antipathy was no secret. They had rows in public. At his forty-fifth birthday party, she refused to sing 'Happy Birthday'. Once she even drove off and left him in the middle of the desert.

During the shooting, Marilyn talked of suicide. She told her press aide Rupert Allan that she had climbed out on the ledge outside her thirteenth-storey apartment in New York in her nightie, determined to jump, but below her she saw a woman in a brown tweed suit.

'I thought if I jumped I would do her in too,' she said. 'I waited there for about five or ten minutes, but she didn't move and I got cold, so I climbed back in.'

Houston had told Marilyn not to take any pills while they were out on location, but she got some from a local doctor. In the middle of the shooting, she overdosed on sleeping tablets and had to be rushed to hospital in Los Angeles. She may have done this deliberately because Yves Montand was in town, but he refused to take her calls. However, Brando,

Sinatra and DiMaggio all visited her in hospital.

Soon after shooting was over, Clark Gable died of a massive heart attack. His wife blamed the stress that Marilyn's tardiness and absences had caused during the filming of *The Misfits*.

Marilyn announced to the press that her marriage was over. Miller moved out of their Manhattan apartment, taking nothing with him that would remind him of her. Years later, Miller said: 'If I had known how we would end up, I would never have married her.'

In fact, her four-year marriage to Miller was her longest and, overall, her happiest. He did get something out of their final humiliating scene. During the filming of *The Misfits*, he met stills photographer Inge Morath, who became his third wife.

The press printed rumours that Marilyn was divorcing Miller to marry Montand, who was due to visit New York. Montand said that he had no plans to divorce his wife and Simone Signoret phoned Marilyn to tell her that her husband's proposed New York trip was off. Marilyn overdosed on sleeping pills again. This time, it was DiMaggio who nursed her through.

Marilyn flew to Juarez, Mexico, to obtain her divorce on 20 January 1961 – the day John F. Kennedy was inaugurated. The idea was to keep Marilyn's divorce off the front pages. It failed, though humorist Art Buchwald was one of the few to link romantically Marilyn with the new president.

She had already been to bed with him long before he entered the White House. They had met at a party when Marilyn was still married to DiMaggio, who was immediately suspicious and had to drag his wife away from the handsome young senator. JFK became obsessed with her when he was totally immobilized after an operation on his back when someone had thoughtfully taped her nude picture on the wall opposite. Their affair began after her divorce from DiMaggio and continued, sporadically, throughout her marriage to Miller. They met in his 'playpen', his suite in New York's Carlyle Hotel, or in Peter Lawford's Santa Monica beach-house.

She appeared at the party to celebrate his nomination at the 1960 Democratic convention in Los Angeles. Kennedy had her flown from New York for the occasion and, to allay suspicion, got Sammy Davis Jnr to escort her to the party. Even the bartender noticed the young Jack Kennedy, fresh from his 'New Frontier' acceptance speech at the Los Angeles Coliseum, move in on Marilyn. At a dinner afterwards, Jack put his hand up Marilyn's dress under the table, to discover she was wearing nothing underneath. Later, they went nude swimming in Santa Monica. The affair intensified during the election campaign.

The day following Kennedy's election, Buchwald urged the president-elect to stand firm on the Monroe Doctrine.

'Obviously, you cannot leave Monroe adrift,' he wrote. 'There are too many greedy people eyeing her.'

He was right about that. Marilyn was still seeing her long-standing confidant Henry Rosenfeld, and she was extending conjugal privileges to DiMaggio and Bob Slatzer. The maid often heard giggling from Marilyn's room when her handsome young masseur visited.

'He has the best hands in the world,' she said.

Her Italian chauffeur, a Rudolph Valentino lookalike, turned up at her apartment whether she was going out or not and they would lock themselves in her room for the afternoon. Yul Brynner's young son Rock once found Marilyn naked in his father's bedroom. Billy Travilla was still on the scene. There were brief flings with director Nicholas Ray and agent Charlie Feldman. There were persistent rumours that she was sleeping with mobster Bugsy Siegel and columnist Walter Winchell. And, it was said, the studio had paid off a famous actress who had claimed to have had a lesbian affair with Marilyn.

Her obsession to go naked reasserted itself. She loved to

walk the streets or go to the movies wearing nothing but a mink coat, a thrill she shared with her neighbour Jeanne Carmen. Together they flashed at comedian Jack Benny in the street. All three of them would go to the nude beach, north of Santa Monica. Benny would disguise himself with a false beard and Marilyn would wear a black wig.

She went steady with Frank Sinatra who, she said, was 'the most fascinating man I ever dated'. She hoped they would marry and got deeply depressed when he dropped her for another woman. After that she took to having casual one-night stands with anonymous men who never dreamt they would ever meet Marilyn Monroe, much less sleep with her. She told her maid that she would go with anyone, irrespective of their looks, provided they were 'nice'. One of them was young scriptwriter José Balaños who followed her to Mexico where he had her serenaded at her hotel by half-a-dozen mariachi bands. After she died, he claimed she was planning to marry him.

Her only steady date during this period was the man she called 'The Prez', the President of the United States, John F. Kennedy.

Jackie Kennedy hated the West Coast, so Jack and Marilyn were safe in California. They would stay together at Peter Lawford's place or Lawford would drive her up to Bing Crosby's home in Palm Springs if Kennedy was staying there.

If the President had more urgent need of her, Lawford would accompany her east on board Air Force One. In New York, Kennedy would leave the nuclear button behind in his aide's charge to sneak into the Carlyle to have sex with Marilyn. Mickey Rooney even saw her in the Rose Garden at the White House and Jackie Kennedy complained about the blonde hairs she found in the presidential bed.

The affair was the talk of Los Angeles. Hollywood insiders would be invited to discreet pool parties at Bing's Palm Springs home, to be greeted by Kennedy with a tipsy and sometimes barely clad Marilyn.

Marilyn began to believe that, after his first term of office, Kennedy was going to divorce Jackie and marry her. She called the First Lady on the President's private number and told her so. Jackie graciously responded that Marilyn was quite welcome to the job if she was up to living in a goldfish bowl. Of course, she was not.

The FBI had Peter Lawford's beach-house bugged and J. Edgar Hoover used the tapes to keep his job when Kennedy tried to sack him. Hoover also dropped into the conversation that someone else was bugging the beach-house – the mob, who Kennedy had crossed during his election.

Robert Kennedy, JFK's younger brother, was a womanizer who often took on his brother's cast-offs. He was Hoover's boss and, as Attorney General, he was also determined to break the Mafia. He warned his older brother that he must give up Marilyn. The mob could use her to break him.

Despite herself, Marilyn knew that Jack Kennedy wanted her, not for herself, but as Marilyn Monroe, movie star. Some in Hollywood thought she was important to him. Washington insiders knew: 'Marilyn Monroe was just another cup of coffee to Jack.'

Jack wanted to ease out gently. He allowed Marilyn her last moment of glory. On the President's birthday, Peter Lawford brought her to the Democratic Party fund-raiser, where she sang 'Happy Birthday, Mr President' in a gown which veteran diplomat Adlai Stevenson described as 'skin and beads – only I didn't see the beads'.

John Kennedy said: 'I can now retire from politics after having, ah, 'Happy Birthday' sung to me in such a sweet, wholesome way.'

It was Marilyn who was being retired. At the party afterwards, Bobby Kennedy moved in. Marilyn had one last night with the President in the Carlyle, then it was RFK all the way.

Robert Kennedy was a little prudish compared with his

older brother, but Marilyn soon took care of that. She and Jeanne Carmen took him to the nude beach in Jack Benny's false beard. He was so thrilled that no one had recognized two such famous people in the nude, they laughed all the way home.

Meanwhile, Marilyn was filming *Something's Got to Give,* written by her old friend and sometime lover Nunnally Johnson. In the movie, she is supposed to be nude in the swimming pool, trying to lure co-star Dean Martin in with her. Director George Cukor found that it was impossible to shoot the scene convincingly and hide the flesh-coloured bodysuit Marilyn was wearing. So Marilyn took it off.

Once the news that Marilyn was doing a nude scene got around the lot, there was a stampede. Cukor closed the set, but Marilyn invited in the photographers. *Playboy* magazine paid an unprecedented $25,000 for the most revealing shots. Tamer pictures were circulated to other magazines. It did not make up for her lateness and frequent absences from the set and she was dropped from the picture.

Marilyn was mortified. She tried to put a call in to the President, but he did not return it. Instead Bobby Kennedy flew to LA to inform her that her affair with Jack was over. She was distraught. He comforted her. One thing led to another. Soon they were deeply in love with each other. They talked of marriage. The FBI had the whole thing on tape. So did the mob. But Bobby did not care – until she became pregnant, that is.

Although she had been seeing other men, Marilyn was sure that the baby's father was either Jack or Bobby Kennedy. She called Bobby at the Justice Department and told him so. His response was to change the number of his direct line so she could not phone him again.

Peter Lawford was left to sort out the mess. He took Marilyn to Lake Tahoe where she had an abortion. There is some suggestion that she was kidnapped and underwent the termination forcibly, but she was too full of drugs and booze at the time to tell the difference. She attended some orgies with Lawford and Sinatra and was filmed there, possibly to blackmail her if she ever went public about her affairs with the Kennedys. More drink and drugs and wild sex did not help. She was used to drinking champagne all day. Now she started the day with Bloody Marys and amphetamines.

In the early hours of 5 August 1965, the last great Hollywood sex goddess, Marilyn Monroe, died of an overdose. Little is known of what really happened that night. Her death is shrouded in mystery, giving rise to the kind of conspiracy theories that also swathe the assassinations of JFK, Bobby Kennedy and Martin Luther King, not to mention those surrounding Fidel Castro, the Bay of Pigs, the Cuban missile crisis, the Vietnam war, the Mafia, the Pentagon, missing Teamsters Union boss Jimmy Hoffa, the FBI, CIA, KGB and practically every other organization, crisis or unexplained mystery you can think of.

There has been some suggestion that Bobby Kennedy was in Los Angeles that night. A helicopter was heard buzzing overhead. An ambulance was seen waiting outside Marilyn's house before the maid raised the alarm. Marilyn's telephone records and other evidence went missing. Her autopsy report was lost. FBI reports on her death were suppressed and friends of Marilyn's who tried to investigate her death independently received death threats.

She was thirty-nine years old.

SELECTED BIBLIOGRAPHY

Always Lana, Taylor Pero and Jeff Rovin, Bantam, New York, 1982

Ava, Ava Gardner, Bantam, London, 1990

Ava, Roland Flamini, Hale, London, 1983

Ava's Men, Jane Ellen Wayne, Sphere, London 1990

The Casting Couch – Making It In Hollywood, Selwyn Ford, Grafton Books, London, 1990

Clara Bow – Running Wild, David Stern, Ebury Press, London, 1989

Crawford's Men, Jane Ellen Wayne, Robson Books, London, 1988

Jean Harlow – An Intimate Biography, Irving Shulman, Warner Books, London, 1992

Joan Crawford – A Biography, Bob Thomas, Weidenfeld & Nicolson, London, 1962

Joan Crawford – The Last Word, Fred Lawrence Guiles, Pavilion Books, London 1995

Detour: A Hollywood Tragedy, Cheryl Crane, Michael Joseph, London, 1988

Garbo – A Biography, Barry Paris, Sidgwick & Jackson, London, 1995

Goddess: The Secret Life of Marilyn Monroe, Anthony Summers, Victor Gollancz, London, 1985

SELECTED BIBLIOGRAPHY

Grace, Robert Lacy, Sidgwick & Jackson, London, 1994

Grace: The Secret Lives of a Princess, James Spada, Sidgwick & Jackson, London, 1987

Greta and Cecil, Diana Souhami, Flamingo, London, 1996

Here Lies the Heart, Mercedes de Acosta, André Deutsch, London, 1960

If This Was Happiness: A Biography of Rita Hayworth, Barbara Leaming, Weidenfeld & Nicholson, London, 1989

Lana: The Lady, the Legend, the Truth, Lana Turner, New English Library, London, 1982

Lana: The Life and Loves of Lana Turner, Jane Ellen Wayne, Robson Books, London, 1995

The Life and Loves of Grace Kelly, Jane Ellen Wayne, Robson Books, London, 1991

Loving Garbo, Hugo Vickers, Jonathan Cape, London, 1994

Lulu in Hollywood, Louise Brooks, Hamilton, London, 1982

Marilyn: The Last Take, Peter Brown and Patte Barham, Heineman, London, 1992

Marilyn Monroe: The Biography, Donald Spoto, Chatto and Windus, London, 1993

Marilyn Monroe: Confidential, Lena Pepitone and William Stadiem, Sidgwick & Jackson, London, 1979

Marilyn's Men, Jane Ellen Wayne, Robson Books, London, 1992

Marlene Dietrich, Maria Riva, Bloomsbury, London, 1992

Marlene Dietrich: Life and Legend, Steven Bach, HarperCollins, London, 1992

Marlene Dietrich: My Life, Marlene Dietrich, Weidenfeld & Nicholson, London, 1989

Marlene: My Friend, David Brett, Robson Books, London, 1993

The MGM Girls – Behind the Velvet Curtain, Peter Harry

SELECTED BIBLIOGRAPHY

Brown and Pamela Ann Brown, Harrap, London, 1983

Mommie Dearest, Christina Crawford, Hart-Davis, MacGibbon Ltd, London, 1979

Platinum Blonde – The Life and Legends of Jean Harlow, Eve Golden, Abbeville Press, New York, 1991

Rita Hayworth, James Hill, Robson Books, London, 1983

Rita Hayworth: The Time, the Place and the Woman, John Kobal, W.H. Allen, London, 1977

Star Billing – Tell-Tale Trivia From Hollywood, David Brown, Futura Books, London, 1985

Survivor: A Long Night's Journey from Anger and Chaos to the Peace of Inner Awakening, Christina Crawford, Donald I. Fine, New York, 1988

Tallulah, Brendan Gill, Michael Joseph, London, 1972

Tallulah Bankhead, Jeffery L. Carrier, Greenwood Press, Westport, Connecticut, 1991

Tallulah Darling, Denis Brian, Sidgwick & Jackson, London, 1972

INDEX

INDEX

INDEX

INDEX

INDEX

INDEX

INDEX

INDEX

INDEX

276

INDEX

INDEX

278